Walter Wager, a graduate of H
former Fulbright Fellow at th
adviser to Israel's Director of
United Nations Secretariat an
A prolific writer, he has contri
magazines, authored eleven cloak-and-dagger novels under a pseudonym, and written television documentaries for three networks and films for the United States Information Agency. He is currently Editorial Director of the American Society of Composers, Authors and Publishers.

Also by Walter Wager:

TELEFON
TWILIGHT'S LAST GLEAMING

Walter Wager

Swap

Futura Publications Limited
A Futura Book

A Futura Book

First published in Great Britain by
Futura Publications Limited in 1977

ISBN 0 8600 7562 1

Printed in Great Britain by
Hazell Watson & Viney Ltd
Aylesbury, Bucks

Futura Publications Limited
110 Warner Road
Camberwell, London SE5

THIS BOOK IS DEDICATED

to my daughter, Lisa.

That which follows is wholly the product of one writer's imagination, a work of fiction about people who never existed. It is the writer's hope that no one—in any land and for any reason—will attempt to emulate these characters or their deeds, for that would be no useful contribution to the very real and serious problem that inspired this book.

W. W.

SWAP

1

The real question was, who was going to get it tonight?

Which of the ambushers would be zapped, Garrison wondered as he peered into the jungle, and how badly?

It was black and it was hot and it was humid, and the Claymores were in place along the twisting trail that snaked through the U-Minh Forest. The Claymores weren't men, they were devices to maim and kill men—three-and-a-half-pound anti-personnel mines, each with 700 small steel balls embedded in a plastic matrix at the front of the curved polystyrene case and one and a half pounds of C-4 explosive behind the matrix. On detonation, a Claymore sprays those flesh-bearing balls some fifty-five yards in a sixty degree fan-shaped arc.

Garrison could have told you all that, even though he wasn't an ordnance specialist. He was an almost everything specialist: jungle fighter, frogman, saboteur, parachutist, and crack shot with all U.S. and Soviet bloc light-infantry weapons. He could set a broken leg, tap out fourteen "code groups" per minute and garrote a foe with chicken wire. If he ran out of food, he knew which berries and insects and snakes he could eat safely and how to trap small animals or fish. If he had no ammunition, it was easy for him to make a bow and arrow—he was an excellent archer—or to fashion a club by filling one of his socks with sand or earth and then urinating on it. His command of German and Russian was only passable, perhaps 900 or 1,000 words in each tongue, but his Vietnamese was good and there was probably no American here in IV Corps area who spoke the dialect of the Meo mercenaries better.

If Captain D. O. Garrison of the U.S. Army Special Forces had any *special* specialty, it was the art of ambush. While his talents at shooting snipers out of trees with M-74 grenade launchers and leading Long Range Reconnaissance Patrols into "denied territory" had won him a certain respect, if not fame, it was his unique skill at setting up ambushes that his superiors prized most. It had no commercial value. It wouldn't get him a job with I.B.M. or Ford or Trans World Airlines and it didn't qualify him for a post on the remedial reading staff of the Department of Health, Education and Welfare, but it was useful here—at this place and at this time.

That was why Garrison was sweating and peering and waiting in the jungle with two U.S. sergeants and a dozen Meo tribesmen—at this place and at this time. He had set this ambush, and if the intelligence reports were correct a supply column of the 119th North Vietnamese Division would walk into it sometime within the next three hours. It ought to work: the Claymores were properly spaced, the automatic weapons correctly located, and the ambush team tough and experienced. The Meo were amiable, ruthless warriors whose hatred for the Northerners went back many centuries, perhaps 300 years—or maybe 1,300—when some women had been raped or some nameless village looted by a raiding party of one side or the other. Nobody remembered how it had started. Nobody cared. The arrogantly civilized French had stopped the fighting for a little while—forty or fifty years—but now the French had gone, and armed Meo were waiting in jungle ambush once again. As for the American sergeants—the big Apache from Arizona whom everyone called Chief and the baby-faced Georgian known as Junior—they were Special Forces professionals who'd fought beside Garrison in a score of previous ambushes.

The men, the weapons, the place, and the plan were right.

It ought to work.

Even when it worked very well, Garrison brooded in the miasmic heat, there were always some casualties in the ambush team. There was always some brave or stubborn or panicky son-of-a-bitch among the foe who squeezed off a lucky burst from his AK-47 or tossed one wild grenade into just the wrong place, just the wrong patch of darkness. The enemy would fight. Even though they were using more young and inexperienced soldiers these days, Garrison knew that the North Vietnamese didn't usually cave in under attack, and he soberly expected them to fight back. That and the casualties on both sides were fairly certain.

The stifling heat and the implacable insects, the snakes and the thirsty three-inch leeches didn't bother him nearly as much as the question of who would catch it tonight, and as Garrison realized this he knew that it was time for him to go home. With his coveralls soaked in perspiration and his tired gray eyes hurting from the hours of squinting into the darkness, he silently celebrated the fact that his tour would be over in twenty-nine days.

No, twenty-eight.

Then he saw the first man turn the corner of the winding trail. Garrison didn't hear anything; the "point man"—like the soldiers who would follow him—was small and light and wore rubber soled sneakers. The scout trotted ten steps down the earthen path, paused to listen and sniff. His eyes swept the tangle of rain forest on both sides, searching for some glint of metal or gleam of teeth that might signal an ambush.

The point man loped on, Garrison exhaled and raised his rapid-fire M-16. The rest of the column would be coming along in a minute or two, first a few more scouts and then, 100 or 150 yards behind, the main force. The Claymores had been placed ninety yards apart, and the sergeants would detonate them when the bulk of the foe was between the mines. The signal would be the tall, tense captain's first burst of fire.

There they were.

To some people, they were nationalists who'd been fighting to free their country from foreign oppressors for more than a quarter of a century.

To others, they were Communist fanatics spearheading a Red thrust to conquer all of Southeast Asia.

To Garrison, they were simply the enemy—dangerous men who'd hurt or kill him if he didn't hurt or kill them first, during the next twenty-eight days.

It was difficult to estimate how many there were in this column, to decide when to fire his M-16 so as to secure the maximum "casualty effect" of the Claymores. If the captain shot either too soon or too late, most of the 2,800 steel balls would fly harmlessly into the lush green walls of the U-Minh Forest and the ambush would fail and the much larger enemy force would fan out swiftly through the jungle to seek violent vengeance. There was no sure way to determine the size of this detachment in time, so he considered, guessed, sighted his weapon on the eighteenth man in the line, and squeezed the trigger.

The Claymores answered immediately, their blasts half-covering the first bursts of the Meo.

Screams.

Shouts.

Cries of pain, curses, and the familiar staccato sound of AK-47 assault rifles.

The enemy was shooting back, tossing grenades into the darkness.

Who's going to get it tonight, Garrison wondered as he finished his clip and deftly reloaded.

At that moment, one of the enemy soldiers who had already passed by raced back and spotted the American captain in the underbrush. It must have been the sound of Garrison's weapon, for the M-16 was equipped with a flash suppressor, or perhaps it was just luck. In any case, the son-of-a-bitch threw a grenade into just the wrong place.

Suddenly Garrison knew which of the ambushers was going to get it.

He knew it for two or three seconds.

Then everything went black.

2

Black.

There was no light, not a sliver, and for a moment Garrison thought he was still in the dark midnight of the dense U-Minh Forest where centuries of tangled vegetation and towering trees conspired to blot out the sun. Then he felt the vibration and heard the noise of the motor, a loud sound that seemed to come from all sides. Now he was swaying, or rather the thing on which he was lying was swaying, and then there was an impact, a bump. He felt it, but he couldn't see anything in the moonless night.

The engine noise sounded a bit different, almost as loud but there was a rhythmic whoosh-whoosh-whoosh of metal cutting through the hot air. "Chopper," his mind registered automatically. He started to sit up to see, but he didn't move at all. He couldn't. A moment later, he discovered that he couldn't talk either.

"Easy, handle him gently," a nearby voice shouted over the helicopter noise.

Somebody was lifting him up, but not by his arms or legs.

He was on his back, in a litter.

"Jeezus Christ, what the hell hit him?" another voice asked from somewhere near his feet.

"Grenade. . . . Watch it. Watch the door, you dumb bastard. . . . Easy. . . . Okay."

They were walking, and he could feel the warmth of the morning sun.

"Not much face left," commented one of the corpsmen as they slid the litter into the open rear of the waiting ambulance.

"That's the least of his problems. He's lost a lot of blood. I think he's had it."

Blind.

Mute.

Disfigured.

Paralyzed.

Probably dying, or perhaps doomed to spend the rest of his life as a hopeless, helpless cripple in a bed in a Veterans Administration hospital—isolated, impotent, forgotten, drifting toward madness in the nightmare of solitary confinement in a ruined body that was now a prison.

Captain David O. Garrison fought against the billowing fear and fury for several seconds before he slipped back into unconsciousness. Eighteen minutes later, he was lying on a table in a large well-equipped field hospital and whole blood was dripping into his left arm. A nurse was taking his blood pressure, showing no emotion at the devastation of his face. She'd seen many ravaged faces, some worse than this. They weren't so bad, if you didn't think of them as faces but just as wounds.

"More blood," the doctor said in the soft tones of Puerto Rico, "and then get him to X-ray, fast. He may be going into shock, dammit. I'll want those X-rays right away. I've put in a call for Major Brodsky, and he'll want to look at them too."

It was going to be very close.

3

Garrison didn't die.

The surgeon arrived in time and he performed a brilliant operation, and when the Special Forces captain came to the next morning he could talk and he could move and he could see out of one eye. The other eye and the rest of his face were covered with bandages, a knight's helmet of sterile white fabric pierced only by slits through which he could peer, breathe, and ingest. "Ingest" was the term the doctors and nurses used for eat and drink, and it amused Garrison that the medical people should have their own jargon that was just as stilted as those of the infantry or the fly boys or even the C.I.A. "spooks."

Nothing else amused David O. Garrison very much. He still hurt in many places and he'd be bedridden for at least a month and he had only half a face left.

"You'll be on a Med-Evac flight back to Travis in about four weeks, as soon as Major Brodsky says you're well enough to fly," announced Captain A. R. Diaz, "and then they'll fix your face in the States."

"Who the hell is Brodsky?"

Diaz shook his head.

"For you, Brodsky is God. Just remember that, he's God. He

saved you, gave you your life back and your body back—everything. He's the man with the magic hands, the surgeon who took those fragments out of your brain. Another great victory for Brodsky in his private war!"

"What war?"

"Brodsky is at war with war," Diaz explained. "He's crazy. He wants to kill death, with a scalpel. Every time he saves somebody, that's one for Brodsky. He's keeping score, you know. It's a personal feud, Bruce G. Brodsky versus the Grim Reaper."

"Who's winning?"

"Hard to say," confessed the pudgy doctor. "Brodsky's not doing *too* badly, considering that his opposition has the entire armed forces of the United States, South Vietnam, North Vietnam, and the Viet Cong as allies. I wouldn't say that Brodsky's winning, but he's holding his own. Anyway, that's *his* war. *Your* war is over. I hear some general's coming by next week to give you a Silver Star and a couple of Hershey bars, and then in a couple more weeks you're heading Stateside to get a shiny new face."

Garrison grunted, thought briefly of Stockbridge, Mass., sighed and indulged in the luxury of permitting himself to slide off into a deep, deep sleep. He hadn't slept that long or that well in a long time, and it felt so good that he did it again most of the next day. It may have been exhaustion or shock or simply his body taking charge, but he averaged fifteen hours of sleep per day during the following week. He got his Silver Star, and twenty days later—three days after he was pronounced fit to walk—he boarded a large U.S. Air Force medical evacuation jet that carried him and fifty-one other patients eastward across the Pacific to Travis Air Force Base near San Francisco.

He was still wearing the bandages around his head when he stepped out of another plane at Andrews Air Force Base outside Washington, D.C., and when four days later the senior plastic surgeon at Walter Reed let him look at his face, Garrison knew why: about a third of his face was ruined. He had his eyes and his ears and his nose, but he'd been so scarred that only a mother could love a face such as that, and his mother was dead.

"We can fix it, Captain," assured the plastic surgeon.

There was no point in crying about it, none at all.

"I've seen worse," Garrison replied truthfully.

"But not much? That's what you're thinking, isn't it?"

"No, not much," Garrison admitted slowly to the balding, neatly-mustachioed colonel in the white hospital jacket. "Of course, I wasn't any movie star to begin with—just an ordinary looking man with dark brown hair and regular features. I seem to recall that my mother used to say that my best feature was my teeth, which isn't saying too much."

Colonel M. L. Parker flashed that warm man-to-man smile he had used for the previous six years to encourage so many seriously disfigured men.

"Don't worry about your face," he advised confidently. "We've had a lot of experience with this sort of thing, you know, and we can make it just as good as new if you'll supply a decent photograph."

He hadn't heard the door open behind him, didn't see the woman enter.

"Or even an indecent one," Parker added with a wink.

The brunette woman with the large green eyes framed in gold-rimmed glasses shrugged, and Garrison guessed that this was one of Parker's standard jokes that she'd endured hundreds of times. The white jacket she wore signalled "doctor," but the striped tan skirt that ended three inches above her knees was plainly unmilitary, so the captain concluded that she was a civilian physician on the Walter Reed staff.

"Good morning, Colonel," she said to announce her presence.

She was quite pretty and, if Garrison judged her speech correctly, from North Carolina or perhaps Virginia.

"Good morning, Doctor," Parker answered heartily as he turned to greet her. "Captain Garrison, this is Doctor Clement, one of the most charming and capable members of the plastic surgery staff."

The sudden gleam in her cool eyes seemed to show disdain for this perfunctory flattery.

"How are you feeling, Captain?" she asked.

Right to the point, and that was a refreshing change.

None of that "How do you do" or "Nice to meet you" or "I've heard a lot about you, Captain"—the mumbled amenities to which most people devote so much of their lives. All she really had in mind was to find out how this patient was feeling, and she said so straight out.

"I'm all right."

He watched her eyes to see whether she'd flinch at the sight of his face. He was reasonably confident that she wouldn't, and he was right. He studied her for a moment, estimated that she might be thirty-one or maybe thirty-four. It didn't matter. What she really was was a lady doctor, with the emphasis very obviously on doctor. As a matter of fact, she probably wasn't a lady at all.

"Have you seen the medical report that came in with the captain from Vietnam?" asked the colonel.

He'd never simply say "Nam," only enlisted men did that.

The woman nodded.

"Grenade, bad. Multiple fragments in face and brain. He's one of Brodsky's boys," she said briskly.

Parker saw the reaction on what was left of Garrison's face, and misinterpreted it.

"That's just an expression we use here, Captain. You had a very fine brain surgeon work on you at that field hospital out there, a Major Brodsky who's made quite a reputation. Quite able for such a comparatively young man."

"The best," said the woman as she approached the head of the bed.

Now she studied his face with no sign of motherly compassion.

"Are you just sight-seeing?" Garrison asked, "or are you going to work on me?"

"Dr. Clement will be part of the surgical team, a very important part. In her field," Parker added, "she's almost as good as Major Brodsky."

"Not really," she corrected in matter of fact tones, "but you could do worse."

For a few seconds, Garrison found himself liking her and starting to dislike this legendary Brodsky. Then he decided that he probably didn't like either of them and that he certainly didn't owe them anything. They were only doing their jobs, just as he'd been doing his with some distinction for so many years. In the world of jungle warfare and guerrilla fighting—in Saigon and the Pentagon and the Special Forces headquarters at Fort Bragg—there were important men who recognized and respected the name of David O. Garrison. He was entitled to good medical care.

While he reflected on these matters, the two surgeons spoke in their private medical language about what might be done to and with his face. Parker seemed to take seriously what the woman said, and the colonel, despite his initial flattery toward her, plainly wasn't the sort to do this out of mere chivalry. For all his smooth bedside manner and diplomatic skills—the skills needed to run a whole staff section in any Army outfit, even a medical one—Parker had to be a competent doctor. Maybe he wasn't a goddam genius like that goddam Brodsky, but he knew what he was doing, or at least what ought to be done. Walter Reed Hospital was no meat market; it was supposed to be the best that the U.S. Army had.

"How long is it going to take?" Garrison interrupted suddenly.

The surgeons exchanged glances.

"What do you think, Doctor?" the colonel said warily. "Two or three?"

"Months?" wondered the man seated on the bed.

The woman shook her head.

"Operations. Maybe we can do it in two. It depends in part on how quickly you heal."

"I'm a great healer. How long will it take?"

They looked at his face, then at each other again.

"Five months, maybe six or seven," she said.

"Yes, yes," agreed the colonel. "If it's only two operations and you heal well and everything proceeds normally, I imagine that you'd be in fairly good shape in six or seven months. Perhaps eight, to be on the safe side."

Colonels always like to be on the safe side. They are almost as cautious as generals.

"Okay, say eight. In eight months, I ought to look human enough so I won't scare any children, right?"

"Yes, although the final healing could take a bit longer. I'd expect that you'd be out of bandages and able to circulate freely outside the hospital in eight months," Dr. Clement said.

"It used to take a lot longer," Parker contributed cheerfully. "Before we improved our techniques it would have taken two or three times as long. Army medicine has come a long way since we started large-scale combat operations in Vietnam."

The woman shrugged, and Garrison sensed that she wasn't at all sure that this progress was worth the price.

"What about the photo?" she asked.

"I was just raising that with the captain when you arrived. Can you supply us with a decent picture, Captain?"

"Suppose I don't want to look the way I used to? Could I have a different face?"

"What for?" she questioned.

"That's my business. Maybe I'm going to be a whole new man, and I want a new face that will suit the new Garrison. I don't know. But if I did want a new face, could I have it?"

Colonel Parker swallowed twice, recovered and flashed his affable manly grin.

"Why not? No extra charge. Nothing's too good for a man with your battle record, Captain."

"Is Captain Garrison a *hero*?"

It was difficult to tell whether she was impressed or sneering.

"Four Purple Hearts, two Silver Stars, and a Distinguished Service Cross," Parker replied.

Garrison decided that he didn't like him either.

"Well, then, I guess Captain Garrison can have just about anything he pleases," the woman replied. "Any face within my modest talents, that is. What did you have in mind, Captain? Something on the order of Gregory Peck or perhaps Peter Fonda, or would you prefer our sincere, boyish John Kennedy model? How about Peter O'Toole, worldly but innocent at the same time?"

Something was going wrong, and Colonel Parker couldn't understand why.

"I'll let you know," Garrison told her evenly. "There's no big rush, is there?"

"Not at all. Not at all," soothed the colonel as he reached out to nudge Dr. Clement—first name unknown—toward the door. "Just take your time, and let us know whenever you're ready."

"We could send up a few of those movie-and-TV fan magazines to give you an idea of what's available," she offered with a girlish sweetness that was just about one millionth of an inch thick.

The man on the bed considered this, wondered why she was reacting this way and whether *she* was available. Yes, the odd ones often were—if you could take everything else that went with it.

"Thanks, Doctor," he answered pleasantly, "but I think I ought to tell you that I don't always settle for what's *available*. I try to get what I really *want*. I only mention this because I know how important it is for a truely up-to-date surgeon, especially a plastic surgeon, to understand the patient and have a real psychological rapport."

She replied with a glance that could fell trees.

"Of course, of course," Parker broke in and quickly guided her out into the wide corridor.

"Dr. Clement, I don't understand what that was all about," confessed the distressed colonel.

"That's right."

"What's right?"

"You don't understand," she said.

"Well, could you explain it?"

She nodded.

"Well?"

"I could, Colonel, but I'd rather not. Let's just say that I'm being a bit emotional because it's the wrong time of the month—the lunar thing."

Parker sighed in paternal comprehension.

"Of course. I didn't realize that you were having your . . . that it was that time of the month."

"It isn't," she replied in tones that were barely civil, something quite unusual for Dr. Clement, and then she did something almost as strange. She gestured to a young Filipino intern, from whom she borrowed a cigarette. She'd stopped smoking eleven months earlier.

"Dr. Clement . . . Elizabeth, is something wrong?" the senior plastic surgeon tried again. He hated this sort of thing—this edgy human thing—especially with women. He was clumsy with women. "You've been with us for two and a half years now, and I've never seen anything like this. If there's something about this case or the patient that bothers you . . ."

She took a second deep drag on the cigarette, and her face relaxed.

"No problem, Colonel. I didn't sleep too well last night, and I guess I'm a bit irritable. I'll get ten hours tonight, and everything will be fine."

"If you'd rather not handle this case . . ."

"Just another case, just another patient," she said before she shifted the conversation to the black platoon sergeant on whom they'd be operating that afternoon. He was in much worse condition than Garrison, having been badly burned when an enemy rocket hit the fuel tank of the Armored Personnel Carrier in which he'd been riding. Four of the other soldiers in that A.P.C. were dead, but that wasn't what the two healers discussed. They talked about two new ears and half a jaw for the sergeant who'd survived. Dr. Elizabeth Clement was her usual sensible, lucid self as she analyzed the problems, and Colonel Parker felt a lot better by the time he left her shortly before noon.

The operation went quite well, exceedingly well.

The entire surgical team was pleased with the results.

Despite this, Dr. Clement slept badly again that night—for no apparent reason. She couldn't blame it on the old nightmares, for they didn't show up, but she couldn't sleep either.

4

Garrison slept ten hours that night, and he was in good spirits when a beaming blonde nurse brought him breakfast. The food at Walter Reed wasn't bad at all, certainly better than the rations he'd tolerated in Vietnam, and the shapely nurse evoked all sorts of pleasant carnal memories because she looked a lot like a passionate Welsh girl who'd been reporting the war out of Saigon for a London daily. The man in the bed noted that superior American orthodentistry had given the nurse better teeth, but he decided that she was probably inferior to the spirited journalist in other *important* ways.

After his second cup of coffee, two doctors came in to examine his face and change the dressings. Colonel Parker didn't appear and neither did the brunette Dr. Clement of the gold-framed glasses. He read the *Washington Post* and a three-week-old copy of *Sports Illustrated*, and then he wondered about the ambush in the U-Minh Forest. Had it been successful? There was no one to ask here, and far away in IV Corps area nobody cared anymore. There must have been a score or more ambushes since that night and there'd be an infinite number of others, he reflected as he got up to go to the toilet.

And not one of them *really* mattered—not *that* much.

They were routine and sound from a tactical point of view, of course, and that was why every military organization of every political persuasion in every part of the world did this sort of thing, but the ambushes probably didn't matter *that* much. They annoyed the other side, and they made work for people such as that bastard Brodsky.

"Latrine philosophy," Garrison said contemptuously to his empty room as he returned from the toilet.

He hadn't really thought it all out, and he knew it. He'd never had any patience for this kind of cheap cliché profundity when he'd heard it in a hundred locker rooms and bars and officers' clubs, and it didn't sound any better when he indulged in it himself. Even the thought that he might well be right in his judgements—right by some lucky flash of insight or inspiration—didn't justify it, Garrison thought as he sat down on the edge of the bed. To a man such as David O. Garrison who'd long ago set rather high standards for himself, this sort of thing was a sign of weakness.

"Next thing I'll be feeling sorry for myself," he brooded aloud as he stared out the window.

"Not you, Captain."

She'd done it again—like a cat.

The brunette in the white jacket—Clement—had entered his room unnoticed.

"You're not the sort to feel sorry for yourself. I'd bet you're not."

There was no edge, no malice in her voice now.

"It's nice of you to come by," he answered cautiously.

"I wanted to see how you were."

She wasn't going to say anything about what had happened yesterday or his new face. She was trying to make peace in her own way, or was it just that she regretted her lapse from the approved professional behavior? Whichever it was, she had an interesting, although tentative, smile.

"I'm all right, Doctor. Adjusting nicely, as they say."

"Good. Of course, career officers usually do. You're a professional, aren't you, Captain?"

She had an excellent figure. He hadn't noticed it the previous day.

"Well, I'm finishing my second hitch in another nine months," he answered noncommittally.

Her face looked tired.

"Say, Doctor, there's one question that I'd like to ask you. It isn't about me. It's about Brodsky."

"Dr. Brodsky? What about him?"

Garrison nodded.

"Exactly. What about him? What do you know about him?"

Now the pretty face narrowed in puzzlement.

"Brodsky? I don't know anything about him. He's a splendid brain surgeon who's been in Vietnam for something like three years. Harvard and Peter Bent Brigham, I think. . . . That's a hospital in Boston," she explained.

"I know that. I'm from Massachusetts. But what about Brodsky—as a person?"

She considered this for several seconds.

"I never thought of him as a person, Captain—just as a surgeon. I think his first name is Bruce. Yes, Bruce Brodsky. He's a . . . a major, as I recall. He might be a lieutenant-colonel by now."

"Where's he from? What does he look like? Does he have a family?"

"I have no idea. I suppose that everyone has a family. Brodsky? No, we never talk about him—just his patients and his skills. Why do you ask?"

Garrison would have told her if he knew, but he didn't.

"Just curious. People keep telling me that he saved my life, so I'm curious about him. I never saw him, you know—not once."

The man seated on the bed seemed to be complaining.

"I'd imagine that he's very busy," she apologized without any idea as to why she should have to defend Brodsky. Brodsky hadn't done anything wrong. Suddenly she felt weary and wanted to yawn, but she fought back the impulse. She looked into the gray eyes of the man who'd been asking about Brodsky, and wondered what sort of a person this Garrison was. The thought rather startled her, for she rarely if ever speculated about the patients. It wouldn't be wise to get involved.

She broke loose by glancing at her wristwatch.

"I'm afraid that I've got a staff meeting," she lied.

"You'll let me know if you hear anything about Brodsky, won't you?"

She promised that she would and left, unaware that Garrison was as conscious as she was of how odd his compulsive curiosity about the brain surgeon was. Two days later—it was a Wednesday—the Special Forces captain called Colonel Parker and showed him a photo of a Dutch missionary in a *Life* magazine report on Africa. The man had a strong, open face, attractive but certainly not theatrical. Parker promised that this model would be followed "so far as possible." The first operation was scheduled for the following Friday. On the day before it took place, Garrison's father and his older brother came down from Massachusetts to see him. It was a warm family visit that lasted two hours and all three of them enjoyed it, but when they departed the captain wasn't that sorry to see them go. It wasn't that he didn't care for them, but his mind was on the operation.

The plastic surgery was a success.

Colonel Parker told him so the following morning.

"You're coming along fine, just fine," he guaranteed jovially.

"Thanks to you and Dr. Clement and Brodsky," Garrison said through the new slitted hood of bandages.

"Thanks to all of Army medicine," the colonel replied modestly.

"Of course, and I'm grateful. By the way, how is Dr. Brodsky these days?"

Parker blinked at the unexpected question.

"I don't know. All right, I guess. We keep getting his patients every week or two, so I guess the old boy's still in business," the senior surgeon chuckled.

"How old?"

"I'm not sure—under forty, I think. He's a brain man, you know, and that's not my field. I know the plastic surgeons, but the brain men are another crowd altogether."

"Does he ever come through here?" Garrison probed.

Suddenly the colonel recalled what Dr. Clement had reported about the Special Forces captain's unusual interest in Brodsky, and he silently decided to talk it over with one of the psychiatrists. Probably nothing to it, but it would be safer to let one of them look into it.

"I don't recall Dr. Brodsky visiting Walter Reed," Parker said truthfully. "Well, you get your rest, Captain, and do some of that good healing that you promised us. As the big fellow used to say in that television commercial, leave the driving to us."

There was nothing you could reply to an inanity such as that, so Garrison simply gestured vague compliance and hoped that the colonel would go away. He did, and the man with the flawed face retreated into the privacy of his bandages. He had his own world inside this shield that hid his thoughts and looks and facial expressions from everyone else, a place where no one could intrude or judge. It was almost like some child's dream of his own secret cave or sanctuary where the grown-ups would never find him, a wonderful change after the many years of communal living in the organized herd—the military mass. They were taking good care of him in this hospital; they owed him that, of course, and he didn't have to think about anything except what he wanted to. He didn't have to worry about getting his clothes cleaned or securing ammunition or taking care of his men. Other people were taking care of him in this clean, safe place, and as he enjoyed that snug recognition he recalled what it had been like when they'd taken out his tonsils when he was nine. This was better, for he had a private room now.

He wasn't the least bit worried about his face—now.

The visceral uncertainties would probably return many times at random intervals and they would tighten and trouble him as they had a thousand times since he'd come to in that helicopter, but the intervals would be greater and the knotted stomach muscles less painful. Unless everyone here was lying to him with a greater skill than usual, he would emerge from Walter Reed as something other than a horror, and he'd be able to resume a normal life.

What normal life? More of the familiar Special Forces world, or perhaps something else? Now he had time to think about it all, and, equally important, the inclination to do so. He could consider alternatives; there were alternatives. No one had pushed him into the all-volunteer Special Forces, and he had enjoyed the challenge and pride of this elite force in which he'd earned respect and reputation. He'd be a major in another seventeen months, a bird colonel by the time he was forty-two. He might have his own battalion to command or, if he stayed in Special Forces, his own Group. It was a logical and attractive future with job security, even if he chose to switch to some other branch of the Army.

As he thought about it, he found himself wondering when the woman with the good body and the gold-rimmed glasses would return. This was the weekend, so if not today probably not until Monday. He had plenty of time to think about her too. Six, no, seven weeks since he'd been with any woman, he realized, and he knew that he'd be thinking about this pretty, puzzling Dr. Clement in the days ahead.

She didn't come on Monday either, but a pipe-sucking, bushy-browed Dr. Bettinger showed up at four o'clock. "Just in time for some coffee," Bettinger had said—among other things. He was an amiable, garrulous man, *deliberately* garrulous, Garrison reckoned as they sipped coffee and "chatted" about "how things are going." This Bettinger had the air of a purposeful "chatter" and an experienced one, so it hardly surprised the wounded man when he finally got around to noting *casually* that Garrison was one of Brodsky's boys.

So that was it.

"That's right," Garrison replied just as *casually*, "but I was an Eagle Scout before that."

Bettinger laughed, not too badly.

"I hear he's one helluva surgeon, Captain," he continued as he relit his briar, "and he may have been an Eagle Scout himself."

"I don't know, don't know anything about him. I was sort of curious about him for a while, but now I've got other things on my mind."

"Yes?"

"You know, Doctor. The next operation, when I'll get out, when I'll get back to my outfit, when I'll get laid. The important things," Garrison fenced as he intermittently sucked his coffee through a straw that easily fit the mouth slit in the bandages.

Then Garrison moved the conversation on to all sorts of safe normal things such as the prospects of the Boston Red Sox, his favorite baseball team, the figures and personalities of some of the nurses, and the comforts that television afforded a hospital patient. Bettinger made one more delicate reference to the brain surgeon ten minutes later, but when Garrison showed no interest in pursuing the subject the conversation began to ebb and at 4:35 the "chatterer" knocked out the last embers from his pipe bowl and left.

She arrived on Tuesday, her face lovely but a trifle thinner.

"On a diet, Doctor?"

"Not by intention. My appetite's been dozing for the past week or two. Does it show?"

The white-wreathed head nodded.

"No harm though," Garrison assured her. "No, you're still a very attractive plastic surgeon, the most attractive I've ever seen. If I end up looking half as good I'll be more than satisfied."

Flirting.

Just the usual male flirting, she judged with relief.

She could handle that all right.

"You'll look fine, Captain. With a little luck, you'll look almost exactly like that picture of the missionary."

"You like that face, Doctor?"

She hesitated.

"Yes."

"But you didn't think I was the missionary type, did you?" he reproved. "My uncle—my mother's brother—was a missionary in Africa for almost twenty years, you know. He's a bishop in Boston now, a real spiritual tiger and full of compassion for his fellow humans."

"So *that's* where you get it from, Captain."

He was pleased to find that she had a sense of humor and he laughed. It sounded odd through the bandages, to him at least.

"A neat turn of phrase, Doctor. You're almost as witty as that clever clown who was in to chat with me yesterday, Bettinger. Do you know Dr. Bettinger?"

"Steve Bettinger? Smokes a pipe? Sure."

"He's a shrink, isn't he?" Garrison accused coldly.

"Yes," she answered without delay.

The gray eyes glared at her through the slits.

"What the hell did you send him in to see me for?"

She shook her head, lit a cigarette. She'd been smoking a good deal in recent days.

"No, I didn't send him in. . . . He's quite a competent psychiatrist, you know."

"Screw him. I don't need any psychiatrists. Do *you* think that I need a psychiatrist, Dr. Clement?"

She shook her head again.

"No, I don't see that you do. As you yourself said, you're adjusting fairly well. . . . I don't know if you need *anyone*," she finished sharply.

"Not right now, I don't, but I will later. That's because I'm a healthy normal American boy who likes people, not crowds but people. Yes, I'll need people later—perhaps soon."

"I can't tell from your voice whether that's a threat or a promise, Captain."

"Both, I'm sorry to say. It's the human condition, isn't it?"

The eyes framed in white looked serious, almost sad, now.

"Probably," she evaded. "I wouldn't know. I'm only a surgeon."

"Yes," he chuckled, "but you're a people too."

"Like Brodsky?"

She regretted the provocation the moment that she'd uttered it, but the masked man was bothering her. Even so, it was a stupid thing to say.

"Yes, just like Brodsky. Exactly like Brodsky."

"Look, this isn't my business. This is all between you and Brodsky," she blurted. "Or you and Colonel Parker. It was probably Parker who sent Bettinger in to see you, but don't tell him I said so. He might not like that."

"I won't tell him, Doctor. I wouldn't want to get you into any trouble."

The whole dialogue, all the conversations with Garrison, didn't exactly make sense to her. Garrison seemed simple and straightforward enough, but the talk was never simple. It was always allusive, with unspoken references and irritating implications. It didn't get any better during the next four months, and five weeks after the second operation she said so—quite bluntly. It was a few days after the bandages were finally removed and they both saw his new face. There were still several scars and raw plaçes to heal, but he was already. a handsome man.

"You've done an excellent job, Doctor," he complimented as he studied himself in the mirror.

"I'm glad you're satisfied."

"But you're not, Doctor Clement, is that it?"

She shook her head.

"With the surgery, yes. But there's something else. You've been fencing with me from the first time we met, and I don't like it."

"How long will it be before I can go outside?" he parried.

"Seven weeks, maybe less. But that's not what I'm talking about, Garrison. Just what is it you've been trying to say to me, and why are you being so clever about it? You've got no reason to needle me, and I wish you'd stop it. Playing word games is Bettinger's routine, not mine. I'm not equipped for it. I wasn't trained for it."

"I didn't mean to bother you, Doctor," he answered.

"And stop that silly 'Doctor' routine. You make it sound like an insult. What is it, Garrison, have you got something against female physicians?"

"You mean am I a Male Chauvinist Pig?"

"I mean what the hell do you want from me, Garrison?"

He thought about that for several seconds.

"What are you offering, Doctor?"

She started for the door, stopped.

"Let's get one thing straight, Captain. I never . . . repeat, *never* . . . sleep with patients."

He nodded, smiled his new smile gently.

"That's too bad, Doctor, because I'd bet you're terrific in the sack."

"Screw you, Garrison," she answered and slammed the door behind her.

It was three weeks before he saw her again.

Two weeks after that he took her out to dinner, and then to her apartment.

He discovered that her first name was Elizabeth, that she was thirty-two years old, a former resident of Durham, North Carolina, and a widow whose doctor-husband had been killed in a 1969 plane crash in Vietnam.

He also discovered that she was a people.
Very much a people.
And a wonder.

5

It is really amazing how efficiently human beings—even inefficient human beings—can ignore what they don't want to notice. Mosquitoes, Siamese cats, bald eagles, or porpoises couldn't possibly do it, perhaps because they're lower on the evolutionary ladder. Human beings can perform this difficult trick quite easily and in a variety of ways, and it comes in very handy for ignoring air pollution or *de facto* school segregation or the breach of a politician's campaign promise or the shocking infant mortality rate among the Indians. The method used at Walter Reed Hospital, an official U.S. Army medical facility that operates more rationally than the Alabama State Police, the British Labour Party or the Egyptian cabinet, is not to acknowledge things *officially*. This doesn't work with multiple cancers or bleeding gunshot wounds, but it can cope with lesser human problems. So *officially*, nobody at Walter Reed acknowledged that Dr. Elizabeth Clement and Captain David O. Garrison were involved in some sort of emotional or sexual relationship.

Dozens of people saw them leave the hospital together in the afternoon or early evening and many people saw them return in her 1969 Volvo in the morning, many mornings. People noticed that she didn't seem nearly as sober and inevitably sensible anymore either, much warmer and brighter and cheerier in some deep contented way. It was as if her center of gravity had been lowered from her head down into her hips and abdomen; she even walked differently.

She spoke more slowly and tolerantly, spent more time talking to the patients and even hummed to herself as she moved gracefully—*so* gracefully—through the corridors.

"Just proves you can't beat sex for straightening people out," joked a lieutenant-colonel on the orthopedics staff.

"I wouldn't know. I never tried," said Dr. Bettinger.

Colonel Parker didn't say anything, because, *officially*, he didn't know anything. Even if he did, there weren't any specific written rules against romantic attachments developing between doctors and patients. Parker was the sort of man who still used tasteful phrases such as "romantic attachments," and he wasn't bad at budget conferences or planning meetings either. Oddly enough, he was also a better-than-average plastic surgeon and the fact that he'd married a general's daughter was only incidental to his rise in military medicine.

Day by day and night by night, the man with the new face and the new woman got to know each other and like each other better and better. They walked, they swam, they ate well and drank a lot of Danish beer and French wine; they talked and they laughed and they made love until they fell asleep exhausted. Sometimes she woke before dawn and reached out tenderly to touch the new face, and sometimes he felt her caress and his arms reached out to take her again and she melted. Sometimes she deliberately awoke and aroused him to meet her need, and when the tigerish passion subsided she slept with her head on his shoulder like a weary kitten.

Of course, there were certain things that she wasn't acknowledging either. She knew that Garrison was very happy with her and genuinely cared for her, it was more than just the wonderful sex, but what would happen when it was time for him to leave Walter Reed? That was the first thing. The second was something that he wasn't speaking about, something that he wasn't ready to share yet with anyone—not even her. She had no firm idea as to what it was, but it was there.

"It's Brodsky, isn't it?" she guessed one sunny morning as he turned the Volvo into the hospital parking area.

"Great day, isn't it?"

"It's Brodsky, you bastard, isn't it?" she pressed.

He sighed.

"Elizabeth Diana Evans Clement," he reproved, "where the hell do you come off using that kind of fucking language? What would your dear dad, the *chairman* of the Latin and Greek department at a great university, say if he heard that you were using words like 'bastard.' He'd be appalled. No properly raised Southern gentlewoman of good family speaks that way, Elizabeth."

"I never did until I started sleeping with you, you bastard. It *is* Brodsky, isn't it?"

"*What's* Brodsky?" he asked as he saw a red Impala convertible nose into the parking space he'd been eyeing.

"Mother," he muttered in casual hostility.

"Your language's worse than mine," she judged, "and don't try to change the subject. You know exactly what I'm talking about. You're still hung up on Brodsky, just because he saved your life."

"You saved my life too, in a different way, and I'm hung up on you too."

There, over between the Triumph and the blue Ford, was a space.

"It's not the same thing, you bastard. I want to know what this means. Living with one man is fine, but two—or one and a ghost—isn't. I want you to tell me the whole story."

He spun the wheel swiftly, cut off an insolent major in a yellow Dodge.

"You want everything, don't you?" Garrison asked.

"You're goddam right, I do. I'm giving everything, aren't I?"

He deftly slid the Volvo into the narrow parking place, and turned off the ignition.

"Not bad, huh? Pretty nifty, I'd say," he boasted.

"You drive as well as you make love, Garrison, but that doesn't answer my question."

She was right and she was lovely, and she was entitled to an honest reply.

"Okay, I'll try to put it simply. I don't like being in anyone's debt. I don't like being under obligation to anybody. I don't like to owe, and I owe Brodsky."

She tried to make sense out of this irrationality.

"*What* do you owe him?"

Garrison shrugged.

"Almost everything. My sight, my speech, my whole nervous system, my brain—even you. I owe it all to Brodsky, and I don't like that. I'm getting to dislike Brodsky too."

"My darling, my beloved," she began earnestly, "I love you, *there*, I said what women aren't supposed to say first because it scares men off and I don't want to scare you off because I need you the way I need arms and legs. I love you, Garrison, but I think you're losing your perspective. Maybe you ought to see genial pipe-smoking Steve Bettinger."

"I don't want to see Bettinger. I want to see Brodsky to settle this thing."

Then he reached over, tipped up her chin, and kissed her.

"I think I love you too, Elizabeth," he said slowly, "and that's something I never said before."

She beamed.

"Of course I never went out with a girl named Elizabeth before," he added.

"Bastard, bastard, bastard," she replied without rancor, for she sensed that he did love her.

"That's no way to talk," he advised as he opened the door of the car. "Ben Franklin recommended that a man should go out with older women because they're sexually experienced and grateful—and that doesn't sound very grateful to me."

He walked around, opened her door.

"You *are* a bastard, Garrison," she repeated, "but you're *my* bastard."

And it would all be perfect, or reasonably perfect, if they could get rid of the spectre of Major Bruce Brodsky. She thought of this, giggled.

"What's so funny?" the man with the new face asked as they walked toward the nearby main building.

"I've got to lay the ghost of Brodsky," she laughed. "It isn't enough that I'm laying Garrison, but I've got to lay Brodsky's ghost too."

Her lover shook his head.

"Now you didn't get *that* kind of dirty talk from me," he insisted.

"No, to tell you the truth I acquired that from a young man at the College of Physicians and Surgeons of Columbia University. I never used it before now."

"I prefer your genteel 'Flower of the Old South' number. You stick to that, and leave Brodsky to me."

At three o'clock the next afternoon, the Special Forces captain was returning to his room with two books he'd just borrowed from the library when he saw Elizabeth Clement and a tall graying man in the uniform of a major. He was tan and thin, and he strode with a grace that suggested he'd been an athlete—perhaps a basketball player. As they drew near, the man with the new face noticed that the stranger was wearing Medical Corps insignia. It was difficult to tell whether he was thirty-five or perhaps forty, but Garrison did know one thing about him.

This was Brodsky.

It had to be.

There was something about his manner that communicated authority and power and commitment, qualities sometimes found in the best of senior officers but somehow different in this man. There was something wary—yes, courteous but definitely *wary*—in the way that the woman related to him.

He had to be Brodsky.

"Captain Garrison," she said in her best professional voice, "I thought you'd want to know that there really is a Major Brodsky after all. Major Brodsky, may I introduce one of your former patients who's now one of *my* patients, Captain David Garrison?"

"Good to see you, Captain."

Mechanical. He didn't even remember.

"I'm better to see than I was when you had your last look at me, thanks to Dr. Clement. I don't suppose you recall that though. You've got so many patients."

Brodsky shook his head.

"I remember you quite well, Captain. Special Forces. Hit by a grenade in a night ambush. Fragments affecting sight, speech, and the central nervous system. Severe loss of blood and facial damage. You were on the verge of shock when they brought you in."

"Do you remember all your patients?" Garrison asked.

The brain surgeon nodded, and Garrison decided that he'd been right to dislike this son-of-a-bitch.

"Well, I'm glad to see you're coming along so nicely, Captain," announced the man whom Diaz had called God, and he reached out to shake hands in farewell.

"If you've got two minutes, Major, there's something important that I'd like to discuss with you."

"If it won't take too long. I'm just leaving Washington tonight on my way back to IV Corps, and I've several appointments here and in the Pentagon."

"Two minutes," Garrison assured and gestured toward the door of his room.

She wanted to stop him from whatever it was, whatever crazy thing he had in mind, but she'd learned enough about this man to know that her effort would be a waste of time. She excused herself on the pretext of a telephone call, watching them enter the room.

"Yes?" said the brain surgeon.

"They call us Brodsky's boys, and they say you're God."

"I'm flattered on both accounts, although neither is true. I'm a doctor, not a divinity. Of course, you knew that, Captain."

"Yes, I knew that."

"But that isn't what you wanted to talk to me about, is it?"

Garrison shook his head.

"No, it's about what I owe you," he announced.

"You don't owe me anything. There are no fees in the Army. I get a salary just like any other officer. You don't owe me a thing," Brodsky explained.

"I owe you all those things you fixed, and I mean to pay my debts."

Brodsky studied him curiously.

"A friendly thank-you would be more than enough, Captain."

"Not for me."

"You could buy me a drink sometime?"

"No."

Garrison was grimly serious.

"I can't think of anything else, certainly not money."

"I wasn't thinking of money, because money wouldn't pay for this sort of thing. No, I'd like to do something for you, something of an equal magnitude. You used your special skills to help me, and I'm offering my special skills to help you."

"I don't quite understand."

"If there's something important that you want done, something difficult that a man with my training can do but you can't, tell me. I'm not talking about killing your wife or anything like that, you understand."

Brodsky nodded thoughtfully.

"You do have a wife, don't you?"

"Yes, and two children—and a family problem of sorts," the surgeon answered. "Maybe you could help with it. Just what are your skills, other than the jungle and guerrilla warfare ones?"

"I'm a frogman, paratrooper, saboteur, radio man, medic—you name it."

Brodsky digested all this.

"Any language skills?"

"German, Russian, Vietnamese, and the Meo dialect."

Something was happening somewhere in the back of the surgeon's deep brown eyes.

"Maybe. I don't know. Maybe you're the man. I'll have to talk to somebody else about it, Captain. It might be dangerous. It's rather private, and *unconventional*."

"Unconventional warfare is my profession, Major."

Brodsky looked at him in unconcealed evaluation.

"No, I'm not crazy," Garrison responded to the unspoken question. "A bit odd and a bit driven, but far from crazy. I'm just an old-fashioned Yankee who likes to pay his debts."

"And you keep your promises?"

"That's the way I was raised."

Brodsky smiled for the first time.

"Yes, you and the old man ought to get along fine," he predicted. "He's like you in a number of ways—a bit odd, a bit driven, pays his debts, and keeps his promises. And he plays a helluva game of pinochle. That's a card game not many people play anymore."

"Never heard of it."

"Maybe he'll teach it to you," the surgeon speculated. "Well, I appreciate your gratitude, Captain, and I'll be in touch with you soon. Within forty-eight hours, I'd imagine."

The two men shook hands, and Major Brodsky turned to go.

"Did you ever play basketball, Major?" Garrison asked.

The surgeon smiled again.

"Yes, I did. At college."

"Were you any good?"

Brodsky nodded.

"I wasn't bad at all. Considering that I was only six feet two, I was pretty damned good. I was All Ivy League my senior year. . . . You play basketball?"

"No, I fenced."

"Any good?"

Now Garrison smiled.

"Intercollegiate saber champion my senior year."

It really wasn't surprising, Brodsky decided. It fit.

"Give me a call if you ever come by IV Corps area again," the surgeon invited. "Come by and you can buy me that drink."

"You expect to be out there for a while, Major?"

"As long as they'll let me. I'm a bit driven myself."

After Brodsky had gone, the woman entered and looked expectantly at Garrison.

"Thanks, Elizabeth. How did you find him?"

"I saw a notice up that he was giving a lecture on combat surgery. What did you talk about?"

Garrison considered, yawned.

"My gratitude, some old man who plays a card game called pinochle, his years as a basketball player, and the fact that I was intercollegiate saber champ."

"I didn't know that," she accused. "Is it true, Garrison?"

"Scout's honor."

Even if he wasn't lying, she decided, he probably wasn't telling the whole truth.

"What old man?"

"Major Brodsky didn't say."

"What else?"

Garrison paused to phrase his reply.

"I told him how I wanted to repay him and he asked what did I have in mind and I told him how terrific you are in the sack. I offered him my most precious possession—your fabulous body."

"You know you really are a bastard, and you know I don't believe that for one minute."

He sighed in mock melodrama.

"I'm sorry to say that he wasn't interested, Elizabeth. Nothing *personal*, you understand."

"You're crazy, and I shouldn't have done it. It was a mistake to bring him to meet you," she lamented. "God knows what the hell you said to him. I should never have done it. I thought that it might help, but I've probably made things worse. . . . Well, what came of it all? How *are* you going to get even with Dr. Brodsky?"

"Get even?"

"That's what it sounds like to me. You resent the fact that he fixed up your brain, although he apparently didn't do a complete job. Just what are you going to do to punish him?"

Garrison put his arm around her shoulder affectionately.

"Honey, I'm going to buy him a drink when I get out to IV Corps area again—if I ever should pass that way."

Now her anger turned to fear.

"You're not crazy enough to go back to Vietnam, are you, Dave?"

"No, I have no intention of returning to that part of the world and I very much doubt that they'd ask me to. I've served two tours out there. Anyway, I've lost interest in that war. As a matter of fact, it doesn't make that much sense to me and I may cancel my subscription."

"You want to translate that?"

"I think I'd rather watch it on TV, since Walter Cronkite actually handles it a lot better than I did. Maybe I'll put in for the Command and General Staff school out in Kansas, or take that training job the C.I.A. offered me last year. Pays $18,000 a year, and it's right down in Virginia."

Garrison succeeded in diverting her attention from his talk with the brain surgeon, and then he was very warm and charming for the rest of the day. It was 4:30 the next afternoon when the telephone call reached him. A woman named Margery Martin explained that she was calling at the suggestion of Major Brodsky or rather at the request of the major's father, Mr. Harold Norman Brodsky. She had a British accent and she spoke as if Garrison ought to know who Harold Norman Brodsky was.

"Executive secretary," Garrison thought aloud.

"Yes, I am Mr. Brodsky's executive secretary," she answered with cool civility. "Would it be possible for you to come up to New York tomorrow—at our expense, of course?"

"I think so."

"Good. If you take the 2:30 Eastern shuttle flight out of National Airport, there'll be a car waiting for you at LaGuardia when you arrive. You'll be in uniform, I presume?"

"Yes, U.S. Army uniform."

"Of course," she answered scornfully and terminated the conversation.

In the hospital library's copy of the 1970 edition of *Who's Who in*

America, Garrison discovered that Harold Norman Brodsky was indeed the father of Bruce G. Brodsky as well as of Claire and Jeffrey Brodsky. He was also the president of Amalgamated-United Stores, a member of the board of directors of the First Merchants Bank, the Federation of Jewish Philanthropies, and the Museum of Modern Art. He was a member of the Yale Club and he'd finished three years of naval service in World War II as a commander. He had homes in New York City, Easthampton, and Ocho Rios, Jamaica.

Big money.

He was married to the former Jessica Guggenheim, almost surely the *rich* Guggenheims. Money married money, Garrison knew.

It all added up to many millions, but one thing didn't quite add up—seemed amiss. Harold Norman Brodsky was only fifty-six. Was he the old man who played pinochle, or was it someone else?

6

The Eastern shuttle flight was only half full, which wasn't unusual for the middle of the afternoon, but it was on time. A bright May sun was beating down on the great city as the jet touched down at LaGuardia, and Garrison was not surprised by the temperature when he stepped out of the aircraft. It was eighty, according to the stewardess's announcement three minutes earlier. Yes, just about eighty Garrison calculated as he walked toward the shuttle terminal in the shapeless shuffling column of disembarking passengers. Comfortable in his summer uniform, he made no effort to hurry or even look around for whoever was waiting to guide him to the car.

They would find him.

That was the way they'd set it up, and he didn't mind it at all.

"Captain Garrison?"

She was broad faced, blue eyed behind oval horn-rimmed glasses, slim and endowed—you could almost say decorated—with an extraordinary bust that the proper linen suit couldn't quite suppress. Her sandy hair was done in a neat bun and she wore no lipstick. She didn't need any, Garrison decided, not with that body.

"Yes," he acknowledged.

"Miss Martin. Thank you for coming," she said in a tone that communicated correct manners but a total lack of enthusiasm for his presence.

"This way, please," she stated briskly without waiting for him to reply.

Garrison wasn't used to taking orders from women and this woman was plainly used to giving them, but he said nothing as he trailed her through the crowded bustling terminal out to the portico where a large, black Cadillac was waiting. Actually the big limousine wasn't waiting, but the dark capped chauffeur at the wheel was.

"Nice car Mr. Brodsky has," the Army officer tested.

"This is not his car. Mr. Brodsky does not use such ostentatious vehicles," she answered in that clipped B.B.C. speech.

Garrison's eyes flicked to the license plates, noted the Z that marked it as a rented car.

Now why would Harold Norman Brodsky send a rented car, when he and his companies probably had a fleet of their own?

Miss Martin marched to the Cadillac, stood near the rear door and glared until the chauffeur dashed around to open it.

"Thank you," she said without any trace of appreciation.

She got in, gesturing to Garrison who followed. Some ninety seconds later, the limousine was rolling onto the Grand Central Parkway toward Manhattan. She said nothing for several minutes, then blinked in remembrance.

"Might I please see your identification, Captain?"

Garrison showed her his I.D. card, which she studied carefully and returned.

"I'm cleared up through *Top Secret,* if that matters," he announced.

She declined to be provoked.

"It doesn't," she answered.

She pressed the button that turned on the air conditioning, and they rode on into the city in cool silence. The Cadillac crossed the

Triborough Bridge, cruised down the East Side Highway, and finally pulled to a stop at the corner of 84th Street and Fifth Avenue. The chauffeur opened the door, and she stepped out onto the sidewalk.

"Captain?"

When Garrison stood beside her a moment later, she turned once more to the driver.

"Thank you," she said.

She waited until the rented car was a block away before she extracted the two envelopes from her leather shoulder purse.

"Mr. Brodsky asked me to give these to you, with a message. He wanted you to know that he completely disassociates himself from this entire venture, which he regards as utterly improper, and he urges you to do the same," she recited.

"That sounds promising. I'll keep it in mind."

She thrust the two envelopes at him.

"Does Mr. Brodsky play pinochle?" Garrison asked as he accepted them.

"I should say not. Mr. Brodsky, if it's any of your business, is an exceptional bridge player, a tournament bridge player until a few years ago. Good-bye, Captain."

A discreet dark gray Bentley—just the sort of car that Harold Norman Brodsky ought to own—slid up to the curb, and before Garrison could think of anything insolent to say Miss Martin entered it and it moved south. He shrugged, looked at the square white envelopes. He opened the first, found four $20 bills clipped together with a piece of memo paper on which someone had typed one word—expenses. The other contained two of the memo sheets. The top one had two lines of typing.

Charles Jacob Brodsky.
3 East 82nd Street.

The second sheet bore a single handwritten sentence.

"This is a foolish project, but if you attempt it there must be no violence—HNB."

The words "no violence" were underlined, and the initialed signature was inscribed in a very executive scrawl.

Across the street the fountains were beckoning rhythmically outside the imposing facade of the Metropolitan Museum of Art and the green of Central Park loomed behind it, but Garrison resisted the distraction and walked the two blocks to 3 East 82nd Street. It was a handsome stone town house, four stories high with its own garage at the street level, and it didn't take a real estate expert to gauge that it was worth $400,000 or $500,000. There were heavy wrought iron grilles over the lower windows and the front door, but no nameplate above the bell.

The man with the new face pressed it anyway.

Neither Harold Norman Brodsky nor his executive secretary were the sort to make mistakes, he knew, although he had no idea as to what sort of person Charles Jacob Brodsky might be.

A powerfully built black man in his late forties, and in his shirt sleeves, opened the door.

"Mr. Brodsky?"

"He's expecting you, Captain."

Garrison trailed him into a marble floored foyer, past a staircase and down a paneled corridor lined with a number of small paintings. There was a Chagall, two Soutines, a Modigliani, and two Baskin drawings.

"Very nice," Garrison approved.

"Aren't they, though?" agreed the Negro. "He's got this thing about Jewish artists. There's a fine Epstein statue in the back garden."

There was, and two people seated at a card table beside it. One was an Oriental woman in a nurse's uniform, pretty, about twenty-five and probably of Japanese ancestry. The other was a white-haired old man, wrinkled and tanned and hawk-faced in a way not unlike the brain surgeon. He was thin but big boned, and you could see that he'd been a large, probably heavy, man at one time. He sat in a wheelchair, with a five-inch cigar in one hand and a group of playing cards in the other.

"Captain Garrison," announced the black man.

"Pinochle?" challenged the man in the wheelchair.

"Mr. Brodsky?"

The old man in the elegant silk robe nodded.

"Do you play pinochle?" he pressed impatiently.

"No, but I know you do."

"Harold told you that, I bet."

"No, I haven't spoken with him. Is he your son?"

"My son the art lover—a schmuck."

"A real schmuck," agreed the nurse as she rearranged her cards.

"He doesn't know anything about art," grumbled the old man. "He buys jokes—paintings of tomato soup cans and drek like that—and he gives it to museums. And those idiots take it."

"They're schmucks too," judged the nurse.

The old man coughed, puffed on his cigar.

"In case you haven't met my art-expert-in-residence, I'd like to present Miss Takeda. Miss Shirley Takeda."

She had an attractive smile.

"I know plenty about art," she defied. "I took two years of art courses—modern, medieval, oriental—at college. Nineteen credits of art, all As and Bs."

"Some crappy cow-college in California," the old man dismissed. "My other associate you've already met. You met Solomon at the door, right?"

The black man nodded twice.

"He does everything twice," Brodsky chuckled. "Even his name, Solomon P. Solomon. He'd never tell me what the P stands for."

"None of your business," snapped the nurse. "Why don't you offer the captain a drink in this heat? Your manners are getting worse every day, C.J."

"I keep her around because she plays a good game of pinochle," the old man confided. "A lousy nurse but not bad at pinochle. Not *that* good either. As a matter of fact, she cheats."

"I cheat because you cheat, you dirty old man," she snapped.

They seemed genuinely fond of each other.

"How about a beer, Captain?" offered Solomon P. Solomon.

"He doesn't have to drink beer. *He* can drink anything. I'm the one those doctors won't let have hard liquor. They're schmucks too."

"No, they're not, C.J.," Miss Takeda corrected.

"A beer would be fine," said Garrison.

Solomon opened four bottles of cold dark Carlsberg and poured the brew into tall beer glasses. Then they all sat down and began to drink.

"I used to drink slivovitz when I was younger," reminisced the old man with a wide, crinkled grin. "You ever try it—made of peach pits, a sort of cognac? My mother used to make it. It was like fire, fire."

"I had it in Munich once, and it was like fire," Garrison agreed.

"Yes, like fire."

His eyes glowed as he remembered the long ago, more than half a century ago.

"I still eat well though," the old man announced. "Solomon is a fine cook, and a very intelligent man. He knows about life, plenty. He was a policeman for twenty years, a detective. Now he's got a contract with a book publisher to write his memoirs."

"It isn't anything as grand as that," Solomon disclaimed. "Memoirs are for statesmen and world figures. I'm doing a rather simple autobiography, a personal thing."

"Put in a lot of sex and violence and it'll sell," predicted Miss Takeda as she finished her beer.

"I won't have to *put* any of that in," the ex-detective philosophized. "New York City did that for me. . . . Excuse me, Captain, would you be ready for another beer?"

"He's ready for a talk," broke in the old man. "That's what he's here for—to talk to me. You didn't talk to Harold at all?"

"No."

"He didn't meet you at the airport?"

Garrison shook his head.

"He sent a hired car with Miss Martin," he replied.

"Martin?"

"The one with the big boobs," said the nurse.

"Oh, *her.* Okay, I'll have to explain the whole thing, if these pinochle players will give us some privacy. About half an hour."

"You'll ring if you need anything?" Miss Takeda asked protectively.

"No, I'll blow the shofar."

"You Jews are so good to the help," she counter-punched.

"That's a very old joke," complained Charles Jacob Brodsky as he reached for another cigar.

"You're a very old man."

Having had the last word for the moment, the nurse led Solomon P. Solomon into the house and the lord of 3 East 82nd Street smiled.

"I am a very old man, not as old as they think, but old," he admitted. "I'm old and I'm *rich.* I'm very *rich.* Do you know that nobody uses that word anymore? It's a dirty word. Harold would never tell anybody that he's rich, but he is. I gave him the stores, big stores in sixteen cities. He's worth about twenty-five or thirty million dollars. I gave my other son, Ben, most of the real estate, and he's worth fifteen or twenty million. Good stuff, office buildings and shopping centers—no slum tenements. I grew up in those, and I hate them. My father was a peddler, you know. He had a pushcart. A good man, tough and stubborn and religious. I'm not too much on religion, formal religion, even now when I'm dying."

"I didn't know," said Garrison quietly.

"They don't think that I know, but I *know*. It's all right. It's about time. I'm eighty-one, and I've had almost everything I wanted. I've had some great fights and I've won almost all of them. I had a good wife, and we lived twenty-four hours a day. We didn't waste any time arguing or social climbing; we *lived*."

He handed Garrison a cigar, and the man with the new face lit it carefully.

"Now I'm dying, Captain. . . . I hear you know something about dying."

"I've seen a lot of it, and I almost tried it a few times. It didn't appeal to me."

"It doesn't appeal that much to me either, Captain. I'm not looking forward to it—not till I've tidied up one or two loose ends. . . .Say, how do you like the cigar?"

"Excellent."

"Cuban. I get them mailed in from Switzerland. It's illegal. Harold wouldn't do it . . . smuggling . . . illegal, but I do it. Anyway, that's what I want to talk to you about. There's something that I want done, and my grandson says that you might be able to do it. He tells me that you've got some kind of idea that you owe him one for operating on you in Vietnam."

"Yes, I owe him one."

The old man shook his head.

"Meshuga. That's Yiddish for crazy. . . . You don't owe Brucie anything, and you certainly don't owe *me* anything. So far as I'm concerned, you squared it with my grandson when you came up to see me. The account is closed out, and we start fresh. Agreed?"

Garrison puffed on the smuggled corona.

"No, I still owe him one."

"Listen, Garrison, I do a cash business and I expect to pay for this. Charlie Brodsky has always paid his own way. I'm not that old."

Pride.

A tough old man's pride.

All right.

"Just what is it you have in mind, Mr. Brodsky?" he surrendered.

"Two hundred fifty thousand dollars plus expenses. Twenty-five in advance, so you'll know I'm not just cocking around. It's not an easy job. We checked you out. Brucie has friends in the Pentagon and I got a senator who owes me more than one. We checked you out from A to Z, Captain, and they say you're a one-man army—with brains. This is going to take brains."

The vagueness, the mystery, was beginning to get irritating.

"Now. Right now, Brodsky, what is it you're asking me to do?"

The white-haired man reached into a pocket of the robe, took out a small photo—perhaps three by five inches—and pointed it at Garrison. The captain walked the four steps to get it, studied the picture for several seconds. It was a girl of about twelve or thirteen. She had full blonde curls, an earnest look and clothes that were not American. Girls in the U.S.A. or Western Europe hadn't worn summer dresses like that for twenty years.

"Eastern Europe?"

"Right, Garrison."

"The Soviet Union?"

"Right again. Her name is Sonya. Sonya Brodsky. She's fourteen years old now. That picture was taken two years ago. She's my brother's granddaughter, the only one left. The others are all dead. Her father, he was a chemistry teacher, died of cancer two and a half years ago. Her mother died three years before that. Sonya's in an orphan asylum in Moscow."

"I see."

"She's the only one left, the only member of my family still alive in Russia. For the past twenty-three months I've been trying to get her out, to bring her over here. We've applied for exit permits, used all sorts of political connections to bring pressure, appealed and pleaded to every Soviet official and diplomat we could find. No, they all say no. They will not permit this child to leave the U.S.S.R., ever. They've made it clear that this is their final answer. They refuse to discuss it any further."

Garrison looked at the photo again, then at the old man.

"Go ahead," he urged the surgeon's grandfather.

"They're right. There's no point in discussing it any further. I don't really have the time to discuss it anyway, Captain. I've only got six months at the outside, which means you've got less. I'll answer your question now. I'm asking you to go into the Soviet Union, a police state with some of the most heavily guarded frontiers in the world, and bring out Sonya Brodsky—illegally."

So that's what was bothering Harold Norman Brodsky.

"Will you do it, Garrison?"

The man with the new face considered the difficulties and the dangers, the unreality of the sentimental multi-millionaire's notion that one determined and inventive man with courage and money could overcome the massive security system of one of the great paranoid powers.

Suicide mission.

A silly suicide mission.

"Yes, I'll do it," Captain David O. Garrison replied.

7

"Good, good. Then we've got a deal, Garrison?"

"We've got a deal."

The old man grinned and the whole wrinkled face was transformed.

"You think it's foolish, don't you?" he challenged.

"Foolish? That's your son's word. Take a look," Garrison invited and handed him the note.

The old man found his glasses, scanned the memo sheet.

"Foolish . . . uh, uh, uh, uh . . . no violence," he read aloud. "Can you do it without any violence?"

Garrison shrugged.

"Maybe."

"But no killing anyway?"

The soldier nodded.

"No killing, unless they're about to kill me—or us. It could be us. I may find that I'll need some help."

"I figured on that. It's in the budget, as Harold would say. I can do more than put up money help though. I can put you in touch with some people who've had plenty of experience with the Russians, probably with the question of getting people out of Russia."

C.I.A. or N.T.S.?

Probably the latter, as the Central Intelligence Agency wasn't available for such private jobs.

"Do you mean the N.T.S.?" Garrison asked.

"I never heard of them."

"They're an organization of Russian exiles with headquarters in West Germany. The Soviets believe, and they're probably right, that the N.T.S. draws most of its money from Washington, that the N.T.S. is a C.I.A. auxiliary. The Soviets send assassins across every once in a while to hit N.T.S. leaders with tricky cigarette cases that shoot cyanide gas or poisoned bullets."

"And what does the N.T.S. do, Captain?"

Garrison paused to take off his jacket and hang it on the back of a wrought-iron chair.

"A number of things that I probably shouldn't talk about, classified things. Let's get back to the people you were talking about, the ones who might know about entering and leaving the Soviet Union."

The old man mopped his brow with a linen handkerchief.

"Shin Beth—you know them?" he tested.

"Know of them. The main civilian intelligence agency of Israel.

Very smart and very rough, and well thought of in the trade. The Eichmann job was theirs. You think they'll help you?"

"They ought to, Captain. They owe me a lot, a lot more than one. Back in 1947 when the Haganah needed weapons desperately, Charlie Brodsky gave them five hundred thousand dollars. That wasn't all, but you wouldn't want to know about dummy corporations and forged export permits and airplanes sold to Cuban companies that didn't exist. Let's just say that there's a man named Issachar Doron who's still in the Shin Beth. I checked on that last month. He ought to remember. Doron could help, and I can send word ahead that you're coming on my behalf."

It was hardly ideal—certainly not the way the C.I.A. would mount such an operation—but it was better than nothing.

"I gather you want me to fly to Israel. If I do, how do I make the contact?"

"I'll let you know, or they will. They're very careful, the Shin Beth, and, as you said, smart. This man Issachar is practically a walking encyclopedia. To get down to brass tacks, Captain—say, do I have to call you that?"

"My name is David."

"Fine, and you can call me Charlie."

"She, the nurse, calls you C.J., I noticed."

"A joke. They used to call me that when I ran all the stores, so she thinks it'll cheer me up to use it. David, you'll need a passport and a visa and money, that's the easiest. *Shirley! Shirley!*"

He looked around for the bell, found it on the table, and rang it loudly.

"I thought you were going to blow the shofar, C.J.," she reminded as she appeared in the doorway.

"Get the checkbook—my personal account," he answered.

His hand was not too steady, but ninety seconds later the man with a new face held a check made out to David Garrison for $35,000.

"The other ten is for expenses. There'll be more if you need it. Now Shirley, get the judge on the phone and tell him that I want to see him, right away. He ought to bring a secretary with him. It's important."

"He's not a judge anymore," Brodsky confided when the nurse left to make the call, "but he was—a federal judge—for eleven years. The money was lousy, so he's back in private practice at about $250,000 a year. Simon's been my lawyer for thirty years. A fox. No, a wolf."

It was 5:30 when the elegantly attired attorney arrived with a fattish secretary, who glanced rather pointedly at her wristwatch, and 6:20 when they left. In that interval, Brodsky explained what sort of agreement he wanted drawn and his distinguished white-haired lawyer told him that he didn't quite understand why the contract had to be drafted "so hastily" and the text was dictated, discussed, and signed. It was a rather simple agreement. David Oliver Garrison agreed to deliver Miss Sonya Brodsky of Moscow (U.S.S.R.) to New York City in exchange for $250,000 to be paid him by Mr. Charles Jacob Brodsky, identified as the brother of Miss Brodsky's grandfather. The "judge" had inserted this just so that Garrison couldn't deliver some other girl or woman named Sonya Brodsky. The contract specified that Garrison was to receive a first payment of $25,000 on signing, plus $10,000 in expense monies, and provided that Garrison could secure additional expense funds "up to a total of $250,000" upon request.

It also stipulated that the transaction be completed within six months, and stated that if the girl were not delivered within that time David Oliver Garrison could retain the initial $35,000 as "compensation for time and effort expended." The lawyer took one copy with him, the old man kept one for his home safe, and the third was handed to the soldier.

"Now it's all neat and legal. And fair, I hope," said the man in the wheelchair.

"Very fair, although I doubt that a formal written contract was necessary. Your grandson said that you pay your debts and keep your promises, and I believe that."

"That's true, but you're no businessman, Captain. Suppose I'm dead by the time you get her out? Do you think that my executors are going to pay out that kind of money on your word? Davey, I think you need a business manager to look after your interests."

Garrison nodded.

"I think there's a candidate for the job," he answered wryly.

"A woman? Your eyes say it's a woman."

"You're a pretty smart old man, Charlie."

C.J. Brodsky laughed.

"I'm a very smart old man, Davey, and I was a pretty smart young man too. You don't put together a fortune of—well, let's say more than eighty million dollars—and keep it without being smart. But smart's not going to keep me alive, so I'm counting on you to finish this soon. As soon as you can. No more than six months anyway."

"And no killing?"

"No killing. If you're as smart about your line of work as I was in mine, you ought to figure out some way to do this thing without killing."

"Okay, I'll be creative. You'll get what you want, Charlie. I imagine that you usually do."

"Almost always, but I've always been willing to work for it and pay for it. The hardest part is deciding what it is you want. You know that."

Garrison nodded.

"I'm still working on that," he admitted.

They both saw Solomon in the doorway.

"Maybe you'll work better on a full stomach," suggested the millionaire. "What have we got for dinner?"

"Cold borsht, crab cakes, and pot roast. Apple strudel for dessert."

"He makes terrific borsht, even better than my wife used to. You'll never taste better crab cakes either."

"They're Maryland style, Captain," explained the black man. "My mother's recipe."

Elizabeth would be waiting, the soldier reckoned, but if he stayed he might learn more about the grandson. There had to be more.

"All right, but I ought to phone someone in Washington," Garrison agreed.

He called and explained that he'd be back at eleven, and then there was time for one more drink before an excellent dinner. The old man spoke of many things, a tenement without hot water on a street named Rivington, of working seventy hours a week and earning eleven dollars, of his wife, his first store, his struggles and his adversaries and his victories, his children and his grandchildren and his five great-grandchildren. He told many earthy anecdotes—only two about the brain surgeon—and he told them with skill and charm and gusto. As the old man spun his web of lusty life, joyous battle, human comedy, and unforgotten passion, the others ate their way through the excellent dinner and enjoyed the saga almost as much as he did. When Garrison left at 9:10, he didn't know that much more about Major Bruce Brodsky, but he felt considerably closer to the surgeon's grandfather.

"You'll let me know what happens, how things are going?" the senior Brodsky asked as Garrison was at the front door.

"I'll drop you a postcard from Tel Aviv, Charlie. It'll probably take a week or two to get there, since I've got to get a passport and some leave."

"Apply for the passport tomorrow, in the afternoon," ordered the millionaire, "and you'll have it in forty-eight hours."

"Nearer two weeks."

"Davey, when I say forty-eight hours don't argue. I'll make a phone call at ten o'clock tomorrow morning. These things can be arranged. Shirley, get some phone numbers where we can reach the captain in Washington.".

The old man turned the wheelchair, rolled away down the corridor into another room at the end. Garrison watched him until he was out of sight, and then gave the nurse the two telephone numbers: the room at the hospital and Elizabeth Clement's apartment.

"I'm not going to ask you what he talked to you about because that's none of my business," Miss Takeda announced. "I've only got one thing to say to you, Captain. He's on his way out, and there isn't that much time left."

"He told me—only six months."

She hesitated and something troubled her face, something internal she couldn't suppress.

"No. Three. Maybe four, but certainly not six," she said in a taut voice.

"I didn't know it was that tight."

"He doesn't either," she replied, and for a moment Garrison thought she might cry.

She didn't.

"Don't tell him. You mustn't tell him," she said fiercely.

"You've got my word."

Now Solomon P. Solomon appeared, offered to drive the soldier to the airport. Sensing that the former detective wanted to talk,

Garrison accepted. There were two cars in the garage, a large maroon limousine at the back and a blue Thunderbird convertible near the door to 82nd Street.

"We'll go in my car, if you don't mind," said the black man.

He drove smoothly and surely and prudently, and as the convertible moved north on Madison he began to speak about the old man. The old man was honest and fair and decent, never patronizing or subtly "kind." The old man had guts and wit and wisdom; he never condescended to the poor or the black or the uneducated or anyone else except the smug or the stupid. The old man couldn't stand the arrogant or the stupid or the bigoted.

"He doesn't hate anybody, you understand," Solomon explained as the cool breezes soothed them on the Triborough Bridge, "but there are a number of people that he doesn't quite love either. Some people aren't that easy to love, Captain."

"I've met a few like that, more than a few."

"I've met *a lot* like that, Captain. . . . Say, that thing Shirley said about the pinochle. It isn't really true. He doesn't cheat; he doesn't have to. He plays a great game of pinochle."

The traffic was light, flowing quickly.

"You like him. Is that what you're saying, Solomon?"

The man behind the wheel nodded soberly.

"A lot, and not just for the things he's done for me. Not because he pays me three hundred a week or because he's putting my youngest brother through M.I.T. or anything else like that. No. He's my friend. He's a good man and a good friend, a good human being."

They could see the lights and hangars of the airport, and the blinking wing lights of a big jet swooping in to land a mile away. Neither of the men spoke again until Solomon pulled to a halt in front of the Eastern shuttle terminal.

"Thanks for the ride. And the talk," Garrison said as he prepared to climb out of the car.

"You're welcome, Captain. My pleasure. I wanted you to know what sort of man he is. He's a lot better than most, and he's counting on you."

"You know what he wants me to do is illegal?" Garrison asked the ex-detective.

"Yes, we talked about it for hours. Don't let him down, Captain.'

"I won't."

They shook hands, and Garrison entered the terminal in time to catch the ten o'clock flight to National Airport.

It was 11:30 by the time he reached the apartment. They kissed, embraced, and he could feel the tension in her fingers. He kissed her again, but that didn't help much.

"Easy, honey, take it easy," he advised softly. "There's nothing to get so up-tight about."

"What did he want?"

Garrison smiled his best smile.

"Let's have a drink and I'll tell you all about it," he promised.

"I've had a few. Make yourself one."

He did, and then he told her what the brain surgeon's grandfather had asked.

"That's crazy. Impossible and crazy. You're not going to do it, are you?"

Her eyes were large, angry and yet imploring.

"I'm going to try."

"It's ridiculous! You know why his son sent a secretary in a hired car, why she dropped you two blocks from the old man's house? Because Harold Norman Brodsky has enough sense to disassociate himself from such a ridiculous hare-brained scheme!"

"That's the way I figured it," the man with the new face agreed.

"But you're going to try it! My brain-damaged lover's going to play the comic book hero. James Bond and Superman and Mighty Mouse all wrapped up in one! You've got delusions of grandeur, Captain!"

He sipped at the vodka-and-tonic.

"I'm a pretty talented fellow. After all, I wooed and bedded you—and that wasn't easy."

"Listen, you bastard, I haven't taken all the risks of falling in love again to have my man go off to get killed. You may be a hero with lots of medals, but you're not good enough to get that kid out—and you know it."

"Maybe my new face has gone to my head."

She didn't even smile.

"Honey, I have no intention of getting killed. I'm going to study the situation—the terrain, the defenses, the enemy's order of battle—and then I'll *try* to work out a plan. I'm pretty good at this sort of thing. I was trained for it and I've done it many times, with a minimum of casualties. I'm not a Marine. I don't storm hills hell-for-leather into the enemy's crossfire. I'm Special Forces, unconventional, sneaky, hit and run."

"That's what you're doing with me, hit and run. Well I don't want to be left by the side of the road all bloody, another memento that Captain Garrison passed through."

He cupped her chin in his hands.

"Honey, if I can't come up with a plan that seems reasonably feasible and if I can't assemble the strike force it requires, I won't do anything. I'll write it off, and I'll come home, with twenty-five thousand for my trouble. That's not bad money for a few weeks."

She shook her head.

"No, you won't. You're all hung up on your debt to Major Brodsky. You'll end up dead or in a Russian prison, and the U.S. Government isn't going to exchange anybody for you. You'll rot, and I'll curse you. I'll curse you and I'll cry and the old man will die, and nobody will give a damn after that."

She started to weep and that was worse than her anger, and it took him half an hour to convince her that he would abandon the mission if his "recon" indicated that it was impossible.

"And if it's possible—it could be, Honey—we'll have that extra $225,000," he reminded.

Her head was on his shoulder; that helped.

"You'd probably blow it on something silly. The old man was right, Dave, you're no businessman. What would you do with $225,000 if you had it?"

He patted her hair gently, stroked her neck.

"I'd spend it, Honey, like that Indian maharajah."

"What maharajah?"

"I'll tell you. This is a true story. There was an immensely rich Indian maharajah who fell ill and died, and as soon as he was pronounced dead his greedy relatives ran into his treasure room and grabbed the crown jewels, about four million dollars worth. The next day his body was put on the cremation pyre, but as the flame rose—to everyone's amazement—so did the maharajah. He wasn't dead, just coming out of a very deep coma. But the heirs wouldn't return the jewels since he was legally dead, so he sued them. The case dragged through the courts for three years, finally reached the Privy Council in London. There, a brilliant Queen's Counsel won a final judgement for the maharajah."

His hand moved down her back, and he felt her respond.

"After his client thanked him, the lawyer confessed that he'd been wondering why the maharajah, whose total fortune was known to exceed two hundred billion dollars, had devoted almost three years of his life solely to litigation involving a mere four million. After all, the maharajah would only get cash now for the jewels had been sold and resold. It was a matter of principle, explained the righteous client. 'And what will you do with this money, your highness?' asked the barrister. 'Why I'll spend it, of course,' answered the maharajah. 'Might I ask on what?' said the lawyer. 'I'll spend it the way any ordinary man would,' responded the maharajah, 'on women and elephants!' "

She shivered as his hand caressed her hip.

"You'll spend *our* money on women and elephants?" she gasped.

"Mostly on women," he assured her gravely.

Then he kissed her many times and stroked her lovingly and they didn't talk anymore for nearly an hour. It was two A.M. before they fell asleep in the big brass bed, the woman cuddled against him possessively in the night.

8

In the morning, Garrison applied for a sixty day "rest and rehabilitation" leave, and hand-carried Colonel Parker's letter of approval to an office in Ring B on the third floor of the Pentagon.

In the afternoon, he had photos taken and applied for a passport at the Department of State—not the main building but the branch over near the White House.

"That'll be twelve dollars and about seven days," announced the clerk.

He paid and departed.

At three P.M. the next day, the telephone rang in his hospital room.

"This is Miss Shulman, Captain," said a crisp New York voice. "The senator wanted me to let you know that your passport can be picked up anytime after ten tomorrow morning. Of course, if you'd like us to send it out by messenger. . ."

"No, thanks. I'll collect it myself. Thank you and the senator very much."

"Not at all. The senator wanted me to ask if there's anything more that we can do."

Charlie Brodsky must have been a very generous contributor to several campaigns, for this was the V.I.P. treatment that Garrison had only seen generals receive.

"Not a thing, thank you," the captain answered and hung up without learning which senator it was who was being so helpful. The old man probably had several friends in both chambers of Congress, perhaps in both parties.

"With his money he could start his own party," Elizabeth Clement jested as she unlocked the apartment door that evening.

"He's too smart for that," Garrison answered.

They heard the phone ringing. She turned the key, hurried in to pick up the instrument.

"Hello. . . . Yes, he's here. . . . One moment, please. . . . It's for you, Captain."

"It's the old man," guessed the soldier.

He was wrong.

It was an unfamiliar voice, a young man with some sort of blurred foreign accent.

"Captain Garrison?"

"Speaking."

"I have that Tel Aviv telephone number that Mr. Brodsky requested. It's 833-61, extension 12."

"Just a moment. I'd better write it down."

He pulled his ballpoint from his shirt pocket, set down the number on a pad beside the phone.

"833-61, extension 12," he read back to the caller.

"*Tov.*"

And that was all, aside from the terminal click.

"What was *that* about?" she asked as he turned to face her.

"Phone number I'll need. Say, do you speak any Hebrew? He said something just before he hung up, and I think it was Hebrew."

"I picked up a few words from an Israeli doctor who spent six months at Reed."

"Do you know what *tov* means?"

She nodded.

"Good. It means good. *Boker tov* means good morning, *laila tov* means good night. Thank you is *todah raba* and please is *b'vakasha* and May 11th is their Independence Day, Israel's Fourth of July."

"You're a real mine of information, aren't you?"

"Wouldn't you like to hear about the Hisadrut's health service?" she challenged.

"I doubt it, since I don't even know what the Histadrut is."

She shook her head in mock despair.

"That's their central federation of labor, one of the most important organizations in the country. You're quite ignorant, aren't you?"

He hung his jacket on a chair, dropped onto the couch.

"Yes, I don't know much aside from how to lay ambushes and lady doctors, but my heart is pure."

She sniffed scornfully.

"Your heart is filthy, Garrison, and your mind is a disaster area."

He took off his shoes, removed his tie.

"It didn't used to be. I got A's in Elizabethan Literature and Greek Drama and Twentieth-Century American Novelists—and Biology. I loved Biology," he reminisced.

"I'll bet you did, you lewd brute," she jeered as she unzipped her skirt.

"But I wasn't that great at Math, and I didn't care much for the military history and other crap we had to take in the Reserve Officers Training. It was boring."

"Your mind was probably on sex all the time," she suggested as she took off her blouse, then her shoes.

"Not really. I'd had plenty of that since I was seventeen. Those were good years, the college years, even though I've forgotten most of what I learned. That's too bad. A lot of it was interesting, much more interesting than shooting strange little men in sneakers in some stinking jungle, come to think of it."

With her brassiere half-off, she paused to look at him.

"You never said anything like that before, Dave."

"Don't stop now," he evaded, "unless you're practicing to be a stripteaser."

"I don't tease and you know it, but what's this new Garrison philosophy?"

"Take off the bra and I'll tell you."

"You're getting crazier by the minute," she complained.

She dropped the brassiere on the floor.

"Well, sex maniac?"

"You know you have some wonderful spiritual qualities, Elizabeth," he complimented.

"Now who's teasing, Captain?"

"I think you're putting on a little weight," he observed thoughtfully.

"I think you're putting me on. Talk seriously."

He shrugged, patted the couch beside him. She sat down, looked up expectantly.

"Please don't expect any profound insights on the nature of man or existential wisdom," he began. "It's just that I've been thinking that there are other things to do besides setting ambushes or attacking supply depots. I'm not saying there's anything wrong with that line of work. It's honest and I suppose it's necessary."

"And it offers a lot of fresh air and exercise."

"Don't get bitchy, Honey. It's not your style. No, I'm comfortable with the military life and I'm good at it and I've got a pretty solid future in it."

"You could start an army of your own, go into business for yourself. That's what you're doing for Brodsky, isn't it?" she challenged.

He sighed, reached out for her, but she pulled back.

She had no intention of permitting him to deflect her with sex this time.

"No, it isn't, and you damned well know it," he answered.

"Besides, I'd probably lose money at it if I set up my own army. Everybody seems agreed that I'm no businessman. Anyway I'm not complaining about what I do, not really. Maybe I'm getting too good at it, so it isn't very challenging anymore."

"Don't get discouraged just because the Viet Cong are starting to bore you, Baby," she soothed. "Maybe there'll be a new war somewhere else soon, and you can start from scratch."

He finished the drink.

"It isn't the Viet Cong that's beginning to bore me."

Several telling and clever answers flooded to her lips, but she didn't articulate any of them. It wasn't that she was afraid—although she was—but rather that she sensed that her lover didn't want to go any further with this now. He wasn't ready, and she was wise enough not to force the issue. She knew a lot of well-meaning women who always had the last word and a few more besides, righteous rigid types who talked about respect and attended a lot of lectures and concerts and read books on the place of the woman in contemporary society. They dressed well—but lived alone.

"I didn't mean to nag, Dave, but this is important."

He nodded, smiled.

"You weren't nagging and I suppose it is important. We'll talk about it some other time."

He saw the question in her eyes.

"When I'm finished with Sonya Brodsky," he promised.

He reached for her again, and this time she didn't pull away.

"You know . . . we're really extremely compatible," he told her two hours later after they'd finished dinner. "I don't just mean physically, although that's important."

"You're mad about my mind?"

He hesitated.

"Yeah, as a matter of fact I am. I even like your taste in clothes and furniture and records and poets and perfume and toothpaste. You're intelligent and you're clean and you despise the same TV shows that I do. Aside from this funny hang-up you've got about the army . . ."

"That's *your* hang-up, Dave, but go ahead with all the sweet talk," she urged.

"And I respect you, Elizabeth. I deeply respect you, much too much to even dream of taking advantage of your innocence and virtue," he continued with mock earnestness. "I know you're much too fine a lady for such indecencies. Someday when I've got a good job with the Post Office, maybe with a Special Delivery route in a clean suburb and a nice little second-hand Volkswagen of my own, maybe then we could go steady?"

"You're a true blue bastard, Garrison, and if that's not bad enough I've gotten used to you. Your bulk beside me, your skin, your terrible sense of humor—the whole thing. . . . I'm probably lucky that you're going away now. You will come back?"

"You can count on it. But I won't be going for a few days yet. I've still got to cash the check, get the leave approved, and buy my ticket."

It took three days for the check to clear, and on the fourth the leave papers arrived. When he purchased the TWA ticket she took it well. She accepted the inevitability of his journey, demonstrated this by presenting him with a heavy, handsome attaché case of dark tan leather as a going away gift.

"That looks rather expensive," he said after he thanked her.

"It ought to—eighty dollars worth. It'll help you look more like a businessman. You can pack your razor and overnight things in it and carry it with you, just in case they misplace your suitcase or send it to Cairo by mistake. I don't want my man to arrive in the Holy Land looking like a bum."

"It isn't that long a trip, Honey. Paris, Athens, Tel Aviv—about ten hours altogether if the Arab terrorists don't get us. Don't look so scared," he advised when he saw her frown. "They never attack American planes. They know the big oil companies wouldn't like it."

"I hope you're right. And while we're on the subject, will you write—just to let me know you're alive?"

"I give you my word as an officer and a gentleman," he answered and then he began to pack his clothes—his civilian clothes bought at Washington's best men's shop with Brodsky's money—into his Valpak. She drove him to the airport beside the Potomac for the flight up to New York where he'd transfer to the trans-Atlantic 707, and she didn't make a scene as he left her at the gate. The trip up to John F. Kennedy International Airport was uneventful, and Garrison found that he had enough time between planes to telephone the old man that he was on his way. The old man wished him good luck, the overhead loudspeaker announced that TWA flight 621 was now loading at gate 33 and he found he had enough time to buy a box of Canary Island cigars at the Duty Free Shop.

The takeoff was on time, smooth, and graceful.

The stewardesses in the First Class compartment—Charlie Brodsky would have wanted it that way, Garrison told himself—were also smooth and graceful, but they didn't seem nearly as warm as those attractive models who play the parts in the airline commercials. They were deft, businesslike, and automatically attentive and they all used a discreet but effective mouthwash. They were better looking than the Air France girls but not nearly as pretty as the leggy blondes of SAS, judged the man with the new face. They probably wore clean underwear and spoke enviously about the rumored promiscuity of the B.O.A.C. and Lufthansa girls, and when they were off duty they all used hairsprays and French perfume bought at some duty-free airport. This was speculation—informed speculation, to be sure—but what was certain was that they served hors d'oeuvres and drinks quickly and generously to the First Class passengers. Garrison knew that by the time the plane was fifteen minutes off the Kennedy runway. Their skirts may have been tight but their hearts were not—or was it the keen competition on the Atlantic routes?

Garrison had a pleasant and uneventful flight, but he wasn't bored. He wasn't tense either. He was simply and deliberately relaxing as does a veteran professional athlete before a major game, preparing for the inevitable shocks and surprises and impacts that lay in the clash ahead. He was already in a danger zone, for he had no idea as to who were these well dressed people in the half-empty First Class compartment. It was like the start of a Long Range Reconnaissance Patrol into "denied territory": there was no certain way of knowing where the "friendlies" ended and the VC began. He had to be careful. He had to be ready. He drank champagne rather than stronger spirits and ate sparingly so he wouldn't become too drowsy too soon, The food was good but the movie was one he'd seen in Washington, so he finally slid off to sleep shortly before midnight.

Sunlight.

The warm sunlight streaming in through the window woke him, and for a moment he thought he was back in the U-Minh Forest.

Then he smelled the perfume and the vague deadness of the recirculated air of the sealed cabin.

"Coffee, sir?" asked the stewardess in that flat sincere Iowa voice.

She was standing beside him, and he could feel the body heat she radiated. She was smiling, of course. Her hair was neatly combed and she was smiling. He knew that before he opened his eyes.

"Yes, thank you."

"Black with one sugar," she recited to let him know that she hadn't forgotten.

"Very good," he complimented disinterestedly.

And he thought about Elizabeth Clement as he watched her walk away. Elizabeth Clement always looked so serene and woman-sleek and lovely in the morning, a short woman who somehow looked longer uncoiled beside him. Then he thought about Bruce Brodsky, the courteous but remote brain surgeon who couldn't understand why a patient might want to meet or thank him—or repay him. He was very different from his grandfather, Garrison brooded as he rubbed his chin and considered the electric razor in the lavatory. Yes, it was quite odd how different the two Brodskys seemed.

There were still some tender places where the scars would have been if Elizabeth Clement and the other plastic surgeons hadn't been quite so skillful, but he decided to shave after he'd had his wake-up coffee. When he returned to his seat feeling mildly triumphant—he'd hardly hurt at all—it was time for a big breakfast. After that, the plane touched down at Paris Airport for forty minutes to disembark two or three dozen and pick up a few more than that. A new crew came aboard, the ashtrays were emptied, and the fuel tanks refilled. Then the 707 headed southeast for Athens. The walk around the "In Transit Area" at Orly had helped a bit, but Garrison still felt somewhat stiff as the plane knifed across central France at 550 miles per hour. It wasn't the seats, for they were ample and comfortable, but just the fact that he wasn't used to sitting so long or being enclosed for such an extended period.

Lunch.

Then the voice of the captain announced that they'd be on the ground at Athens in four minutes, and they were.

The big transport whined to a stop less than 50 yards from the terminal building, and after the usual amenities the passengers descended to stretch their legs and scan the local souvenirs. Some were leaving altogether, and apparently the stewardess thought that Garrison was one of those "terminating" here.

"Your case, sir," she said victoriously as she hurried to hand him the costly leather going-away present that was to make him look like an executive.

Rather than argue or hurt her feelings, the soldier took the attaché case and thanked her and walked down the steps to the concrete. The case was heavy, heavier than an M-16, he noticed, but he swung it easily as he followed the other passengers toward the building. There was a uniformed policeman at the door, gesturing that this was the entrance for disembarking travelers. Some 200 yards away another large jet—blue and white—was moving up toward the terminal slowly, but Garrison gave it only a casual glance as he plodded on in the warm midday sun.

It happened very quickly.

The guard at the door crumpled under a blow struck from behind, and two small men raced out toward the blue and white airliner now only 100 yards away. One charged forward with what looked like a large airline bag while the other drew something metallic from beneath his light raincoat.

Son-of-a-bitch.

Satchel charge.

The one up front was carrying a satchel charge, a prepacked bundle of explosives used by demolition men and sappers.

Machine-pistol.

The other one was waving a 9 millimeter machine-pistol, a Stechkin or somebody's copy of it. All the Red Bloc armies used them.

Garrison suddenly realized that the blue and white jet was an Israeli airliner, that these were dedicated Arab commandos intent on destroying it.

It wasn't any of his business, not by the *wildest* stretch of anyone's imagination.

Even if it was, he was naked, without a weapon.

It would be stupid, perhaps fatal to interfere, and it would attract attention to him and his journey. There were undoubtedly other guards at this airport, he reasoned, and in a moment they would surely open fire.

They didn't.

But the bastard with the machine-pistol did, squirting two bursts at the Israeli craft.

Somebody had to do *something*, dammit. There were probably scores of passengers, maybe women and children, in that goddam plane.

Son-of-a-bitch, where were the Greek police?

Garrison ran forward, raised the attaché case and threw it at the man with the automatic weapon. The heavy piece of luggage struck him in the back of the head and he reeled, dropping the Stechkin.

Amateur.

A soldier might have staggered under the impact, but he would have held onto his piece somehow. This man let his weapon fall to the concrete apron, letting out a shrill cry of surprised pain as he put both hands to his head. Garrison was upon him in four or five bounds, battering the dazed attacker with a series of brutal judo chops that dropped him like a steer struck by a slaughterhouse sledgehammer.

Then the man with the new face grabbed the Stechkin, a weapon he knew all too well. He'd test fired it at Bragg a dozen times, used captured Chinese models in Vietnam even more. He dropped into a shooting crouch, swung the machine-pistol toward the other man with the satchel charge.

At that moment, a door in the fuselage of tne El Al transport opened and a man stood silhouetted in the opening. He had an automatic pistol. He fired four times. The commando with the satchel charge fell limply to the runway. Then the Israeli pilot reversed his engines and moved the plane away from the terminal. The blue and white transport was more than 200 yards from the satchel charge when it exploded.

Then there was a great deal of shouting and screaming, and a dozen policemen ran out bellowing orders and questions in Greek. Garrison couldn't understand a word of it but he put down the machine-pistol and stood motionless, listening to his heart pound and hoping that he wouldn't be shot by mistake.

What he'd done was romantic and stupid.

It would be even more stupid to be gunned down by some excited and confused airport security guards who took him for one of the commandos, and he'd never get to pay the debt to Brodsky. The man who had dropped the Stechkin was moving and moaning now, sobbing as he tried to get up and couldn't. Garrison saw his face for the first time—thin, dark, earnest, young. He was seventeen or eighteen, perhaps nineteen at the most.

Strictly amateur.

9

"I hope that you understand how delicate this situation is for me," Captain Rossides said with an engaging blend of sincerity, worldliness, and Eastern Mediterranean sophistication.

"Of course," replied the man with the new face.

It was quiet and calm here in the office of the airport's security chief, but it was very different outside in the corridor. Excitement, babbling voices, edgy guards, animated journalists and photographers, minor officials and shaken air travelers all boiled and swirled, speculated and complained, asked foolish questions and made up fantastic answers about what had happened.

"And it is delicate for my government too," the curly haired Greek officer with the dapper black mustache added.

"Of course."

Rossides looked at the American, nodded.

"Of course, you understand. You're a soldier too, and you know how unpleasant and infuriating these international political messes can be," he said to the U.S. officer.

"They're unmilitary."

"Exactly, Captain Garrison. You've put your finger on it exactly. The whole thing is unmilitary—and unfair. Why should these vile Jews and Arabs fight their squalid little fights on Greek territory, threatening our tourist trade? The tourist trade is quite important to our economy, and this sort of violence is embarrassing. It certainly doesn't make my existence comfortable, not a bit."

Garrison nodded sympathetically.

"I'm sorry that I caused all this trouble," apologized the New Englander. "It really wasn't any of my business, but I guess I reacted automatically, as a soldier does."

Captain Constantine Rossides smiled fraternally, pleased that this U.S. combat veteran was speaking to him this way.

"It might have been much worse if you hadn't intervened," Rossides assured the American. "Suppose that Palestinian had hit the plane with the satchel charge? Fire? All those civilian passengers? People of a dozen nationalities—including forty women and children? A mass slaughter—here—in my airport?"

Garrison began to feel better as he recognized that the man across the desk from him was just like some hundreds of other public servants and military officers, a thoughtful humanitarian keenly concerned about saving his own ass.

"And that was well done, the way you took out the younger one who had the machine-pistol, Captain," complimented the security chief.

"Thanks. I'm glad that I didn't have to drop the other one. The man who fired from the plane saved me that."

Rossides lit a filter-tipped cigarette, blew out a puff of aromatic smoke.

"Would you like one?" he offered. "We grow the finest tobacco in Europe. It's our biggest source of income, even larger than tourism."

"Thank you."

"That man who saved you the embarrassment of shooting the Arab with the explosives was an Israeli security agent. They carry one on all their planes, and every one of them is a dead shot. Whatever anyone might say about the Jews," Rossides judged as he flicked his silver lighter at the tip of the cigarette he'd given the American, "they shoot well. Four rounds and four hits, you couldn't beat that on the range at Fort Benning, could you? My cousin took the Ranger course at Benning, you know. Did you ever come across him, by any chance?"

"I'm afraid not, although I know the name Rossides. One of our fine colleges—Columbia—had an All American football player named Rossides some years ago."

"We're third cousins," said the security officer proudly.

"Last I heard he was an Assistant Secretary of the Treasury in Washington—a very important man."

The Greek captain beamed. This American was really very decent and likable.

"Well, to get back to the situation here, Captain Garrison, I want you to know that I appreciate your help in preventing a terrible loss of life. I'm afraid that it may take a day or two to get all the legal details straightened out, but you should be on your way again within seventy-two hours."

"I had hoped to go on immediately. I'm on my way to visit the Holy Places in Jerusalem and Bethlehem and Nazareth—a pilgrimage."

"Ah, a pilgrimage. A religious pilgrimage. Of course. A good soldier is a good Christian, I should have remembered that. I've always dreamt of making such a pilgrimage myself."

Captain Constantine Rossides was obviously sincere.

"And I want very much to avoid any personal publicity about this incident," Garrison explained, "since the involvement of an American officer in such an affair would obviously embarrass *my* government."

"It was much simpler fighting the Red bandits in the jungle, wasn't it?" philosophized the security officer.

Garrison nodded.

"It would be bad, bad for my career, if my name and picture got into the papers," he reasoned glibly, "so couldn't you say that the man who knocked down the gunner was a Greek security agent in plain clothes? Or it could be a Canadian police sergeant named Morrison? I'm sure that you could work it out with TWA, and none of the passengers on my flight could contradict the story because I didn't speak to any of them."

Rossides seemed to be interested.

His eyes wandered up the wall past the calendar decorated with the Parthenon photo, and he blew a wonderfully thoughtful smoke ring.

"A Greek security agent?" he reflected.

"And there wouldn't be that much flak from the Arabs since it was the Israeli in the plane who did the only killing," Garrison pointed out helpfully.

"Actually, I rather admire the Israelis," confided Rossides. "They've got the guts to fight for their freedom, as the Cypriots did. I'm half-Cypriot, you know. . . . Yes, one of our own daring agents. Cool, courageous, and resourceful without too much violence. . . . Maybe . . . I've nothing *against* the Arabs, by the way. Their struggle isn't my struggle though."

"Nor mine, and I don't want to wreck my military career on it. As one captain to another, I'm sure you understand. I'm expecting a promotion, I'm half-way to a good pension. Well, *you know*."

Now it was Rossides who nodded, for he did know.

He smiled, and he suddenly became very brisk and purposeful. "Right. I'll do it. There's an Olympic Airways plane leaving for Tel Aviv in twenty or thirty minutes, and you'll be on it. We can get you out through the back door of my suite, through the cargo area and over to the gate without anyone seeing you. I'll arrange everything, if you'll give me your ticket. You can pick up your bags at Lod Airport when the TWA flight to Tel Aviv arrives an hour later."

"I can't thank you enough, Captain," Garrison said truthfully.

"It is only professional courtesy. After all, you'd do the same for me if you were in charge at Washington Airport and I got into some mess there."

"I'd try."

"If you should by any chance run into my third cousin, the Assistant Secretary of the Treasury, you might give him my regards. Say hello from Captain Constantine Rossides."

"I won't forget," vowed Garrison as he puffed on the cigarette. "Say, this is a fine smoke," he added.

"The best tobacco in Europe," beamed the security officer patriotically. "Take the pack with my compliments, and may your visit to the Holy Land be a wonderful one."

"I'll say a prayer for you," promised the American who'd last been in a church in 1963.

They shook hands, and Garrison left by the side door. He was airborne on the Olympic flight half an hour later, and shortly after four he stepped out into the hot glare of an Israeli afternoon. He looked around for several moments, not at the modern terminal that was similar to a score of other such buildings at other Asian airports but at the dimly visible line of Judean Hills on the horizon. Somewhere over there to the East was Jerusalem. Although he didn't consider himself a religious man, the naked thought of that city stirred something within him. Startled by this unexpected emotion, he paused in the ninety degree heat to wonder what it might be.

"This way, this way," announced an airport policeman.

The policeman was a woman, very pretty in a snug, tan miniskirt but quite businesslike too. She saw the surprise in his face, smiled.

"Welcome to Israel," she said in greeting, "and come in out of the sun. As Noel Coward wrote in the song, only mad dogs and Englishmen stay out in the midday sun."

"But it isn't midday," Garrison replied as he noticed the revolver holster on her right hip.

"And you aren't English," she joked back cheerfully "American? Yes, American. Come inside, *Adon* American."

Adon.

He'd seen the word in a book. It meant "Mister."

"Thank you. Are all the police here so pretty?"

"You're American all right," she chuckled and pointed again to the door.

It was cool inside, and there were more armed police. There were also the usual immigration and customs and public health officials, and signs in English, French, and Hebrew designating which portals and lines led to each. Actually the officials weren't quite the usual ones at international airports, for they were all beaming warmly and the passengers queued up before them appeared to be equally happy. There was a good deal of noise and bustle, all oddly joyous as if there was a large family reunion in progress. It was probably because many—perhaps most—of the inbound passengers were either Israelis or coreligionists from other lands, the Special Forces officer reasoned.

The entry formalities were brief and pleasant, almost informal, and there was nothing in the atmosphere that suggested a nation under siege. The great diversity of faces—dark Yemenites, Europeans, husky, native-born "Sabras," North Africans, and some plainly American—hardly suggested a nation at all. The Old

Testament prediction of the "ingathering of the exiles" seemed to be a visible reality in this building.

"*Shalom*. Nice of you to drop in," said the bronzed immigration official with the imposing handle-bar mustache as he reached for the American's passport.

Garrison thought, remembered the Hebrew words for "thank you" that Elizabeth had recited back in the Washington apartment.

"*Todah raba*," he answered.

The man said something else as he flipped open the green plastic-bound passport, and Garrison shrugged.

"I'm afraid that I didn't get that," he confessed. "I only know about seven words in Hebrew."

"So you'll learn. It's a terrific language, Baby. . . . Surprised you with that 'Baby,' didn't I? I see plenty of American movies—plenty. . . . David Garrison . . . Stockbridge, Massachusetts. . . . That's near Tanglewood where the Boston Symphony plays in the summer. I've got some of their records. You a musician?"

Garrison shook his head.

"Purpose of visit—tourism," read the official as he scanned the answers that the soldier had written on the landing card. "Okay. . . . Duration of visit—one week. Hah, you could spend two weeks in Jerushalaim, I mean Jerusalem, alone. Why not make it a month, Mr. Garrison? We need the Yankee dollars."

Now the man's eyes darted to a clipboard on the desk, and Garrison guessed that the paper contained a "watch or hold" list of undesirables—just like the one that the F.B.I. supplies each week to immigration teams at the U.S. ports of entry.

"You're clean, Baby," said the affable Israeli as he returned the passport. "I hope you've got hotel space booked. It's tight at this time of the year."

"I've reserved a room at the Hilton."

"Enjoy."

The soldier in civilian clothes moved on to the public health inspector, and as soon as the American was out of sight the smiling immigration official picked up the phone and dialed swiftly.

"This is Tsur at Lod Immigration," he reported. "Garrison, David, U.S. Passport number M, repeat M, 9904609, just arrived on Olympic Airlines from Athens. . . . Right. . . . He said he was booked into the Tel Aviv Hilton. He's the one you've been waiting for, isn't he? . . . You're right. It's none of my business. Definitely, it's *your* business and *you* put him on *your* list for *your* reasons—and now *your* mother can worry. *Shalom,* Baby."

All security men were impossible, the immigration inspector told himself as he put down the phone to glance up at the next incoming passenger. His smile grew even broader as he saw the young woman and her passport. She was a Dutch girl in her early twenties, and she had, as they said in the American films, a great body.

"*Shalom.* Nice of you to drop in," Mordecai Tsur said as he reached for her passport, and he forgot all about David Garrison of Stockbridge, Mass.

10

It cost sixteen Israeli pounds for the 14-mile cab ride from the airport across the flat, hot plain into Tel Aviv, and the Moroccan driver—formerly Moroccan—achieved the impossible. Not only did he manage to operate his '67 Ford as boldly as the most creative Tokyo taxi man, but he succeeded in being even more garrulous than the most talkative New York cabbie. Perhaps this was the land of miracles after all, Garrison thought as the hot, dry air from the open windows abused his face. The driver discoursed endlessly on the latest rumors of a cabinet crisis, the superior *humus* and *tehina* served at a restaurant named Yunis in nearby Jaffa, the relative merits of two local red wines named Adom Attik and Ben-Ami and the outrageous cover charge—six pounds—at a Ben Yehuda Street discotheque called Mandy's.

"Not that the Hilton is cheap, not at ninety pounds a day without food," he added as Garrison stared at a tall building that dominated the skyline ahead. "That one—the one you're looking at—that's not the Hilton. The Hilton is only sixteen floors," he boasted. "That's a real skyscraper, the Shalom Tower. Thirty-five stories high. There's an observatory on the roof, and people say it's a great view from up there. You can see about a quarter of our whole country, I hear. . . . This is your first trip, isn't it?"

And he went on and on and on, until the mounting traffic at the edge of the city—it looked like a miniature Tampa or Miami Beach—forced him to concentrate his attention and dialogue on other drivers. But now his accented English shifted to a rich mixture of French and Hebrew, liberally laced with grunts and hisses and eruptions that had to be epithets. Garrison focused on the teeming streets, the modern buildings, the sidewalk cafés, the abundant movie theaters—everything except the swirling streams of vehicles that billowed and eddied around them. It was difficult to realize that this pulsing city of 500,000 was only sixty-two years old, very young indeed in this ancient land.

"Here we are," announced the driver as he finally stopped the taxi. "The beach is right behind it, and there's a swimming pool too."

It was a sleek and not unattractive building, totally contemporary in architecture. Two bellboys started for the cab.

"By the way," the man behind the wheel said as Garrison paid him, "I hope I didn't frighten you when I said ninety pounds a day. That's for a couple. For you it'll be forty-five pounds."

"I'm glad you mentioned that. Ninety seemed like a lot."

"Forty-five isn't so cheap either," countered the driver indignantly.

Aware that he couldn't win with this man, the soldier decided to settle for a draw and nodded noncommittally as he left the cab. The hotel was in the great Hilton tradition, with an imposing lobby that was just a trifle too well air-conditioned. There were eye-catching fluted ceilings, marble floors, and great copper kettle lamps that hinted of the country's history. Clusters of men and women, mostly American tourists, if their clothes and cameras were valid clues, moved briskly across the lobby. Yes, the majority were speaking American English in familiar Stateside accents. It was probably a good thing that he was staying at this hotel, Garrison reasoned as he asked the desk clerk for his room, for in this mass of Americans he was less likely to be noticed.

He didn't know that he'd already been noticed.

The moment that he entered the elevator with the bellboy, the desk clerk was on the telephone.

"Extension 12. . . . Hello, *Adon* Garrison has just checked into the Hilton. Room 817. . . . Don't mention it. . . . I understand. *Tov*, I won't mention it either."

It was a quarter to six by the time that the man who owed Brodsky stood on the balcony of Room 817, looking down at the beach and the blue-green waters of the Mediterranean. The air was hot but the vista was cool and soothing, and Garrison found himself thinking of those Cape Cod shores where he'd worked during summer vacations while he'd been at college. This was quite different, more like Hawaii where he'd twice gone on R&R leaves. No, this wasn't much like that either. Even these sands were covered by a sense of history, of ancient Phoenicians and Hebrews and Crusaders and Egyptians and Mohammedan armies, of Greeks and Turks and nations whose names now lingered only in books.

Then the soldier thought of the man named Issachar, and he decided that it was probably too late in the day to telephone 833-61, extension 12. Government offices here undoubtedly closed at five P.M. as they did everywhere else, so he'd call in the morning. He'd go down to the pool now to unwind after the long journey, to swim and observe the bikinis. Then he might have dinner at the hotel's King Solomon Grill Room, whose massive copper door he'd noticed in the lobby, or he could wander out along Hayarkon Street and stroll into the center of the city to find another eating place—perhaps one of those sidewalk cafés. He liked to walk around strange cities, to wander leisurely and freely, to eavesdrop, to study store windows, to pause for a drink, to buy a snack—to set his own pace. The old man couldn't blame him for taking this first night for himself.

As he reentered the room from the balcony, the telephone rang. Probably the desk clerk with some routine greeting.

"Hello," he said wearily.

"Captain Garrison?"

The desk clerk didn't know that he was an officer.

"Yes."

"There is a very fine view from the Migdal Shalom—the Shalom Tower—now, or would you rather make it tomorrow morning?" asked the slightly guttural voice in the accent that was beginning to get familiar.

"Is this Issachar?"

"*Kenn*, yes—of course. I don't mean to rush you, but I gathered that time was a factor. If tomorrow is more convenient, I'm sure the tower will still be standing. . . . Well?"

The Brodskys wouldn't let him wait.

"Where is the tower?"

"Not far—at the head of Herzl Street, about two blocks from the Great Synagogue. The tower observatory will be open for another fifteen minutes, so you can just make it if you leave immediately. It's on Ahad Haam Street. You can see it from the front of your hotel."

"Countersign?"

"I like that—very correct. Baron . . . Rothschild."

"I'm on my way."

At four minutes to six, Garrison stepped out of the elevator onto the observation deck of the Shalom Tower. The view was everything that had been promised. The city sprawled out at his feet and to the west lay the splendid sweep of the coastline. On the eastern horizon he saw the mass of Jerusalem some 30 miles away. A score of tourists, including half a dozen teenagers, stood around the outer rail, staring admiringly at the panorama and chattering in several languages. Garrison scanned the group swiftly, wondering which of these people was his contact.

"We close in two minutes," announced a dark bright-eyed girl whose dress-uniform meant she had to be some sort of official guide.

It was cooler up here and the breeze from the sea ruffled her hair as the tourists erupted in a final flurry of picture-taking, but Garrison's attention was focused entirely on the question of meeting Issachar or his envoy. It was unlikely that a high intelligence executive would come to meet a stranger. It would be an envoy, an agent.

"*Shesh, shesh* . . . six o'clock . . . *six heures*," the guide called out and the visitors dutifully started for the exit to the elevator. Garrison watched, hesitated until all the others had left the deck. The uniformed young woman walked back to get him, waving her finger reproachfully.

"Come along, come along, Mr. Baron."

"Rothschild," he answered.

"Wait here," she advised and then she joined her flock and the metal doors closed.

Contact.

He was alone in this place with the remarkable view, but his eyes remained fixed on the elevators. In a little while he looked at his watch, 6:04, and then he heard one of the cars rising. The door opened, and two men in their late twenties stepped out. They wore light suits, wary half-smiles.

"Garrison?"

He nodded.

"Are you armed, Garrison?"

"No."

They were. He had no doubt of that. One of them walked to him and searched him for a concealed gun, grunted.

"No gun, Maven," he said loudly.

A third man, large, big featured, wearing sunglasses, stepped out of the elevator. He wore an open shirt, no jacket. He might be fifty or even sixty, but it didn't matter, for he was obviously the man whom the New Englander had come so many thousands of miles to see.

"Good evening, Captain. Welcome to the State of Israel. I'm Issachar Doron."

"He called you Maven."

The heavy man laughed.

"A harmless piece of flattery, a silly nickname. Maven means very wise or well informed, a great scholar," he explained.

"Charlie Brodsky said that you knew a great deal."

The Shin Beth executive chuckled again.

"He was always kind—and generous. A good Jew and a good man. How is my old comrade?"

"Sick. Old and sick."

The Maven's smile faded.

"How sick, Captain?"

"He's dying. That's why I'm here."

Garrison glanced at the two younger agents.

"Guard the doors," ordered Doron as he led the American to the other end of the deck where they could speak without being overheard. There Garrison told him the whole story, starting with the ambush in the U-Minh Forest and ending with his pledge to Charles Jacob Brodsky on East 82nd Street in New York.

"Brodsky's right," judged the Israeli. "You don't owe him anything. I owe him. We, his fellow Jews, owe him something—but you owe nothing. I'm not even sure that we owe him anything. The Bible says that it is a blessing to do good deeds, but that the recipient doesn't *owe* the benefactor. God takes care of all of that. He rewards the good."

"I didn't come all this way for a lecture on the Old Testament. You admit that you owe him something, and if you're a man—not just a biblical scholar—you may want to do something for him. He thought you would, Maven.

Doron shrugged, reflected for several seconds, and shrugged again.

"I suspect you are a sentimental man, Captain," he judged.

"I *know* you're stalling."

The heavy man with the curling gray locks nodded.

"Perhaps, but you are, beyond doubt, a sentimental man. That's not necessarily bad—not necessarily, but often. I do not advocate coldness or immorality, you understand," the Israeli pointed out carefully in that burred slurred accent, "but I can't put much stock in impulsive sentimentality. Let me explain it with a quotation from the Talmud."

The American wouldn't listen.

"No thanks, Maven, I gave at the office. Do you or don't you owe Brodsky, and will you or won't you pay your bills?"

The Shin Beth executive shook his head—probably sadly. It was difficult to tell exactly what was going on behind those sunglasses.

"You . . . *you* can afford to be sentimental, or even stupid . . . to make mistakes. You're a soldier in the large and well equipped army of the greatest and richest and strongest power on earth. I'm the Deputy Director of one of the three small intelligence organizations of a little country."

"Are you appealing to my sentimentality, Maven?" Garrison challenged.

Doron said something in Hebrew—whatever it was it wasn't too pleasant—and one of his young aides replied even more harshly. You didn't have to know the language. The tones told it all.

"I said that it's a miracle you've stayed alive this long. You wouldn't in my business, you know," explained Doron, "and he agreed."

"Brodsky. Charlie Brodsky and Sonya Brodsky, yes or no?"

"You're crazy, Garrison. That's my professional opinion," the man in the sunglasses announced angrily. "You want to get one Jew out of Russia, and we want to get out millions."

"That's because you're a man of morality. I'm sentimental, Maven, so one kid is enough for me. Will you help me?"

Doron walked to the railing, looked out at the city briefly, and then turned.

"I don't have a man or a pistol, not even a penknife, to spare," he replied. "We're coping with the whole Arab world. And even if I had any kind of manpower or equipment to spare, we've got enough trouble with the Russians. I'm not looking for any more—not even for Charlie Brodsky. We named a school after him in Jerusalem, and a forest near Haifa. Well, not a forest but a large orange farm. Maybe we can name one of the new kibbutzes in the Negev too."

"He doesn't want any of that—just the kid."

They all heard the elevator door open, saw the girl in the tour guide uniform step out with an envelope. She handed it to Doron, who tore it open swiftly with his thick stub-ended fingers and scanned the sheet of paper he extracted.

He spoke again in Hebrew—without any bitterness this time—and the others all turned to stare at Garrison.

"What's wrong?" asked the New Englander.

"You really are crazy, Garrison. Really and truly," sighed Doron.

"But brave," said the girl.

"Brave and crazy," said the Shin Beth Deputy Director. "And modest, another Gary Cooper cowboy. I wouldn't have believed it. You should have told us, you know."

"What?"

"I didn't know," continued Doron. "Of course The Maven is supposed to know everything, but I didn't know. We just got word now. I had no idea that you were the man in Athens."

The two younger agents were grinning.

One of them—the taller with the small scar on his chin—said something in Hebrew, and the other answered. Neither of them took their eyes from the elevator doors, however. They were disciplined, businesslike, purposeful.

"That's not very funny," answered Doron.

Whatever they'd said had annoyed the older man.

"We'll talk about your sick jokes later," Doron continued to his assistants. "In the meanwhile, I ought to thank Captain Garrison for saving the plane and the passengers. One of Israel's finest concert pianists was on that flight, you know."

Garrison reached into his jacket pocket for a cigar, and suddenly there was a 9 millimeter M1951 Beretta pistol pointing at his abdomen.

"Easy, *easy*," he advised. "I'm just getting something to smoke."

Slowly and carefully he drew out the petit corona, bit off the end.

"Got a match, Maven?"

Doron said something that caused the young security man to sheath the pistol, and then Doron handed Garrison a box of wooden matches. The American lit the cigar, puffed and handed the box back.

"Keep them, with my thanks."

"I don't want your matches or your thanks, Maven. Just pay me what you owe me—*me*, not Brodsky."

"What are you talking about?"

"You owe *me* one Boeing 707 and about 110 or 120 passengers—including a concert pianist. You may not owe Brodsky anything, but you owe me, and I don't give a damn about any schools or public toilets being named in my honor. I'm not *that* sentimental, Maven."

Doron shook his head, took out a pipe from his pocket and sighed as he filled it from a worn brown pouch.

"Can I have my matches, please?"

Garrison handed him the box, watched him ignite the tobacco.

"I want to get paid, Maven."

"You know, Captain," Doron replied as he sucked at the pipe, "the great twelfth-century Jewish philosopher, Moses Maimonides, once said . . ."

"Stick it," Garrison interrupted coldly. "Stick Maimonides and the twelfth century and your whole wise-man number. This is now, the twentieth century, and I'm neither a philosopher nor a theologian. I'm just a simple-minded soldier from the Diaspora, a foreigner of limited sophistication."

"You're a . . ." Doron began, faltered and finished in Hebrew.

"How do you say it in English?" he demanded impatiently of his young aides.

"A thorough son-of-a-bitch," one of them translated cheerily.

Garrison nodded.

Doron puffed on the briar, shrugged.

"I can't make any promises," he finally answered. "I will speak to some people, and perhaps they will speak to other people. If those other people are willing—and I can't promise that—I should have word for you in a day or two. I mean positive word. In any case, you'll know within forty-eight hours. I give you my word, Captain."

"Your word is good enough for me. Brodsky told me that you're a man of honor."

The man with the pipe said something more in that stuttering guttural tongue of ancient prophets and kings.

"The Maven says that that is true," the girl translated dutifully, "but you are . . . a . . . a pain in the ass."

"And he's right," agreed the American. "Yes, the Maven is always right. Well, I'd better get back to my hotel. You can reach me there."

Doron glanced at the girl, decided.

"I wouldn't want you to spend two days sitting in a hotel room waiting for a telephone call, Captain," he said. "Why don't you see something of our wonderful old-young country? Shoshanna is a registered tour-guide, and she can show you many places of historical and archaeological interest. You can get a car and visit Nazareth and Jerusalem and Beersheba, Haifa and the Sea of Galilee, King Solomon's mines and the ancient fortress of Masada."

"Masada shall not fall again!" said the girl in oddly defiant tones.

"Masada shall not fall again!" repeated the two young security agents.

It was some sort of a chant, a litany with special meaning.

"Masada, the Jewish citadel down in the Negev that Rome's Tenth Legion besieged back in the first century," Doron explained. "967 Zealots—that's what they were called—held out against an entire legion for three years."

"And then when they couldn't resist any longer they all killed themselves—men, women, and children," recalled Garrison. "Yes, I read General Yadin's book."

"Then you should enjoy your visit. The Dead Sea is quite nearby, and Shoshanna knows the whole area well."

Garrison nodded.

"I guess it would save you a certain amount of money if Shoshanna came along in the car I rent," reckoned the American, "because otherwise you'd have to use one of your own cars and your gasoline to tail me."

"We have to be thrifty, Captain," Doron agreed amiably, "for we are not a wealthy country such as yours. It is more than economical for us; it will save you the cost of a guide. But more important, it is practical—for all concerned."

There was no point in arguing with him.

"All right. When does this economical-practical tour of Israel start, Maven?"

"Why not now? You haven't seen Tel Aviv yet, and my younger associates tell me that it . . . what's the American expression . . . yes, *really swings*. That's it, really swings at night."

Garrison couldn't help smiling.

"Shall we go, Captain?" she invited.

They went.

11

They went down in the elevator to the lobby and then they went out into the street, and then she turned right and led him two blocks east to the Great Synagogue.

"This is Israel's largest place of worship, Captain," she explained in the rhythmic sing-song of the professional guide. "You must wear a hat when entering, of course, for it is our religious law that one cannot enter such a house of God bareheaded."

Garrison studied the impressive structure, then looked at the girl.

"Why don't we leave all the holy places until tomorrow?" he proposed. "I don't intend to be disrespectful, but I'd rather start with the city, get the feel of it and the people."

He smiled, and she couldn't decide whether his remark was simply a turn of speech or a deft proposition. She was a progressive young woman who wouldn't have been bothered by such an overture, but the uncertainty, the withdrawn quality of this apparently outgoing soldier, troubled her.

"You're not very religious, are you?" she tested.

"I don't know."

"But I thought there were no atheists in foxholes, Captain?"

He shrugged.

"I didn't bring my foxhole with me. Nobody wears them anymore. We use flak-jackets and nylon body armor instead. Much cleaner. Let's walk."

They turned left to stroll north along what had been named Allenby Road during the British Mandate era and crossed the Shield of David Square to the large open-air Carmel Market. She led him through the Yemenite Quarter, filled with small restaurants and people who looked wholly Oriental, Arab.

"No, they're all Jews. Very devout too," she told him. "They were airlifted in from Aden in 1951 and 1952. They'd never even seen airplanes, you know, but they took it all quite calmly because the Bible had predicted they would return to The Promised Land on the wings of angels. They settled for some surplus C-54 transports we bought from the United States. My brother saw them getting off the planes at Lod. He told me that they kissed the runways."

"Am I supposed to get all choked up by that?" Garrison asked.

"I did, but I have no idea what you might do. You might do anything. I never heard anyone talk to The Maven like that," she told him truthfully. "Yes, you might do anything."

She was quite romantic, the New Englander judged. He was, of course, touched by her account of the Yemenites and, despite all the misery he'd seen in Southeast Asia, touched by the ordeal and oppression that had produced this extraordinary little nation. He wasn't going to tell her that, and he wasn't going to sleep with her either. She might be willing—either out of that romantic view or out of some silly emotion generated by the incident in Athens or perhaps because the Shin Beth might want her to—but Garrison wasn't going to make it any easier for Issachar Doron. He had to remain at arm's length, reserved.

"Yes, I might do anything," Garrison agreed. "I might even ply you with costly food and drink—if you'll pick the place."

"Is that all?"

"Why don't we start with that, and we can build from there?"

They walked south all the way to the former Arab city of Jaffa, the ancient port used by the Crusaders. Separated from Tel Aviv by a half mile No Man's land—a rubble left from the 1948 fighting—it had been handsomely restored and was now an artists' and handicraftsmen's quarter with galleries, shops, cafés, and several churches and mosques. There was also a French restaurant named Toutoune, where Shoshanna Hayin was well enough known to get an excellent table in the roof-top dining room. The filet bearnaise reminded Garrison of the Saigon cuisine, and the local wine wasn't that bad—it wasn't that good either. They ate and imbibed heartily, wandered about Jaffa's twisting streets and managed to stop off at two cafés and a nightclub in Tel Aviv before Garrison went to bed—alone.

They rented a car the next morning and spent the day in and near Tel Aviv, turning toward Jerusalem early in the afternoon. It was much smaller and quieter and older, and more majestic. The holy places of three faiths and many centuries of history did something to this legendary city of pinkish golden stone. Garrison couldn't revere it, but he couldn't resist it either. *Something* moved him. When they left the golden domed Mosque of Omar, she drove him out to a stark building beyond the city limits, a modern structure she called the Vad Yeshem. The floor was covered with writing, and there was a flame burning that had to be some sort of memorial.

"Those are the names of the martyrs who died in the Nazi ovens," she said soberly. "The six million we cannot forget."

He let his eyes wander over the names. Despite all the dead he'd seen—actually seen—this place bothered him and angered him.

"There's been a lot of stupid vicious killing, hasn't there?" he thought aloud.

"You have a gift for Yankee understatement, Captain."

"It's only one of my many talents. Killing is another one," he replied coldly.

For a moment she was stunned, silent.

"Nobody's going to be butchering Jews anymore," she answered defiantly. "Not here, anyway."

Garrison looked at the names of the six million and he shook his head.

"Let's go," he said.

The sun was going down as they stepped outdoors, and he paused to look at the sprawling city on the nearby hills.

"We can see the Dead Sea Scrolls and Herod's Citadel in the morning," she suggested.

He didn't reply, silently scanning the horizon.

"And the Tomb of the Virgin Mary and the Damascus Gate built by Suleiman the Magnificent in 1537," she continued conscientiously.

His eyes moved across the spires and domes of a score of churches, mosques, convents, and shrines—all looking oddly appropriate despite the modern apartment and office buildings sprinkled among them.

"You're not listening, Captain."

"Just barely," he acknowledged. "I guess I've had enough for one day, Shoshanna."

Of course, she thought. It was time to rest. Tourists get shrine-groggy after a certain point, she told herself. Their feet hurt and their backs ached and their minds couldn't absorb any more history or grandeur. And they grew thirsty. It was only human. Even the healthy young West German visitors with splendid muscled bodies and all that fine unspoken guilt gave out by this time of day, she remembered.

"Why don't we check into the hotel and have a cocktail?" she suggested with the assurance of a veteran guide who knew a good deal about Americans—that wonderful species who wore wash-and-wear everything and consumed strange alcoholic mixtures.

"Something a little less Miami Beach—the hotel, I mean," he answered.

"We're booked into the King David. It's an older hotel, very gracious and . . . patrician, that's the word. It has a Near Eastern quality and a Victorian touch too, which isn't too surprising since it was built during the British Mandate here. Excellent cocktails on the terrace."

The cocktails were excellent and the service on the terrace overlooking the vaguely Oriental gardens was pleasant, and later the beef stroganoff in the hotel's brick-paneled Regence Grill was clearly the work of an above-average chef. As they sipped their sweet, strong, Turkish coffee at the end of the meal, he began to relax—a little. Perhaps it was fatigue or the wine they'd consumed, but the tension started to flow away and she could see it.

"Good. You're looking less grim, Captain," she complimented. "Much more easy, and handsome. You've got a fine face, you know."

"It isn't mine. I'm glad you like it though. I picked it out myself."

She frowned uncertainly.

"No, it's no joke," he told her. "I left my face—a good piece of it—in a jungle in Vietnam. This is a new one that some Army surgeons put together for me at a hospital near Washington."

"I'm sorry."

"Don't be. I'm not ashamed of it. I really did pick it out, you know. I saw a picture in a magazine, and I asked the doctors to give me a face like it. I'm quite used to this face now. As a matter of fact, I barely remember the old one any more."

For a few seconds she wanted to cry. She almost reached out for his hand, but then she feared that it might offend this soldier, so she didn't. She smiled warmly, then brightly.

"I was a soldier too, Captain," she said cheerfully. "I was a corporal, a radio operator with a tank brigade. My brigade was one of the spearhead units in the Six Day War."

"I hate war stories," Garrison said truthfully.

"I don't have any, and besides it was a very different sort of war."

"I had the impression that they were all the same, Corporal."

"This was nothing like yours in Vietnam. It was all out in the open, no jungle, and there was practically no damage to any civilians and it was all over in six days. Besides, it's much easier to fight to protect your homeland. It's more inspiring."

Was it her language or her innocence, he wondered.

He shrugged, feeling depressed and paternal at the same time. "After a very short time, say a bit longer than six days, war isn't that inspiring. Not any war to any one, unless you're a romantic or an idiot or a professional who enjoys the challenge. I'm not putting down patriotism, Corporal, but I know that you can be a patriot and/or a good soldier without finding battle inspiring. Exciting—that's another matter."

"Our boys were inspired in 1967—by desperation, if you like," she answered stubbornly. "Maybe because they knew that if they lost they had no place to go."

Garrison sighed.

"Shoshanna, in a war nobody ever has any place to go. . . . Don't look at me that way. I'm not belittling the courage or the skill of your remarkable army, and I'm not minimizing its' extraordinary achievements. It moves fast, hits hard, does a lot of damage with a minimum of casualties. Good intelligence, good officers, good morale, and a lot of guts and imagination—a highly successful military organization."

The waiter arrived with the two brandies Garrison had ordered.

"But you're not impressed by this little country's army?" she accused the American.

"Impressed, but not inspired. However, I'll drink to the brave soldiers of the Israeli army," he proposed.

They toasted the Israeli army, then the air force, and finally the navy—all with the acceptable but basically mediocre local brandy. After that they had another round, and suddenly the pretty young woman smiled mischievously.

"To be frank, Captain," she confided softly in tones edged with the intimacy of alcohol, "I can understand why our odd citizen-army may not exactly overwhelm a professional soldier. Not so long ago, a French journalist was down in the Gaza Strip getting a story on the Israeli occupation. One of the Arabs was telling him how harshly our troops treated the civilian population there, and the Frenchman asked about the number of cases of rape. The embarrassed Arab had to admit that there had been no rapes at all. 'O My God!' sneered the Frenchman, 'and they call *that* an army!' "

Garrison chuckled, as he was expected to.

"Yes, we do call *that* an army," she announced with visible pride, "even if it doesn't seem like much to Washington or London or Moscow."

"All right. Now, how about calling *this* a night?"

"I don't understand."

"It's an idiom—an American usage," he explained. "It means the evening is over, sort of like the British pub keeper's 'Time, gentlemen' when he's ready to close."

She stood up, shook her head.

"I'm not ready to close, Captain. I'm ready to dance," she declared with a nod toward the nearby floor where a dozen couples were moving rhythmically to the beat of a competent quintet.

She was a fine dancer, quick and strong and graceful and warm. Her supple young body—very shapely and very alive—radiated an attractive animal heat, and once again Garrison decided that he'd better be careful with this desirable woman. She was almost surely an agent, no—surely. He couldn't afford to desire her if he wanted to, even if Elizabeth Clement or Sonya Brodsky wouldn't mind. They probably would mind. Women, even the most emancipated, always did. The ones who cared always did.

Thinking all this, knowing all this, he still found her very attractive—and that was why he lied and told her that he was tired shortly before eleven o'clock. He was alone in his room fifteen minutes after that, but he didn't fall asleep for more than an hour and he got little rest. The whole night was a series of fragmented dreams, bits of ambush, a dozen different bloody ambushes, in the Ashau Valley, the U-Minh Forest, the D.M.Z., and the Delta and places whose names he couldn't remember. The images and the sounds and the smells, the passions and the terrors were brilliantly clear—but the names were all jumbled now. The names didn't matter, only the tactics and the foe's reactions and how the "play" worked, counted. The mistakes counted, for if they were recognized they wouldn't be repeated in the next ambush. Like an athletic coach endlessly rerunning the films of last season's games, Garrison lived and relived each small savage battle all through the night.

He was awake at dawn, an obvious reversion to the routine he'd absorbed over so many years. They toured the city again until noon, then drove south on the Hebron Road to Bethlehem where they visited the Grotto of the Nativity—the subterranean cave sacred as the birthplace of Christ. He listened silently as she delivered a commentary she must have recited hundreds of times before. Beth Lehem—in Hebrew, The House of Bread. A fertile area. Church above the grotto built by Constantine in sixth century, reputedly oldest Christian house of worship still in use. Bronze doors inside brought by the Crusaders. That niche, at the eastern end of the cave, was where He was born.

She finished her familiar text, waited.

He said nothing.

His eyes moved to the ancient tapestries on the walls, the light cast by the silver lamps, the niche with its Latin inscription. He opened his mouth as if to ask a question, but a party of Canadian pilgrims arrived and Garrison sighed instead. When they stepped out through the church's strange four-foot high door into the midday warmth of Manger Square, he thanked her and suggested that it was time for lunch. Whatever he'd thought or felt he'd locked away now, so they ate and talked of other things and then pointed the car toward Hebron, the 5,000 year old City of Abraham. As he drove, he found himself studying the terrain as if it were a sandbox model or a military map. He was annoyed to discover that he was scanning it like a soldier, like a commander planning an attack. Vineyards. Olive groves. Twisting road across the valley floor to the town.

Ambush terrain.

"There is a legend that Adam and Eve lived in this valley after they were expelled from the Garden of Eden," said the girl, "and, of course, it was here that David was proclaimed king."

"Of course," Garrison replied mechanically as he tried to ignore his obsession. It was a stupid preoccupation, an ugly one.

There.

Up ahead about three-quarters of a mile.

That would be the place.

If the VC or the North Vietnamese were operating here, that's where they'd put their goddam ambush.

The road would be mined, and there'd be a 7.62 millimeter RP-46 light machine gun off to the right and an RPG-2 bazooka concealed somewhere over there, on the left.

Those were the standard tactics, straight out of the Russian and Chinese manuals—and quite effective. The bazooka rocket would knock out the command car after the mine had blasted the lead vehicle, and then the machine gun would sweep the column for two or three minutes before the ambushers escaped. Of course, there were no ambushers here. He glanced off to the right where the machine gun would be, saw nothing. Then he looked ahead along the hill on the left side of the road.

The afternoon sun glinted on something.

Whatever it was, it was placed *exactly* where the bazooka should be.

12

It could be anything, an irrigation pump or the corrugated metal roof of a toolshed or a farmer's parked jeep.

Or an RPG-2 bazooka.

Shoulder-fired, smooth-bore, projecting an 82 millimeter shaped-charge warhead capable of penetrating 8 inches of conventional armor.

Capable of gutting an armored personnel carrier or a light tank at a range of 150 yards, a rocket weapon evolved from the German *panzerfaust* of World War II.

A bit old-fashioned, simple, and nasty.

All these thoughts ran through his mind as he slowed the rented car's speed from 30 to 20 miles per hour.

"It is a beautiful valley, isn't it?" she said, misunderstanding why he'd reduced speed.

"Beautiful. Any Palestinian guerrillas active here?"

The needle on the dashboard continued to drop.

"Not usually."

There was a curve, masked by an olive grove.

He stopped the car.

"Maybe we're just lucky, lady, or maybe I'm paranoid—or maybe

I attract violence," he speculated, "but there may be an ambush up ahead. I could be wrong, but I've got a feeling for these things."

She didn't argue.

"I suppose you saw something, Captain?"

He nodded.

"Yes, I saw something where a bazooka ought to be if somebody was using the right training manual—the P.L.A. book. It's almost as popular as Chairman Mao's book of quotations, they say."

She translated quickly: P.L.A.—People's Liberation Army—was the regular ground forces of Communist China.

"You could be right about the ambush," she replied. "There are a few Chinese instructors with the Arab guerrillas, and some of the guerrilla officers went to Peking and Hanoi for training."

He considered the situation for several seconds before he thrust his right hand toward her.

"I'll need a gun, Shoshanna."

"Captain, what makes you think . . ."

"No games," he interrupted. "I don't have time to screw around with you. Even if we sit it out here, there may be an army truck or a school bus or a big limo full of dumb fat tourists moving in from the other direction. You're an agent, and you're armed. Give me the goddamn gun."

She opened her shoulder purse, removed a small pistol and handed it to him.

"Nice. Nine millimeter Beretta semi-automatic," he identified. "Eight rounds—a nice handgun. Of course, an Uzi would have been better but beggars can't be choosers."

"An Uzi? *Sorry*, Captain, I can't fit a submachine gun in my purse."

He was already out of the car.

"I'm going to snake through the grove, cross-country over the ridge to catch them from behind," the American explained. "If that number works and they really are holed up with a bazooka, I'll try my hand with the machine gun crew on the other side of the road next."

To her credit, she didn't say "Good luck" or "Be careful."

He would have been disappointed if she'd said either of those, for such remarks were unnecessary between two professionals.

"*L'hitra-ot*," she said instead.

"What's that?"

"Be seeing you."

"*L'hitra-ot,*" he echoed as he started toward the grove.

His Special Forces men wouldn't have used that expression, he thought as he moved into the trees. Junior would have probably said "Watch your ass, Captain" in that quilted Southern drawl, and Chief wouldn't have said anything. Sometimes the Apache muttered "Geronimo!" before going into combat, but that was a jest, a put-on parody of the paratroopers' jump cry. Garrison moved quickly now, shedding all such abstract rumination as he hurried between the rows of olive trees.

There wasn't much time, not if those were Arab guerrillas up ahead.

They'd be alert, scanning the road in both directions.

They'd probably seen the car approaching, and now they'd be wondering why it had stopped out of sight.

At the edge of the grove he stopped, listened, and then moved up the ridge slowly. He had to be careful now. The raiders might have scouts out protecting their bazooka unit. That's what Garrison would have done. That's what the VC always did, and these boys were presumably using the same tactics that Victor Charlie had applied so regularly. Just before he reached the crest he halted, dropped into a crouch, and advanced warily.

He peered over the top, saw the scout.

Checked Arab headress, camouflage battle coveralls, Kalashnikov rapid-fire gun.

Standard outfit, and the man wasn't any brighter than the usual infantryman in any army but he was alert. In the argot of the Special Forces School at Bragg, he was motivated. Junior—Sergeant Arnold Culpepper, Jr.—would say that he wasn't sitting around with his thumb up his butt, which added up to the same thing. It wasn't that surprising that this sentry was alert and motivated, Garrison decided, for he'd heard that these Palestinian guerrillas were all volunteers and many of them high school or college graduates.

Of course, that socio-cultural data wasn't what mattered at the moment.

What mattered now was the AK-47, the weapon that was often called a submachine gun by those not sufficiently sophisticated to realize it was actually an assault rifle that could be set to fire either fully or semi-automatic. The AK carried a thirty-round magazine, and at 100 yards was twice as accurate as the U.S. M3A1, the British Sten, or the Israeli Uzi. They all used pistol cartridges, but the AK fired 7.62 millimeter rifle-type cartridges. Such an efficient, familiar, and accurate weapon would be much more useful than the Beretta pistol he held.

All he had to do was get it, without getting it in the belly himself.

The bushes.

He could crawl through the bushes, slowly and carefully—a yard or two at a time—moving only during the intervals when the nervous sentry was looking elsewhere. Crawling through underbrush was no problem for David Garrison. He was almost as good at it as he was at the art of ambush, two qualities that were proving increasingly useful in the second half of the twentieth century. Any state senator, corporate vice president, college dean, or adolescent revolutionary could confirm it. He tensed, saw his chance and wriggled over the crest quickly.

Then he froze, waited for a burst from the goddamn AK.

Nothing.

It was hot and the bushes had thorns and he wasn't dressed for this sort of thing—a short-sleeved sport shirt, slacks, and moccasin loafers—and the glare of the sun didn't help either. But he stole another brief look, moved forward another 8 feet. Then he paused again, his body rigid in implicit resistance to the impact of those 7.62 slugs.

Nothing.

He was breathing heavily, sweating and focusing on the stranger still 50 or 60 yards away. It was all quite impersonal, he told himself a few minutes later after he'd closed half that gap, and had nothing to do with the man's nationality or politics. Garrison was long past the stage where he cared about his enemy's courage or convictions. For the past two years or so he'd been much more impressed by a foe's professional skills and by the urgent realities of the immediate combat at hand. Those things were considerably easier to deal with, to face, judge, and handle.

Then—inexplicably—his wall of detachment and expertise cracked.

He suddenly found himself wondering what he was doing out *here,* why he was stalking *this* anonymous adversary.

The questions lasted but a moment before he brushed them away, renewed his crafty advance toward the scout. That cloth headdress—that was good. Good for the attacker, for it would have been much harder to club a man in a metal helmet. It wasn't going to be that easy in any case, for this man seemed better trained than the one at the Athens airport. He held the AK as if he knew what to do with it, he looked around often, he didn't seem nearly as young or green.

But he dropped just like the other one when Garrison struck him with the Beretta. Garrison hit him again, then swore softly when he saw that the man wore no belt or grenade bag. He smiled when he saw the canteen, used its canvas belt to tie the man's wrists together. He tugged loose one of the sentry's sneakers, pulled off a smelly tan sock to jam into the raider's mouth as a gag.

Then he moved on with the AK across the small ravine to the next low crest, peered down at the three men with the bazooka. There was no detonating box in sight, so the mine was either the usual pressure type or it would be fired by the machine-gun crew on the other side of the road. The mine itself would probably be something cheap and simple, one of the basic models with ten or twelve pounds of TNT and an MV-5 pressure fuse that went off under forty-four pounds of weight. Or it might be one of the nasty DM "road mines," those ugly little bastards that were set off by the vibrations of a passing vehicle and couldn't be neutralized by hand.

Whatever it was, he had to take the bazooka team first.

How do you say "Hands up!" in Arabic?

He should have asked the girl that. She'd probably know, for Shin Beth agents were likely to have some basic vocabulary in Arabic. It was too far and too late now, so all he could do was to hope that at least one of these reputed high school graduates had picked up a little English before he joined the Palestine Liberation Front. If the educational achievements of these patriotic guerrillas had been overestimated, there was a distinct possibility that one or all of them might die.

Unlike the now unconscious sentry, they were all looking at the road—which made it easier for Garrison to crawl toward them. One of them took out a cigarette and was reaching for a match when another—perhaps the leader—said something. Looking a bit sheepish, the raider muttered a brief reply as he shrugged and put the cigarette back in the pack. Garrison wriggled on until he was within 15 or 18 yards, buoyed by the confidence that at this range the AK could chop down all three of them in one or two bursts. The way they were bunched up around the RPG was very helpful.

If they would only be sensible instead of political, they'd be all right. Garrison had no wish to, no need to hurt them, but he would if they tried to hurt him. Hundreds of Arab guerrillas were already in Israeli prisons, he recalled, and maybe these would have the practical wisdom to accept the same fate. If they didn't, there'd be three more martyrs and a dozen expended shells on this thorny hillside.

Garrison moved up between two boulders, rose to a half crouch, and pushed the assault rifle's safety selector level to the middle position marked by the two Cyrillic letters AB. Now it was set to fire "automatic"—to spit out its thirty rounds in three or four seconds. They'd have very little time to enjoy their martyrdom. With the laminated wood stock against his right shoulder and his finger on the trigger, Garrison spoke.

"Don't move," he said in a low clear voice. "I'm behind you with an AK, and I'll shoot if any one of you makes a move."

He saw them tense.

"Hold your hands out away from your bodies and your weapons. . . . Okay, you can turn around slowly."

They were whispering now.

"Turn around . . . easy . . . nobody's going to get hurt if you do what I say."

One of them turned, saw the weapon, and said something softly.

"That's right, Sonny. You tell 'em it's an AK alright. As a matter of fact, it's one of the newer models—the AKM. Six hundred rounds a minute, and she's on automatic."

The man who'd turned—he was twenty-four or five—shrugged.

"Tell 'em, dammit."

The guerrilla spoke again, and his two comrades turned around.

"Zionist pig!" one of them said angrily.

It was terrible, just terrible.

It was depressing to believe that anyone actually said things such as that anymore. With the exception of characters in pre-1950 films, comic strips, and Egyptian musical comedies, nobody had used that sort of language seriously in two decades or more.

"I'm going to ignore that baby talk. Put your hands up, and walk toward me . . . about four steps. . . . That's fine. Stop."

And then the same raider—the pudgy one with the large nose and the very big black eyes—said that awful thing again, and added a few more trite epithets and slogans.

"I'm going to gut-shoot you if you don't shut your fucking mouth," the Special Forces captain promised.

"All of you," he added a moment later.

Another of the guerrillas muttered something, and the stupid dialogue halted abruptly.

"Good. You're in command of these yo-yos, I gather?"

"Yo-yos?" the man who'd ended the stream of slogans wondered in a rather tasteful British accent.

"Cowboys. Troopers. Soldiers. Heroes. Anything you like. Are you Number One?"

The man nodded.

"All right. I'd rather not zapp anybody if I don't have to, but I have a limited sense of humor. If any of you tries anything comical I'll cut him in two. *Zapp*—is that clear?"

"Yes. . . . You speak like an American?"

"Just a tourist passing through. All I want to do is get rid of that goddamn mine and the machine gun across the road, and then I'll move on."

The man shook his head.

"I don't believe you're a tourist."

"All you've got to believe is that I know how to chop with an AK, and you'd better believe that, Sonny. Now you boys are going to unbuckle your belts and bandoleers, drop them, and then turn around to face the road. Fast but *nice*—is that clear?"

"Yes, but I don't believe you're a tourist at all."

Then the senior guerrilla told his comrades and they obeyed the instructions, and Garrison moved up behind them as quietly as he could. He stunned two of them with swift blows with the Beretta before the third began to react. That raider was spinning with a knife he'd pulled from a boot. He turned quickly, then doubled up when the Special Forces captain rammed the muzzle of the AK into the pit of his stomach. For a classicist, the next move was obvious. Kick him in the head two or three times, and then in the groin. It never failed to impress people, and it always ended discussions or disagreements. Feeling sad and unconventional, Garrison hit him in the head with the pistol and watched him drop.

He collected all their guns, jerked out the magazines, and threw them into the brush. He looked across the road, tried to spot the machine gun and cursed. Then he looked south along the highway, saw something moving and swore again. A large vehicle—probably a bus or a truck—was moving closer. It was probably a mile away, maybe less, heading right toward the mine.

He had to knock out that machine gun.

Otherwise it would cut him down if he tried to stop the approaching vehicle.

He seized the bazooka, peered left and right and then left again.

There.

Nicely camouflaged, but there it was.

He raised it to his shoulder, aimed, and squeezed the trigger.

Explosion, flame, smoke, screams—in that order.

"Sorry about that, Suh," he said in mechanical imitation of the Georgia sergeant who always used the phrase in such situations.

His glance flicked south, picked up the bus only 300 yards away and still rolling.

"Son of a bitch!"

200 yards.

He discarded the bazooka, took up the AK, and squeezed off two bursts.

And that did it. The bus shuddered to a halt, and several people leaped out onto the road.

"Stay in the bus!" Garrison shouted as he stood up and waved the Russian assault rifle. "Stay in the bus! There's a mine down there in the road! Stay in the bus!"

He walked down the hill, drenched with perspiration and hoping that nobody in the bus would panic and shoot him. It would be idiotic if that happened. He trudged through the brush, paused to mop his brow and wave "friendly" at the people in the vehicle.

Good.

They were staying inside, obeying his warning.

At least somebody believed him.

13

Any American general would have been impressed.

Richard Burton or whoever commands the British ground forces today would have been thrilled to pieces.

For a low-budget military organization, the Israeli Army certainly came on like gangbusters—swiftly and aggressively.

Youth—that was the key.

Two truckloads of bronzed young men, very agile and purposeful fellows whose average age couldn't have been over twenty, and the officer in charge—*Segen* Batsur—was only three or four years older. They seemed to have plenty of confidence and experience, especially the demolition expert who found and defused the road mine in about eleven minutes.

"*Tov, tov*, Mordecai," congratulated the *Segen*-lieutenant in the sunglasses.

It was a strange little army all right, with the officers addressing soldiers by their first names.

"Mordecai's handled a few of these before, I gather?"

"Nearly a dozen."

"Good man."

"You're not so bad yourself. Let's see: you captured a bazooka team and knocked out a light machine gun. Two enemy dead, one wounded. We picked up that scout you tied up. Unfortunately the bazooka crew seems to have escaped, but they won't get too far."

The American shrugged.

The guerrillas who'd been manning the RPG hadn't meant

anything to Garrison, but there was probably no point in explaining this to the husky, young *Segen.*

Shoshanna said something in Hebrew, and the Israeli officer nodded in comprehension.

"*Aha,* Green Beret," he identified in tones of respect.

"I'd rather wear a steel pot anytime," Garrison answered.

Then one of the soldiers hurried over from a truck, spoke briefly.

"One of the bazooka crew has been killed by a helicopter patrol, I'm told, and the other two are being pursued toward the frontier," announced Batsur.

"You wouldn't have some water, would you?"

The Israeli handed him a canteen, and Garrison sipped four or five half-mouthfuls. An untrained man who was that thirsty would have gulped down much more, but Garrison drank like a man who was used to conserving his water. Then he passed the canteen to the pretty Shin Beth agent beside him, and when she was finished Garrison returned it to Batsur.

"Thanks. Can we go now, Lieutenant?"

"Of course. *Shalom,* Captain."

"*L'hitra-ot.*"

The lieutenant smiled.

"Your Hebrew's not bad," he complimented.

"But I'm better with an AK-47. See you."

The next day, at 3:50 P.M., he saw the man called The Maven.

They were driving south from Beersheba—the girl at the wheel—when she stopped at a gas station, and even as the car halted he saw the helicopter blossom on the horizon. It touched down beside them a few minutes later, and the Shin Beth executive stepped out and waved.

"I hear you had a busy day with some Arab visitors," Doron began.

Garrison wondered whether he'd also heard about the night after the ambush with the girl in Beersheba's Hotel Zohar, decided that it didn't really matter. It was as unimportant as why Garrison had changed his mind about going to bed with her.

"Our Army was impressed, and so was the Minister of Defense," Doron continued.

It was probably untrue, or at least exaggerated.

From what Garrison had heard, it would take a great deal to impress Israel's one-eyed Minister of Defense.

"Glad you liked it. I'll put it on your bill," the American answered.

"Bill?"

"One 707 jet transport, one RPG bazooka, one light machine gun, and a couple of AK-47s—you're running up quite a tab."

Doron laughed, said something in Hebrew and laughed again when the girl answered.

"Shoshanna is impressed with you too, Captain."

Garrison studied their faces, concluded that she hadn't told him and wondered why—for about three seconds.

"That's lovely, but I'm not planning to run for office here. How about our deal?"

Doron nodded.

"*Kenn*—yes, you've got a deal, Captain. Maybe not a very good deal, but it's the best I can do for you."

Then he paused, lit the pipe, and puffed until a mini-cloud of aromatic smoke rose from the bowl.

"I'm listening," Garrison prodded.

"Officially, we can do nothing. We certainly can't put any of our intelligence networks at your disposal, but we can give you an agent who knows a great deal about Russia. He's operated there frequently during the past thirteen years, speaks the language perfectly and has been in and out nine or ten times. He's been the best man in our Soviet section, the very best. We've just retired him."

"What's the kicker?"

"Kicker?"

"The catch, the problem. What's wrong with him?"

Doron sighed.

"Like yourself, Captain, he's been involved in a good deal of violence. When he was eleven—no, twelve—he fought his way out of the Warsaw Ghetto when the German Army was trying to exterminate the Jewish population there. I don't know how many Nazis he killed—some with his teeth and bare hands, some with broken bottles, rocks, hammers—on his way out, how many more on his way south through the Balkans. He worked for the British in Turkey for two years, then came here to join the Stern Gang. Do you remember the Stern people?"

"They were the roughest of the Jewish underground units, I'm told."

The older man nodded.

"Very rough, very brave, and a little frightening. A small violent organization that some called dedicated, others called fanatical. . . . Well, they went out of business in '48, and since 1950 the man we're discussing has been associated with the Shin Beth. Until last month, anyway. We had to retire him on a pension because he'd lost his objectivity."

"Translation?"

"He's . . . well, he kills too much, too fast."

Garrison shook his head.

"Dandy. That's just *dandy*. Old man Brodsky, wants me to avoid violence and killing, and you're offering me a goddamn homicidal maniac. If you'll pardon the sacrilege," the American muttered, "Jesus H. Christ!"

"I'm really not prepared for theological discussions, Captain. The man I have in mind . . . a very clever and effective agent of great determination . . . we called him *Sahkeen*. In English that means 'knife.' A code name, of course."

"Is he or isn't he a goddamn homicidal maniac?"

Doron's eyes wandered off across the desert.

"That would be an exaggeration, Captain. Do you think I'd offer you a homicidal maniac?"

"Only if it suited the noble purposes of the State of Israel."

The older man smiled, puffed on the pipe.

"I'm glad we understand each other. To quote the great Jewish philosopher Spinoza . . ."

"I wish you wouldn't," Garrison interrupted. "I don't think I could take any epigrams, medieval philosophy, references to the U.N. Charter, or agricultural production figures right now. . . . Tell me more about your kosher assassin."

"Eliahu is not an assassin!" protested the girl.

"His proper name—his legal name—is Eliahu Livneh," Doron

explained. "I believe he could be useful to you because he's used to operating with a minimum of help, with a minimum of that expensive and complicated hardware your C.I.A. seems to favor. He can pass for a Russian, a Pole, a Frenchman, a Greek. He is what you would call . . . a loner. No wife, no children, no known living relatives. The Nazis destroyed his whole family, some in Warsaw and the rest at Auschwitz. Parents, brothers, sisters, uncles, aunts, cousins—all butchered. . . . And as for who's crazy, I wouldn't exactly call your project the most rational operation I've heard about recently."

The hot wind moving across the sand was picking up speed.

"There's a difference. I've got a hang-up, an obsession about settling my bill with the Brodskys. That may be *compulsive* or *neurotic*, but it certainly isn't *psychotic*."

"Let's not argue, my friend, and let's not waste time with this kind of cocktail-party psychiatry. You need a man who knows Moscow and the Soviet Union, who knows the Russian security systems and frontier defenses. I am offering you such a man. He's not perfect—I wish he were—but he's good, maybe just right for this operation."

A truck went by, but they ignored it.

"What have you told him about the operation?"

"Only that you wanted to get a Jewish child out of the Soviet Union, an orphan."

"And what did he say?"

"He said he would try to help you. It was his own decision. He's not under my orders anymore. He's a private citizen now."

The sweat began to bead on Garrison's brow as he considered.

"Why would your Eliahu risk his neck again to help me?"

Doron shrugged.

"Maybe he's as crazy as you think he is, Captain, or maybe he has a . . . what did you call it, a *hang-up* about orphans. You can ask him and find out for yourself."

"All right. I will. About this killing . . ."

"Yes?"

"He doesn't kill people at random, does he? He's not trigger-happy or anything like that?"

The older man shook his head.

"No, nothing like that. He has never slain anyone who wasn't an enemy, but he has killed. Why don't you ask him about it?"

The girl said something fast and urgent in Hebrew, and Doron shook his head again.

"No, Shoshanna, your friend, Captain Garrison, your *good* friend, has a right to know."

Just as Doron knew.

He knew about the night in the Beersheba hotel.

Well, you'd expect The Maven to know a lot—even about sex. Maybe he even knew why Garrison had changed his mind about sleeping with this girl.

"I'd like to meet this Eliahu—as soon as possible."

"How about now? The helicopter can drop us off at the kibbutz in the Galil where he lives—not far from Haifa, and we can be back in Tel Aviv for dinner."

"What about the car?"

He looked at the girl as he asked, and she suppressed her woman-smile.

"Don't worry, Captain. Soshanna can drive it back herself before darkness. We're a small country, you know. Even with the territory we've held since the '67 war, Israel is no bigger than your state of Indiana."

"Only 34,943 square miles," she confirmed in her best tour guide voice.

She didn't want him to leave her, but she wasn't going to say it in front of Doron.

"Have a good flight, Captain," she said as she put out her hand. "*L'hitra-ot.*"

This time she smiled.

He squeezed her warm soft hand, then took his suitcase from the trunk and followed Doron into the helicopter. The Maven spoke, and a minute later the noisy little French machine was airborne. They flew north at 2,500 feet through a clear empty sky, with only an occasional cloud defiling the naked perfection. At one point Garrison saw something flash across the edge of the horizon, off to the left along the coast, and he automatically registered F-4 Phantom. One of *ours*, no, one of *theirs*, a plane sold to Israel's ferociously effective little air force. These were the supersonic fighter-bombers that had zapped the entire Egyptian air force in five or six hours. Now the Phantom was gone, and Garrison looked down at the land below. There was undoubtedly a lot more history in those towns, but it was too noisy in the chopper to speak.

Twenty minutes later he saw Tel Aviv, and thirty minutes after that another large city loomed on the coast.

"Haifa?" he mouthed silently to Doron.

The Shin Beth executive nodded, pointed toward a large green-covered peak.

"Mount Carmel . . . Mount Carmel," Doron identified.

He spoke slowly, articulating carefully so the American could read his lips.

Now he gestured off in the opposite direction—inland.

"Na-za-reth . . . Na-za-reth," Doron repeated, and just in case his meaning wasn't clear The Maven crossed himself twice—with no trace of embarrassment.

Some way to see the Holy Land.

It certainly wouldn't have satisfied the chief security officer of the Athens airport.

The helicopter pilot changed his course, flew northeast until a large body of water appeared.

"Sea-of-Gal-il-ee," Doron announced.

Then the pilot pointed to something, The Maven peered down and nodded and the whirlybird began to descend. Garrison saw a spread of low buildings, tilled fields, and what looked like a swimming pool. There were guard towers too, with fences between them marking the perimeter. Like the other kibbutzim in the Galilee, this one had its own defences. The helicopter rotored down onto the concrete of a parking area near a structure that had to be a storehouse or a garage, and half a dozen men and women in short sleeved shirts and khaki shorts came from the building.

There was a brief flurry of the inevitable *Shaloms* and then Doron spoke a sentence or two, and two of the men replied, speaking almost simultaneously. One of the women said something, and the Shin Beth official answered in tones that were both courteous and authoritative. He wasn't ordering, but his voice made it clear that he knew he had the power to do so. But the husky fair-haired woman was unimpressed—emphatically unimpressed if her massive shrug was any clue—and she answered again to demonstrate her independence.

"*Todah raba, Geveret,*" Doron acknowledged as he led Garrison away.

"What was that all about?"

"About? About Eliahu. He's busy. The lady says he's busy teaching the children how to play the flute, and we're not to interrupt him—of course. The children come first—of course. . . . Come on, come on . . . he'll be finished in a few minutes. Please, no jokes about Jewish mothers."

"I wouldn't think of it, Maven."

Doron shook his head.

"You would. I know you would," he grumbled.

Two buildings away and around a corner, they found the man who killed too quickly sitting in the shade of a large shed with a dozen boys and girls. The children appeared to be between ten and thirteen years old. As for their teacher, he was slim, curly haired, brown eyed, and gentle. His speech, his movements, his manner—all gentle in a way that was almost sad, certainly shy. His hands were big, strong. He might have been forty or forty-five, a poet or a stonemason. He played well, Garrison noticed as they watched and listened to the lesson, and he taught well too. The children obviously responded to him.

When the lesson was over and the children dispersed, Doron and the retired Israeli agent exchanged greetings.

"You are looking well, Eliahu," Doron judged in English a few moments later. "I think the life of a kibbutznick agrees with you."

"It does, and so does the teaching. The children and the quiet and the farm life, all good. . . . Excuse my bad manners. You must be the American. Welcome to Kfar Nepthali. Would you like a cold drink?"

"He means soda or fruit juice, Captain," explained the Maven with a smile. "No gin and tonic here."

"We have beer, if you like, Captain."

"A cold fruit juice would be fine, but I'd better introduce myself first. I'm here as private citizen David Garrison, not as Captain Garrison. I don't represent anybody but myself."

The man who'd been code-named "knife" put out his hand.

"*Tov*, we meet as equals. I too am a private citizen now, a man who speaks and acts only for himself."

They shook hands, and Garrison was not surprised to find his grasp firm and direct.

"The Maven says that he's told you about what I have to do, Mr. Livneh."

"Yes. You'd better call me Eliahu. Yes, he spoke about the young girl in Russia, but I didn't know that you *had* to get her out."

"There is no choice. It is a debt I must pay to a man who saved my life."

The ex-spy nodded in comprehension.

"That's good, David. Good. You *care* about the mission. That should help. You are a man of principle. Good, I will help you if you desire."

For a moment Garrison wondered how to say it.

"The mission—it will require considerable planning and delicacy," he began.

"Of course. The Soviet security system—both at the frontier and elsewhere—is quite good," Livneh agreed.

"We'll have to find holes in it, cracks in the wall, you might say."

The former Shin Beth operative nodded.

"I'm glad that you understand. Yes, it has never been easy to move in and out of the Soviet Union."

Garrison exchanged glances with Doron, who immediately understood but said nothing.

"Oh, I see. You're being polite," judged the man who played the flute so well. "That is kind of you, but frankness would be better. I was retired from the security service of my country because I killed two men in Munich. They were . . . not *relevant* to the mission. They were former S.S. officers who had served at Auschwitz."

"He knows about the camp," Doron said.

"No, he doesn't know anything about it at all. Maybe he read about it," declared the bitter survivor, "but that's not the same thing. He doesn't know anything about Auschwitz, and you don't either."

Then Livneh turned to the American.

"Where were you when they were butchering my family in 1944? Playing football somewhere?"

Garrison shook his head.

"I was five years old—in a kindergarten in Stockbridge, Massachusetts."

Livneh's gaze wandered, returned.

"I'm sorry. I really can't blame you for any of this, Captain. As I was saying, I killed two men for personal reasons and this non-professional behavior could have endangered the mission. . . . I shouldn't have done that."

"I think I understand. I've never seen Auschwitz, but I visited Dachau a few years ago, and I think I understand."

Livneh eyed him appraisingly.

"Why did you visit Dachau?"

"So I'd understand a little better."

"And do you?" tested The Maven.

"Maybe—maybe a little."

Silence, perhaps twenty seconds.

"I'm not sorry about those two butchers in Munich," Livneh announced, "but I wouldn't do it on your mission. The little girl will come first—above everything—if you decide to take a chance on me."

"You're taking quite a chance yourself."

"For a good cause. A man who risks for a good cause isn't really taking a chance, Captain, is he?"

"Maybe not."

More silence, and then The Maven spoke.

"Well, yes or no? I feel like some sort of marriage broker with two nervous clients. Are you going together to rescue Sonya Brodsky, or not?"

The two younger men studied each other, finally shrugged at the same instant.

They shook hands.

They smiled, warily.

"When can you leave?" asked the American.

"Not me—*we*. We will need papers and cover stories, and we will need airplane tickets and then train tickets for the last leg. Three days . . . yes, three days should do it if The Maven helps."

"I'll help," promised Doron. "Anything to get Captain Garrison away from here and out of . . . out of my hair."

Then they spoke in Hebrew again—obviously making schedules and arrangements.

"*Tov*, at four o'clock. Now, about the money, Captain?"

"Yes?"

"You'll cover all expenses, I assume?" Doron pressed.

"Yes, and I can pay Eliahu too."

"I'm not doing this for money," protested the man who'd killed too quickly.

"Be quiet. If Charlie Brodsky is paying our friend well, then the captain can afford to pay you. How much? Ten thousand dollars?"

"Well . . ."

"It's worth at least ten thousand," argued the older man.

"For the kibbutz," interrupted Livneh. "Nothing if I come back alive and well, but if I don't return then let him give the money to the kibbutz."

"Now I know you're crazy. All right, ten thousand to the kibbutz. Is it agreed, Captain? Ten thousand dollars?"

"Agreed. Would you want it in writing, Maven? I have a strange hunch that you just happen to be a notary public, right?"

"We have shaken hands. That is enough," said Livneh.

"Now I'll take that cold beer."

The local beer wasn't at all bad, Garrison decided, and he had a second bottle before the helicopter rose to carry him and Doron back to Tel Aviv. It was sunset by the time they reached the Hilton. The rented car stood in the driveway where the Israeli girl had left it, but Doron was tactful enough not to comment on either the vehicle or the woman who had driven it.

"I will call you tomorrow, about eleven," promised The Maven. "There are a lot of details, a lot of things we must attend to—properly."

"I'm sure you know just what we've got to do."

"Of course I know. I'm The Maven," joked the older man before he returned to his own car. He was about to get in when he paused for a final remark.

"And I know about Auschwitz too. I know a lot about Auschwitz, despite what Eliahu says—about all those camps," he asserted.

"I assumed that you did."

"I wasn't always an official behind a desk, you know," said the Maven defensively. "I did my share of the dirty jobs, of the dangerous missions, of the rotten ones."

Garrison nodded sympathetically, showing more compassion than he actually felt. It wasn't that he disliked Issachar Doron, but the American was hot and tired.

Maybe that was why he couldn't resist the temptation.

Couldn't or wouldn't?

It hardly mattered.

He didn't.

"Maven, I'm grateful for your help, but there's something I ought to tell you. Actually I ought not to tell you, but I want to be completely frank with you."

"Aha, I *knew* there was a catch in it somewhere."

"No, not a catch, but there is one thing that even The Maven didn't know. It's about the money."

"The ten thousand dollars?"

"Yes. You thought you did such a great piece of bargaining. I don't mean to hurt your feelings, but I would have paid double that."

Doron considered this—very briefly.

"I think you did mean to hurt my feelings, Captain," he replied without rancor, "but you didn't do it, I'm still ahead on this transaction. A Boeing 707 and a bus and a whole Arab guerrilla team—I'm ahead all right."

He smiled triumphantly.

"You really ought to learn to keep your mouth shut, Captain," he advised in fatherly tones.

"I just wanted to see what you'd say. No hard feelings?"

"Certainly not. Of course, if you'd like to raise the fee from ten thousand to . . ."

"Eliahu and I will work it out."

Doron shrugged dubiously.

"He's no businessman, Captain."

"That's funny. People say the same thing about me."

"So you're not the canny Yankee trader?"

Garrison shook his head.

"*Tov*—eleven tomorrow," declared The Maven in suddenly brisk tones, and then he drove away.

Garrison and his baggage were conveyed to the room that Shoshanna Hayin had so thoughtfully reserved for him, a cool impersonal Hilton room with effective air-conditioning and an adjacent bathroom that had plenty of hot water in its shower. As the warm stream poured over his body a few minutes later, Garrison closed his eyes and thought about the carnal collision in the hotel in Beersheba.

Then he thought about the woman in Washington.

She was probably still asleep, her long hair flowering and flowing on the pillow and that earnest smile glowing from her open face.

He was going to have to do something about that woman, something serious.

After he brought out Sonya Brodsky.

14

Some hospitals use bells or chimes.

Some use electrical display systems, light bulbs behind a doctor's number on a call board.

Well-financed medical institutions, such as Mount Sinai in New York, supply the house staff with miniature Motorola beepers, little breast-pocket radios that sound when the wearer is wanted on the telephone.

Most hospitals—including Walter Reed—rely on overhead speakers.

"Dr. Clement . . . Dr. Elizabeth Clement," summoned the metallic voice as she walked out of the staff cafeteria, and she stepped back inside to the telephone at the cashier's desk.

"This is Dr. Clement."

It was Colonel Parker.

"Elizabeth, there's a long distance call for Captain Garrison—one of his men, I gather—and perhaps you could speak to him. He wants to get in touch with the Captain, I think, and he seems concerned about the Captain's health. Would you want to talk to him?"

"Yes, I suppose so."

"I'll have the call transferred."

She hung up and smiled mechanically at the fat woman behind the cash register. She exchanged nods with Steve Bettinger and another psychiatrist as they paused to pay their checks. Then the phone rang again.

"Hello, yes, she's right here. For you, Doctor."

"This is Doctor Clement."

"M'aam. This is Sergeant Culpepper. Sorry to bother you, M'aam," drawled the lavishly Southern voice, "but I'm calling about Cap'n Garrison. Cap'n David O. Garrison?"

"You're Junior," she identified.

"Yes, I am."

"Captain Garrison spoke of you—several times. You were with him in that last ambush," she explained.

"*Sheeet*, M'aam . . . I beg your pardon. Excuse the terrible language. Yes, I was with him on a lot of ambushes. A whole bunch of ambushes, the Cap'n, me, and the Chief. That's Sergeant Mendoza, M'aam. He's with me now. We just got in from Saigon about twenty minutes ago. We're at Travis, near San Francisco. . . . How's the Cap'n?"

"I think he's fine. I haven't seen him for a couple of days—four or five—but he was fine then."

She heard him sigh.

"We were kind of worried about him, M'aam. With his face all mashed up and everything. How does he look?"

"Quite handsome. Of course, I may be prejudiced, since I did some of the plastic surgery myself. I'd say he looks very attractive, but a bit different."

"And he's all right? I mean can he see and walk and everything?"

"Yes, everything."

She missed the man and the everything, after only four or five days.

Now she heard another voice, deeper and stronger, in the background.

"I'll ask her. . . . Excuse me, M'aam, but is there some place where we could reach him by phone? I hear he's not in the hospital now. Chief and I are flying east in an hour—on our way to Bragg. Then we've got thirty days leave, and we'd sure like to see the Cap'n."

"He's gone away on a little vacation, Sergeant, and I'm not sure when he'll be back. Would you want to leave a phone number where he can reach you?"

Culpepper gave her two numbers, one for his home in Gainesville, Georgia, and another in Arizona where the Apache's family lived.

"Sorry to bother you this way," apologized the soldier, "but Chief and I hadn't heard from him for about two months, and we got kind of worried. Oh, we'll be at Bragg first. That's Fort Bragg, North Carolina. We'll be there a couple of days, just a couple of days."

"I'm sure he's all right, Sergeant," she assured as the transcontinental conversation frew to a conclusion.

It was untrue, for she wasn't sure at all.

She hoped-wanted-hungered that he was all right, but she certainly wasn't sure. Not knowing where Garrison was or what he was doing—and with whom—was disturbing. It was more than that. It was unnerving, and she didn't want to spend the rest of her life like this.

"It isn't fair," she said softly a moment after she'd put down the phone.

"What?"

Elizabeth Clement glanced at the cashier, nodded noncommittally, and smiled her best meaningless-polite smile. She didn't do it nearly as well as Colonel Parker, but it was adequate. As the plastic surgeon walked out of the cafeteria, she thought about her strange attractive lover and made up her mind.

She would have to do something about David Garrison, something serious.

If and when he returned.

15

The message reached Peking at eleven A.M., but it didn't come to the desk of Colonel Feng until four that afternoon. The delay wouldn't have bothered him that much even if he'd known about it, for he was a patient man who took the long view, the Chinese view, about almost everything. He would have understood about the time it took the courier to come into town from the airport, the time required to decode the dispatch, and the time involved in carrying the sealed pouch from the communications center to Feng's office. Everything took time, as it always had and always would, but that didn't matter. After all, the Chinese People's Republic had all the time in the world—centuries if need be—to achieve its inevitable triumph. With unlimited supplies of time, workers, correct ideology, and Chairman Mao's wisdom, it was certain to prevail.

There might be minor defeats or delays along the way, he assumed, setbacks such as the one reported in this message from Moscow. Plan One for the covert operation designated Salt Fish had failed, and the agent had been taken into custody by security police. It was believed that he had used the cyanide pill before interrogation, and it was believed that Salt Fish itself had not been "blown."

Colonel Feng, an earnest trim man with steel-rimmed glasses and no resemblance to any character actor who ever appeared in a James Bond movie, sighed philosophically. He picked up the small metal bell on his desk, shook it twice to summon Lieutenant Chen.

"Salt Fish," Feng said.

"Yes?"

"Proceed with Plan Two," ordered the colonel as he handed the dispatch to his aide.

Plan Two was quite different from Plan One, involving more personnel and another combat area.

Colonel Feng had never had that much faith in Plan One anyway, and Plan Two seemed to have a better chance of success.

If it failed, there was always Plan Three.

And Plan Four.

And Five.

Garrison followed the bellboy out of the Hilton into the afternoon heat, watched him stow the suitcase in the taxi and then handed over a tip of the size that would be commensurate with his role of American tourist—about thirty-five percent more than necessary.

"*Todah,*" acknowledged the uniformed bellboy.

The American groped for the Hebrew equivalent of "you're welcome," gave up and replied with an all-purpose *shalom*. This seemed to be adequate, but it didn't fool the taxi driver at all. He spoke English when he turned to ask for his passenger's destination.

"Lod? The airport, Mister?"

Garrison looked around, slightly irritated that neither Doron nor the girl had come to see him depart. He didn't expect Eliahu, for the ex-agent had left on a morning Alitalia flight, but he had thought that either the Maven or the girl might bid him farewell.

"The airport, Mister?"

"Yeah."

The cab swung into the city traffic, crawled along for fifteen minutes, and then picked up some speed as it neared the edge of the city.

"Where you going?" the driver asked suddenly.

Garrison ignored him, still annoyed at his lonely exit.

"New York, Mister?"

"Pittsburgh," he lied out of petty malice.

"What do you do there?" pressed the prying chauffeur.

"I'm a brain surgeon."

He saw the driver eyeing him thoughtfully in the rear-view mirror.

"You Jewish, Mister . . . excuse me, Doctor?"

"No, I'm the only brain surgeon in Pittsburgh who isn't Jewish, but I'm a great Sammy Davis fan."

The Israeli considered this for at least twenty seconds.

"Is *that* why you came to Israel, Doctor?"

"That's it. I've got all of Barbra Streisand's records too—in stereo."

The driver pondered, decided to change the subject.

"What about Nixon?" he asked briskly.

Garrison shook his head.

"No, he doesn't sing that well. Sammy Davis and Streisand are *much* better."

"I didn't know he sang at all. I thought he only played the piano," muttered the driver.

"He plays the piano *all right*, but *he's no Rubinstein*."

The man behind the wheel nodded just as if he knew what the American was talking about, and there was no further conversation for the next eight minutes. Then—without warning—he pulled the cab off the road and stopped it beside a gray sedan parked in the shade of a two story house. There were two men in the front seat. One was young and familiar, one of the Maven's armed guards whom Garrison had met that first day on the observation deck. The other, heavy, smiling beneath his sunglasses, was The Maven himself.

Doron climbed out of his sedan and joined Garrison in the taxi.

"He says that Nixon can't sing, Maven," reported the cab driver.

"I'll have to remember that," acknowledged the deputy director of the Shin Beth affably.

"This clown one of your men, Maven?"

Doron nodded.

"I should have guessed," reflected the American. "He was asking a lot of funny questions."

"You were giving a lot of funny answers," replied the driver as he lit a cigarette.

"Please, there isn't much time," Doron reminded. "Let's not bicker. I came out to say good-bye, to wish you success, and to give you a present that might be useful. Are you armed?"

Garrison shook his head.

"Too risky to carry anything made of metal. They've got all those detectors and gadgets at the international airports these days," he answered.

"Exactly. That's why we developed *this*—it's plastic. Only a .32 caliber weapon, but it works."

Garrison unwrapped the pouch, studied the small black automatic. He hefted it, found it oddly light.

"It works. Take my word, Captain."

Garrison put the gun in his jacket pocket.

"Thanks, Maven."

"I have a few more words for you. Soshanna asked me to give you her warm wishes for a safe trip. She wanted to come out, but I didn't see any point in that. You understand?"

"I guess so."

"Very well. Now, are we agreed? The debt is paid?"

Garrison smiled, nodded.

"Of course. You don't owe me a thing, Maven. You've paid your bills."

The older man sighed.

"We may not be a rich country, but we always try to pay our bills—if we can. To our friends and our enemies, sooner or later."

Eichmann.

Doron didn't have to say it.

The name just hung there between them, as tangible as a rock.

Eichmann and the others, Garrison thought. He had no doubt that there had been others, had been and would be. An eye for an eye, it was right out of the Old Testament.

"I hear you've got a lot of friends, Maven."

"And enemies too, Captain. It was all decided a very long time ago. We're the Lord's Chosen People, you know."

It was difficult to tell whether he was joking.

"I wonder why God chose the Jews."

The Maven shrugged.

"I often ask that question myself. Maybe nobody else wanted the job."

"Maybe so. There's an awful lot of crap that goes with it."

"Yes, but at least it's steady. It has been for a couple of thousand years, anyway. . . . Well, I don't want to delay you. Give my best wishes to Charlie Brodsky, and to his great-niece—if you ever see her."

"I'll see her—and I'll get her out," Garrison announced firmly.

"You sound completely committed to the rescue of this little girl, Captain."

"Masada shall not fall again. Isn't that the slogan?"

The Israeli considered, nodded thoughtfully.

"Yes, that's it. It sounds a bit odd coming from you, Garrison. No offense meant, but it sounds a little odd. You're not saying that to be . . . amusing, are you? That's a serious pledge in this country."

"I'm absolutely serious . . . *Shalom*, Maven."

"*Shalom*, Yankee Captain."

They shook hands and Doron left the taxi, and nineteen minutes later a porter was unloading Garrison's bag at the airport. When Garrison drew his wallet to pay the driver, the man behind the wheel shook his head.

"Compliments of the Shin Beth," he announced. "We wouldn't want you to think we're cheap. A lot of people think that our people are cheap, and it isn't true."

"I never thought so."

"Well, a lot of people do. We're actually very generous and charitable. It's part of the religion, you know."

"I see. . . . Thanks for the ride."

The driver smiled, leaned out the window.

"It's okay, Garrison. Say, that thing about Nixon? It's true, isn't it?"

Garrison nodded solemnly.

"Absolutely. He isn't a tenth as good as Rubinstein. Not a tenth. That's confidential, of course."

"Of course," beamed the chauffeur who was visibly delighted to be privy to this momentous secret. "I won't tell anyone. I can keep my mouth shut."

They exchanged farewells, and fifty minutes later Garrison was airborne in one of El Al's sleek 707s. It was a quick pleasant flight to Rome, one that seemed even faster because of the deft service by several extremely attractive stewardesses who seemed somehow less impersonal than the young women who'd worked the transatlantic journey. The whole experience was less brisk, less sterile, less mechanical—and one of the pretty Israeli girls had a definite resemblance to Shoshanna Hayin. It wasn't that important, he realized, for he'd probably never see Shoshanna Hayin again.

There was a steward on the plane, too, and as the disembarking passengers began to exit at the Rome airport he handed Garrison an envelope.

"You dropped this, sir," he lied casually and immediately turned his attention to a plump old woman and her graying husband.

Garrison put the envelope in the inner breast pocket of his jacket as he entered the terminal, left it there until he'd cleared through all the customs-immigration-public health checks and paid to have his single bag delivered to a taxi. It wasn't until he'd reached the privacy of his room in the Hotel Continentale—the agreed rendezvous—that he opened the envelope and found his new passport. It was almost his old passport, being an exact copy in every detail except that this counterfeit was adorned with an expertly forged visa authorizing entry into the Soviet Union. Garrison was admiring the skillful work when Eliahu Livneh knocked at the door.

"I'm impressed," announced the American, and he tapped the false passport to make his point clear.

"Yes, they're good at that sort of thing. It's useful, I suppose, but

I can't get enthusiastic about it. I mean, could you fall in love with a watch repairer? It's all technique and technology. Maybe that impresses Americans . . . sorry, I didn't mean to sound unfriendly."

"You didn't."

"To be fair, that visa will save us about ten or twelve days. It would take at least that long to get it approved in Moscow."

"And I notice that there's no Israeli visa in this," Garrison noted. 'According to this, I've never been in the State of Israel."

"What State of Israel?" Livneh asked innocently.

Then he handed Garrison a folder decorated with the name of an Italian travel agency.

"I'll see you in four days, David. You've memorized the schedule?"

"Very carefully . . . Eliahu, thanks. I know you're not doing it for the money."

"I'm doing it for the girl, and because I have no choice—morally. Whether you know it or not, I imagine that you're doing it for the same reasons."

It was a disturbing thought, or at least a disturbing question. Garrison didn't enjoy pondering questions of morality. While he didn't consider himself to be immoral—not even amoral—he felt vaguely uncomfortable when consciously confronted with such grand issues. It was perfectly all right to handle them unconsciously or instinctively, but talking about them made him feel pompous and awkward. He hadn't spoken about such things since college, he realized, and suddenly he wondered why.

Soldiers rarely did, but that wasn't a satisfactory answer. It wasn't the least bit satisfactory, he concluded grimly.

"You look troubled," Livneh noted.

"I'm all right. You want to get some dinner?"

The Israeli shook his head.

"It might not be wise to be seen together—wise for you. I've been operating in half a dozen countries during the past eleven years, and there are people who might remember my face. Have a good journey, David."

The journey began—or resumed—at nine the next morning when Garrison boarded the LOT flight to Warsaw. The Polish airline's Soviet-built Ilyushin transport arrived in time for him to enjoy an excellent lunch at the Europejski—the hotel into which he'd been booked by the official Orbis State Travel Organization. At $15.50 a day for the room and three meals, it was certainly a good buy, and the guided tour of the city—especially the restored old city—was certainly pleasant. Garrison didn't enjoy it much, however, for his mind was on the girl in the Moscow orphanage. He bought her two elaborate folk dolls in peasant costumes the next day before his train headed east for the Soviet capital.

It was cool in Moscow.

As the taxi carried David Garrison from the Byelorussia railroad station toward the lofty white hotel on Gorki Street, he looked out at the city with considerable curiosity. It was all new and strange to him, despite the newsreels he'd seen, for this had not been his team's target area. The Special Forces "A" Team that he'd commanded in Germany had been thoroughly briefed for guerrilla and sabotage operations in the Ukraine, taught the language and the geography and the power plants and the rail lines.

There had been a dam, a big dam.

He remembered it clearly.

A big dam that somebody had code-named Harvey Nine, that somebody else had photographed and still somebody else had calculated could be knocked out with a small atomic warhead of the "Jasper" type.

Garrison had never known who any of these somebodies were, but he still remembered that it had been his team's assignment to take out that dam with the "Jasper"—if and when ordered. There had been another assignment involving the Ukrainian capital of Kiev, and Garrison still recalled much of what he'd learned about that city.

Yes, he'd probably have found Kiev quite familiar after all those hundreds of hours of briefing.

But this busy city wasn't the least bit familiar, and he felt uneasy as the cab halted in front of the twenty-three story tower that had to be Moscow's newest hotel, the Intourist. He wasn't afraid, but it was all new and strange and undoubtedly dangerous. Hazardous or not it was a debt that had to be paid, he reflected, and any notion that Garrison believed in the morality of rescuing this child was pure Jewish romance.

And David Garrison knew he wasn't a romantic or a moralist, no matter what Livneh had said. This thought comforted the American as he entered the glassy lobby, and it wasn't until he reached his room on the eighteenth floor that he found himself wondering what sort of child Sonya Brodsky might be. It had probably been a mistake to buy those dolls in Warsaw, he reflected as he opened his suitcase and saw them staring up at him, for a girl of her age was probably too old for dolls.

"It was stupid," he thought aloud.

And then—quite automatically—his eyes began to sweep the room's handsome Finnish furniture in ritual search for concealed microphones.

16

He didn't find any.

Either there were none or they were too well concealed, perhaps built in during the hotel's construction. It didn't really matter that much because he wasn't going to be doing any dangerous talking here—not in the room or even over the telephone, but he was professionally curious. During the "Soviet Security and Counter-espionage Methods" course he'd taken in Munich back in '70 they'd warned that many of the rooms into which the Russians' official Intourist travel agency booked foreigners were wired, so he felt impelled to try to find the listening device—out of loyalty to his instructors.

No, nothing.

He hung up his clothes, washed his hands and face and then glanced at his watch. It was 5:35, almost dusk and probably too late to visit the Ministry of Foreign Affairs. The Israeli had instructed him to approach the Ministry quite openly and directly, to seek official permission and cooperation from the start. That would help allay any suspicions, and would probably be the quickest and simplest way to get into the orphanage. "Just behave the way any intelligent traveler would in a foreign country," Livneh had said. "Be interested, polite, curious, wary—and respectful—of the other culture. If you find you're under surveillance, you must pretend not to notice it. An ordinary tourist wouldn't. Remember, this is only to make contact with the girl and study the security system of the orphanage—reconnaissance. We're just shopping, not buying, so there's no hurry. Eat, drink, walk around, take a guided tour. Act natural."

Garrison looked down at Red Square—an oddly exhilarating sight—and then he followed Livneh's advice. He dined well in the hotel—the menu was extensive for foreign tourists on the "deluxe plan"—on caviar, Siberian ravioli-like *pilmeny*, skewered mutton, and a half bottle of Georgian *tsinadali* that would cause no insomnia in the chateaux of Beaune or St. Emilion. The service by the black-suited waiters was a bit better than the wine, but Garrison didn't mind the leisurely pace for he was determined to follow the Israeli's instruction not to hurry. The American sipped at a snifter of tolerable "Jubilee" brandy, making it last a long time before he lit a cigar and strolled out into the Moscow night. A number of other people were doing the same thing, and none of them appeared to be paying any great attention to him. He walked down Gorki Street, observed the animated couples entering the Moscow Theater and then wandered on to admire the domes and walls and night illumination of The Kremlin.

No sweat.

No problem, no discernible surveillance, no sweat at all.

He returned to the hotel a little after ten, tried to force himself to read the pompous prose of the official English-language *Moscow Times*, gave up and fell asleep before midnight. After a large breakfast the next morning, he went to the Ministry for Foreign Affairs where he was eventually directed to a minor functionary named Krestovy.

"You wish to see a child named Sonya Brodsky at the Ostankin School for wards of the state? Correct?"

"The Ostankin orphanage," Garrison confirmed.

"There are no orphans in the Soviet Union," said Mr. Krestovy pleasantly. "There are children whose parents have died, of course, but the state is their mother and father. We are very progressive in the care and raising of children, and people come from all over the world to study our modern methods. Not just the Socialist world either."

Garrison nodded, just as if he cared.

"But you're here to see one child," continued Krestovy. "Are you a relative?"

"No, just a friend of her uncle. Her grand-uncle, to be precise. He's an old man and quite ill, and he asked me to see her when he heard that I'd be coming over here on my vacation."

"Your first trip to the Soviet Union?" Krestovy asked warily.

"My first trip to Europe," Garrison confessed with an appropriate display of American modesty. "First trip out of the country at all, except for the week I went up to Montreal for Expo in '67. I don't get to travel much."

"Not even when you were in the Army?"

Krestovy may have been a minor bureaucrat, but he wasn't a stupid minor bureaucrat.

"No, I was stationed in Kansas. . . . This is all pretty exciting to me. Paris . . . Rome . . . Warsaw . . . and now Moscow. Fascinating . . . really fascinating. I'm kind of sorry that I'll only be here five days."

"You can't possibly see Moscow in five days, Mr. Garrison."

The American shrugged.

"Don't I know it. The Kremlin, the museums, the Bolshoi—couldn't see it all in a month. I don't have much time to spend with this little girl, but if I could see her for thirty or forty minutes—say, tomorrow—then I'd have done my duty. I promised the old man, you know. He gave me my first job."

"And you still work for him?"

"No, that was ten-eleven years ago. I've got a bookstore of my own now."

"Of course, you told me. In Boston," Krestovy recalled with a nod.

Nice try.

Nice try, but no balloon.

That's what Junior would have said with a delighted grin, but then Junior found efforts to trick him quite amusing. Garrison didn't.

"Not Boston, Pittsfield," he corrected without any visible trace of the hostility he felt. "Same state, but Pittsfield's in the Berkshires more than 120 miles further west. We're a lot smaller, only about seventy thousand people. Great skiing country all around us. And some fine colleges."

Maybe Mr. Krestovy hadn't been trying to trick him at all, for he didn't ask any more questions but simply nodded again and promised to do what he could to secure permission for Garrison to visit the girl. The New Englander thanked him, went out to look at the great city as a tourist should. Guidebook in hand, he slowly and respectfully went through the impressive towers, museums, cathedrals, frescoes, ikons, weapons collections, jeweled royal costumes, and other historic fantasies that filled the sixty-four-acre compound known as The Kremlin.

The carved walnut throne of Ivan the Terrible and his coat of mail.

Boris Gudunov's splendid carriage and jewel-encrusted ring.

Peter the Great's huge boots.

The huge hall where the All Union Communist Party and the Supreme Soviet assemble in the Grand Kremlin Palace.

Then outside the Kremlin's crenellated red-brick walls to the Lenin Mausoleum in Red Square, where he was courteously ushered to the head of the line along with some other foreign visitors. It was a long day and so was the next one, even with the guide and car he hired. Then, nearly forty-eight hours after his visit to the Foreign Ministry, Krestovy telephoned with word that the appointment had been set for noon.

"And don't worry about the language problem, Mr. Garrison," said the Soviet official. "I'm told that the child speaks some English, and that at least two of the teachers are fluent in several languages. If you should need help, they can interpret for you."

"I really can't thank you enough," Garrison acknowledged truthfully.

"Hospitality to visitors is a Russian tradition, despite all the terrible tales you may have read about us in the foreign press. You ought to read a country's own newspapers and magazines."

"Yes, I should."

"You can get them in the U.S., you know. You might even subscribe. I'm sure that our Cultural Attaché in Washington could help you."

"I'll check into it . . . Comrade."

"That's the spirit. Co-existence and friendly respect. Cultural exchange here, cooperation in space, too. You agree?"

Garrison did, and managed to escape from the conversation just as Krestovy was beginning to suggest that there might be quite a market for Soviet books in the Berkshires. Taking the two dolls from his suitcase, Garrison descended to the lobby to try to find some other gift. Unable to choose from the many handsomely decorated boxes, blouses, bowls, and other handicrafts, he settled for a large box of chocolates as a safe compromise.

He felt a bit foolish as he entered the taxi.

It was almost as if he were going to woo this child.

The Ostankin School was a large four-story building, rather dreary in the square functional design favored by Soviet architects during the 1950s. It was gray and modern, and, by comparison with the gracious older structure next door, somewhat ugly. The ample playground just inside the school fence was filled with swings and other such equipment, but that didn't help much either. The imprint of public institution was unmistakable.

A bell somewhere rang as Garrison approached the front door. He checked his wristwatch, saw that it was exactly noon and pressed the buzzer. Within three minutes, he was in the office of Direktor Fedoskino, the head of the school. It was a pleasant, square, cluttered office, much like the husky woman who occupied it. She had metal rimmed glasses, a motherly manner, and an excellent command of English. She also had about ten minutes to spend chatting with the foreign visitor before she began the tour—obviously the standard tour—of the school. At 12:35, she led Garrison into the large lunchroom and guided him to the table at which nine children and a teacher were eating. One of the children was Sonya Brodsky.

Mrs. Fedoskino—she wore a very plain wedding band—said something in Russian, and all the children replied in what was plainly some courteous greeting. They seemed cheerful and curious, eyeing the *Amerikanski* with unconcealed interest.

"Sonya," said the Direktor, "this is Mr. Garrison from the United States of America. From the State of Massachusetts. He is a friend of your grand-uncle, and he has come here to see you."

The girl smiled cautiously, attractively. She was quite pretty, plainly dressed in the school's blue jumper uniform but definitely pretty. She had large brown eyes, curly blondish hair and an adolescent figure that promised she'd be a shapely young woman in three or four years.

"It was very kind of you to come, Mr. Garrison," she recited, and then she shook his hand, properly. "I hope that your trip was a pleasant one."

She spoke in the serious respectful tones of a well brought-up child, but the voice didn't entirely match the tiny flicker of fire in those large placid eyes. It was there. Something, some secret dream or anger or joy, was there. Garrison had no idea as to what it was, for he knew so little about adolescent girls, but it was there.

"The trip was fine," he answered.

"And how are you enjoying Moscow?"

What the hell was it that she was trying, or perhaps not trying, to hide?

"I'm having a wonderful time. This is a great city, a civilized city so full of history and art," he replied with as much sincerity as he could muster.

The Direktor of the Ostankin School beamed. The visitor had been impressed by her school—he'd said so—and he appreciated Moscow. When he accepted her invitation to join the children for lunch, she sat beside him and told him about other places and theaters he should not miss. She was a tactful woman who knew her job; she made a point of including the children in the conversation from time to time. She wasn't pretending that they were little adults, but she acknowledged that they were capable of intelligent conversation.

Sonya Brodsky spoke several times, at the discreet prompting of Mrs. Fedoskino, but it wasn't until the dessert arrived that Garrison realized what was wrong. She hadn't mentioned her grand-uncle once. She hadn't asked about him once.

It couldn't be bad manners, for hers were perfect.

It had to be caution—or fear.

"I almost forgot the presents. I'm sorry," Garrison apologized as he put down his sweet tea. "I brought these for you, Sonya. They're probably too childish, but I didn't know what else to get."

He handed her the two packages and she glanced at Mrs. Fedoskino; the Direktor urged her to open them.

"Thank you, Mr. Garrison . . . Oh, *chocolates*. I love chocolates," she confessed. Then she remembered and offered candies to each of the other children at the table, as well as Mrs. Fedoskino, and the Direktor beamed again. Marx would have loved it, Garrison reflected as he bit into the piece he'd accepted.

"So this is Socialism," he said in wry admiring tones.

"Don't children share in your country?"

"Yes, but not always so dutifully. Please, I'm not criticizing Socialism or Russia—or you either. Tell me what you think of the dolls."

She opened the box, and she beamed.

"They are childish, Mr. Garrison," she acknowledged, "but they're beautiful. They are . . . what is the word . . . *delightful*."

"You really like them?"

"Our children do not lie," announced Mrs. Fedoskino righteously.

She couldn't help it, Garrison decided.

She was a middle-aged bureaucrat, an administrator, a patriot—and in her own touching way a bit of a pain in the ass. Probably not much more of a pain in the ass than a pious U.S. or British bureaucrat of the same age and organizational loyalty would be, he thought, but still a pain in the ass.

"Yes, I've heard that," the soldier replied. "Tell me something about your life and schedule here, Sonya. Your uncle will want to know, I'm sure."

She explained the daily routine and then—at Mrs. Fedoskino's suggestion—walked the guest through the rooms where she studied, painted, did gymnastics, sang, and lived. The last, a pleasant but slightly bare chamber with four beds, was on the second floor at the rear of the building, near a convenient fire-staircase. Garrison studied the room and the exits thoughtfully, then turned his attention to the photo taped to the wall beside the window.

"That's the Prime Minister, isn't it?"

"Oh yes, there's one in every bedroom," the girl explained in tones devoid of any comment.

"And that watercolor, yours?"
She nodded.
Birds, soaring high and free.
"Nice, very nice," complimented the American truthfully.
"Would you like it?"
"Well, I wouldn't want to . . ."
"Please, I'd be delighted to give it to you—as a souvenir of your visit," she assured him. "I have many others."
She took a large folder from a drawer, showed him more than a dozen watercolors.
All birds.
"Take anyone you want, Mr. Garrison."
He thanked her, selected.
"I guess the artistic taste runs in the family," he observed. "Your grand-uncle has quite a collection of paintings and sculptures, you know."
"I didn't know that. . . . He's . . . he's quite old, isn't he?"
"Yes, and he's not in good health."
Something glowed in her eyes, subsided.
"I'm sorry to hear that."
"He's a remarkable man, your grand-uncle. A big man, in heart and in spirit. Very proud, very decent, very strong, and very loving. You'd like him. . . . Would you like to see him?"
"Of course . . . if he ever comes to Moscow."
Garrison shrugged.
"He's too sick for that. Is there any message that I might give him, Sonya?"
She hesitated.
"Please tell him that I hope he gets well, and that I send him warm Socialist greetings."
"From the peace-loving children of the Soviet Union? Shouldn't I add that to make the message complete and official?" Garrison asked with cool irony.
It was stupid to get angry with this child, but he was half-way there.
"Of course. Yes, and give him this small drawing from me."
She took out another of her works.
"Will I see you again, Mr. Garrison?" she asked as she handed it to him.

Maybe she was trying to say something that she couldn't or daren't say.

"Perhaps. If you like, and if Mrs. Fedoskino likes, maybe we could go to the zoo after classes one afternoon."

She smiled.

"You'll have to ask her. Good-bye, Mr. Garrison, and thank you for coming. For the gifts too, of course."

Then she put out her hand and shook his, and left to join her classmates. He seemed like a very nice sort of person for an American, she thought as she walked away.

If he was an American.

There was really no way of knowing.

He could be anyone—testing her loyalty, perhaps even an agent of the Committee for State Security.

Sonya Brodsky was only fourteen, but she was no fool.

The Israeli had given three rendezvous points.

At 9:45 in the morning, the foot of the huge stone statue of Karl Marx in Sverdlov Square.

At 4:10 in the afternoon, the circular modern building on Kutuzovsky Prospect that housed the "memorial exposition of the Borodino Battle of 1812."

At 10:20 in the evening, the Mayakovskaya "underground station" of the subway system.

There was plenty of time for Garrison to spend an hour in a downtown bookstore and another browsing in the Moskva Department Store on Leninsky Prospect and then buy ice cream from a street vendor before heading for the Borodino memorial. The captain wasn't that interested in the historic clash of arms in which the Tsar's forces had stopped Napoleon's invaders, but it was the crowds of tourists—Soviet and foreign—that made the exhibit hall attractive. With all those visitors moving around the battlefield diorama and displays, it should be fairly easy to contact Livneh without attracting too much attention. The Israeli had explained that and described the building's interior carefully during the final Tel Aviv briefing.

"On September 7th, the foreign imperialists advanced—some 130,000 strong—to Borodino, only seventy miles from Moscow. Here 127,000 Russian soldiers waited, determined to stop Napoleon's brutal assault upon the capital," said the guide who looked nothing like the pretty Israeli girl who'd shown him Tel Aviv and Jerusalem.

They probably had one thing in common though. Garrison looked at the short, one-armed man and guessed that he was an ex-soldier. The American was right.

"At six in the morning, the French began a frontal attack *here*—a great mass attack of infantry," continued the guide.

Garrison saw the Israeli enter the big room, waited as Livneh moved unobtrusively through the crowd toward the big model of the battlefield. When the other visitors shifted in response to something the guide was explaining, Livneh slipped in beside the American.

For nearly ten minutes they listened to the account of the great Russian victory, but they didn't speak to each other until they'd stepped out of the building into the warm afternoon.

"It wasn't a great victory at all, you know," Garrison said bluntly.

"Who cares?"

'They did hold the French for about twelve hours and they inflicted heavy casualties, but they took heavy casualties too *and* Napoleon rolled on into Moscow."

"I know, *Dahveed.* I've been here before."

"Then why the hell do they call it a victory? It isn't as if the Russians haven't had some great victories, some terrific victories. They're fine soldiers, excellent soldiers."

The Israeli shook his head.

"David, forget Borodino. Tell me about the girl. Have you seen her?"

"Yes, at lunch today. Then she showed me around the school. She shares a room with three other girls on the second floor, facing the back. There's a rear staircase right near her door. No guards in sight. No sign of alarm systems."

"Why should there be? It's only a home and school for young orphans, not KGB headquarters," Livneh answered with a smile. "Tell me about the girl herself."

"I don't know. Pretty, intelligent, good manners—but I don't know. She showed practically no interest in her American relatives, the only family she has in the world."

"The key word is *showed*, I gather?"

"I think so, but I can't be sure. Most young American girls in her position would be very interested, would be hungry for some family, maybe even dreaming of getting out of the orphan asylum. This kid didn't seem to care."

"You seem troubled by this," the Israeli noted sympathetically.

Garrison shrugged, then nodded.

"I suppose I am, but I didn't come all this way to worry about some fourteen-year-old kid."

"But that's exactly what you did do," corrected Livneh with a smile.

"I'm here for the old man."

The Israeli shook his head.

"Not me, David. I'm here for the child."

"And the money?" challenged Garrison.

"No, the child. The money wasn't my idea. That was something you and the Maven conceived—your business. I don't do business with children's lives. You can keep the money."

Garrison looked, saw that he was serious.

"I didn't mean to get you angry," apologized the American.

"I know you didn't."

"Okay . . . okay, let's get back to business. Sorry, I mean the mission. Assuming that we can spring her from the school, how do you plan to get her out across the frontier?"

As they walked, Livneh explained that he had received "certain information" during the previous forty-eight hours that indicated a tightening of security on the European land frontiers of the Soviet Union. The airports were always tight, he reported, so they'd have to go out by small boat—either to Sweden or Turkey. Sweden would be easier, certainly easier than last year when that specially-equipped squadron of U.S. torpedo boats had been making "ferret" runs along the Baltic shores to check out the Soviet coastal radar frequencies.

"I thought that was a British operation," Garrison observed as he noticed the policeman across the street.

"Used to be, but not for the past three years. It's stopped now, for the moment, nothing since last November. That's what I hear anyway."

From whom?

Garrison wondered, considering asking and decided that he had no real "need to know." This was the sort of information that would be tightly held, shared only among those with a strong "need to know."

"Can we get a boat up on the Baltic?" he asked instead. "Without stealing it, I mean. If there's any fuss, they'll send out air and sea patrols to blast us—I imagine."

"Correct. Don't worry, David. There is a little port near Riga, and a man there—a *trustworthy* man—who can provide a craft that can get us into Swedish waters before dawn."

Not a bad plan.

If the man was still there.

If the man was still trustworthy.

If he wasn't under KGB surveillance for any one of a hundred reasons.

If his boat wasn't being repaired.

If its motor didn't die in the middle of the journey.

If the night were dark and Soviet patrol craft didn't spot them.

If they didn't hit a minefield or founder in a wild sudden storm.

Not a bad plan at all, Garrison thought with only a trace of bitterness, and certainly no worse than some others that he'd risked his life on in recent years.

"We pray a lot too, I suppose?" he asked.

"It cannot hurt. Yes, we pray a lot, because we are taking a great risk and we are frightened. We pray even though I have done this before and our boatman knows these waters well. Do you object?"

Garrison shook his head.

"Are you saying that you object to praying or you don't?"

The American shrugged, smiled.

"You just tell me what the prayer is. That's all I ask, Eliahu. I've never prayed to the ancient God of Israel before, you know."

"I didn't ask you to pray to *my* God—just to pray. Is there something wrong with *your* God, David?"

Garrison shrugged.

"I'm not sure that he makes house calls anymore," he answered grimly. "He didn't in Vietnam . . . not very often anyway. . . . We'll see. Meanwhile, you'd better see about some travel documents for the kid. If somebody stops us on the way north from Moscow, we'd damn well better have the right papers for her."

"I'll need a current photo of her."

"Check. Tomorrow I'll go back and take a picture of her—to bring back to her grand-uncle. Should be no sweat."

Now it was the Israeli who smiled.

"I think you'll sweat, *Dahveed.*"

"Till I deliver her to Charlie Brodsky," Garrison admitted. "I don't usually get this worked up about a mission though. Must be getting old."

"Tomorrow night at 10:20 you'll bring the film to the subway station, yes?"

"Yes. . . . You don't seem the least bit worried or nervous about the operation, or have you given up sweating for Passover?"

"Passover was in April," the Israeli said calmly.

"You're not answering the question."

"David, I don't sweat. I haven't sweated for many years."

"You're out of practice?" challenged the American.

Livneh considered, sighed.

"Maybe . . . I don't know. All I know is that I haven't been frightened since I reached Turkey at the end of 1944. Is it important?"

There was no answer, none that seemed sensible.

"No, stay cool. Hang loose and watch your ass—to quote Sergeant Arnold Culpepper, Jr."

"A sage?"

"No, a genius at survival," Garrison identified with a grin. "The world champ, you might say. . . . Okay, I'll see you tomorrow night."

They separated without another word or glance, and Garrison walked back to his hotel to reflect on the escape plan. He could handle the details of the break into the school itself, but the departure from Soviet territory was beyond his knowledge or experience. He'd have to rely on a man who was both a stranger and a foreigner, a troubling prospect filled with ambiguities for a professional soldier who'd seen people die doing that.

Unfortunately, there was no alternative.

Not with the old man dying back there in New York.

Dinner at an Uzbek restaurant on Neglinnaya Street that his hotel desk clerk recommended, then some two and a quarter hours watching the Kirov Ballet troupe—the Bolshoi was abroad—and finally a brandy before he returned to his room to prepare for bed. In purely routine fashion, he rechecked for microphones and found nothing. He slept well for three hours, fell asleep for two more, and then dozed fitfully until dawn.

After breakfast the next morning, he visited the masterpiece-crammed Tretyakov Gallery across the river from The Kremlin and emerged somewhat dazed by the fantastic collection of both Russian and foreign paintings. At that, he'd only seen a tiny fraction of the Tretyakov's incredible fifty thousand works when he left at 11:30 to take the taxi to the Ostankin School to photograph Sonya Brodsky.

He didn't take the picture.

He couldn't.

She wasn't there and she wasn't coming back and the Direktor spoke vaguely about the transfer of nine students to "another school—out of the city." Mrs. Fedoskino explained that "The Ministry" had made this decision to move Sonya Brodsky and eight others "to avoid overcrowding," and David Garrison listened without the slightest idea as to whether this was the truth. It was so difficult to determine whether this was some bureaucratic blunder, a real move to reduce overcrowding, or some devious scheme of one of the Soviet security agencies.

"Why don't you write to her? We should have her new address in a few weeks?" suggested the Direktor.

It was probably very easy to get paranoid in Moscow, Garrison judged—even easier than in Washington. Everything *looked* right, but still something *felt* wrong.

"I'll write," he promised.

It was only a hunch, and he kept reminding himself of this on the way back to the hotel. Jungle jitters—the medics had called it "battle fatigue." There wasn't a single sign, not one clue, that anything was wrong, not a shred of hard evidence that might indicate that the mission was blown. If he was under surveillance, they were very good because he couldn't spot one of them—not one.

Of course, it would be easier to spot them in the jungle—*his* terrain. It would even be easier if this were Kiev, a city he'd studied. Still, even if he didn't know Moscow he had his instincts and he wasn't too rigid to respect them. The Apache had taught him that. Trouble. His instincts all predicted it, and his body was already tensing to cope with the nameless danger.

He felt better already.

It was probably very neurotic—that's what the lady doctor in Washington would call it—but he felt better. In a little while he'd know for sure because *they* would certainly make some small mistake no matter how good they were, and then he'd know what to do. He was a veteran commander with years of combat experience in small unit battle. He'd know exactly what to do—when to fight, where to fight, and even when to run. What he didn't know, he realized soberly, was how to find Sonya Brodsky and that was all that mattered. The rescue might still be possible if both Garrison and Livneh hadn't been "burned"—identified as foreign agents by the Sovs. The stock Pentagon designations—Sovs and Chicoms—suddenly struck him as bizarre as any names in *Alice in Wonderland*, and for a moment he wondered what equally weird tags Russian military leaders had picked for the U.S. and Britain.

Then, for no apparent reason, he found himself thinking about Charlie Brodsky and the Nisei nurse and the black man who was writing his book. He thought about them for at least thirty seconds, and then he returned to checking on whether he was being followed. Nothing, not *yet*. When he reached his hotel, he went up to his room to wash before lunch.

Yet.

There it was.

In that first Sov and Chicom Security course back in '67, he'd learned about the eight places where Russian intelligence personnel were most likely to place listening devices and so—quite routinely—his eyes flicked to each of them in the memorized sequence. It was a mechanical precaution with its own rhythm, like checking the seat belt, mirror angle, gas supply, and oil indicator before pulling a car out into traffic. He didn't have to *think* about it, not after all these years. He looked at the floor lamps, then the picture frames, then the wall moldings—and he didn't have to go any further.

It was a standard model, apparently an improved and slightly miniaturized version of The Roach. It probably had a very different name in Russian, of course, but the C.I.A. instructor named Wheeler who'd taught the course had called it The Roach. On reflection, Garrison decided that the C.I.A. man probably wasn't really named Wheeler either since employees of that "other agency of the government" often used pseudonyms—but it didn't matter now.

Garrison had found *it.*

His instincts had been right, and that was all that mattered.

It could be a routine spot-check on visiting foreigners—which would be bad enough. At the very least, that would constitute what Sergeant Culpepper would categorize as "a significant rectal discomfort" or it could be something more serious, "a genuine certified pain in the ass." It might even be a sign that Garrison and/or Livneh had been "burned," which Culpepper would grimly concede to be "an authentic four-star pain in the ass with oak leaf clusters." The situation had to be very bad to rate the oak leaf clusters, very, very bad.

Don't panic.

Garrison didn't. It wasn't his style anyway.

Don't let them know that you know, Wheeler had advised, and David Garrison did exactly that. He washed his hands and hummed, then enjoyed a hearty lunch in the hotel dining room and went out to visit a few more tourist attractions. It was as he left the big GUM department store on the northeast side of Red Square just before five o'clock that he noticed he was under surveillance. He was being followed by a rather dull-faced man of about forty wearing a poorly cut brown suit and an expression that reflected either constipation or an over-tight shirt collar. He'd exhibited the same vaguely unhappy look in the fur department and the rug section, Garrison recalled as he remembered the face, and—understandably irritated—Garrison found himself hoping that it was *both* constipation and a tight collar.

And boils.

With a touch of athlete's foot, and an impacted wisdom tooth.

There was nothing wrong with a little healthy hostility, Garrison reminded himself as he walked back toward his hotel, just so long as it didn't cloud one's judgement. This man was probably a total nonentity, a fourth-echelon fifth-rate agent who'd screwed up in some KGB training school or botched some bigger assignment and was now reduced to serving out his years until pension in such dreary tasks as following low level suspects around Moscow. He didn't even do that too well, just doggedly.

Garrison couldn't shake him.

He tried four times, carefully and discreetly to avoid arousing suspicion, and failed. The man was still with him when Garrison reached the hotel, but he was gone when the American emerged at 9:20 that evening. Garrison set out for the rendezvous warily, moving through the streets with an inner tension that he would never have felt in the jungle. This was a city, a strange one in a foreign land, not his kind of battleground at all. This wasn't even his kind of war, he reflected, as he checked again and again to see whether he was being stalked. Finally, convinced that he was safe, he set off for the subway station where he was to meet Livneh.

He got there five minutes early—a routine precaution—and once more checked on possible watchers. All clear. The American strolled along the passenger platform admiring the handsomely decorated walls, so different from the drab London tubes or Paris metro or the New York network. One minute to rendezvous.

There was Livneh.

Garrison turned the other way casually, as if looking for an approaching train, and then he saw the man who'd followed him from the department store. Maybe he wasn't a first class KGB agent, but he was good enough.

Good enough to have trailed the ambush expert to the rendezvous without being detected.

Too good to let see the contact with the Israeli, an operative who might well be on some Soviet list.

There were—theoretically—several options open, a number of possible responses . . . but in fact there was none. There was only one choice that would not be suicidal, and David Garrison knew that any other course would be much too dangerous. He reached into the inner breast pocket of his jacket as he turned to face Livneh, drew out his wallet and looked into it as if to count his money.

That was the prearranged signal, one of four they'd set in Rome.

Abort.

No klaxons sounded and no bullhorns boomed as they do at Cape Kennedy or Houston when a U.S. space "shot" is canceled or a defective rocket is blown up by a mission controller, but the message was the same.

Danger.

Abort the mission, because it cannot be salvaged.

The Israeli saw the signal from 20 yards away, strolled off toward the other end of the platform. The train arrived and Garrison got aboard, knowing that Livneh would be out of the station and into the street within another minute. The wallet signal meant more than canceling the meeting. It was the maximum danger message, a shorthand version for "Bug out. Run for your life."

Garrison returned to his hotel, and the next morning reserved a seat on the afternoon S.A.S. flight to Copenhagen. He passed through the Danish customs at Kastrup Airport just twenty-one minutes before Livneh's Air India jet touched down outside London.

Now they were more than 1,000 miles from Moscow and they had no idea where the girl was, and Charlie Brodsky was dying by the minute.

17

They met in Paris, but it wasn't the least bit romantic. The rendezvous point that Livneh had selected was impressive and historic, but only a French patriot would find Les Invalides romantic. The Left Bank shrine that housed Napoleon's tomb was grand and Gallic and military, but none of that did anything for Captain David Garrison. The New Englander was taut and bitter, indifferent to the splendor of Bonaparte's crypt and the souvenirs of the past conquests.

"Let's walk," said the American in curt greeting.

"Don't look so grim, my friend. It is, after all, only a battle we lost. Not even a battle, a preliminary skirmish."

Garrison shook his head.

"I'm a lousy loser, especially when I don't even know what I did wrong."

"Maybe *you* didn't do anything. It might have been a spot-check, or maybe they've got a computer matching foreign visitors and visas," speculated the Israeli. "Or maybe our forged visas weren't quite good enough."

"We were *that* close and we blew it, friend. *That* goddamn close," Garrison repeated as he raised his right hand with thumb and index finger an inch apart. "Come on. Let's walk."

They strolled to the Seine, turned right and walked along the quay in the direction of the great cathedral. It was a delightful June afternoon, almost perfect. The warm sun, the barges on the river, the gardens and the Louvre on the other shore all added up to a tourist's dream. Garrison was hardly aware of this, however, for his mind was focused on another city far away.

"Don't be discouraged," urged Livneh. "This sort of thing is quite different from a military assault, different from one of your Green Beret raids or ambushes too. If you're going to operate as a spy, you'll need a more delicate touch and a lot more patience."

"I'm not the least bit discouraged—well, maybe *that* much," the American answered as he held up his hands again with two fingers barely separated. "Don't waste my time with that Old Testament philosophy, friend. I had enough of it from The Maven. We're going to get that damn kid out."

"A matter of principle, David?"

"You could say that. Well . . . my kind of principle."

The man who killed too quickly smiled.

"You are a man of principle, and a friend," he told the soldier, "and I'm grateful."

"What are you talking about?"

"David, why did you give the maximum danger signal that canceled the entire operation? Just because they had you under surveillance?"

"Everything was going wrong, and my instinct told me that it could go a lot wronger—fast. I may be a professional soldier, but I don't have any death wish, you know."

Livneh shook his head.

"No, it was my life that you were worried about. They didn't have anything much on you. The fact they let you leave the country proved that. No, you didn't want to compromise me."

Garrison shrugged.

"I'm going to need you. You're my Russian border expert, you know," he rationalized.

"Thank you, David."

"Leave it alone, leave it alone. I probably should have pushed that son-of-a-bitch under the train instead of pushing the panic button."

"No, you did exactly the right thing. Killing the KGB man would have been a disastrous mistake. . . . That's funny, huh? Coming from me?"

"Not really. Nobody said you were Jack the Ripper, you know."

"I've killed a lot of people, bad people, the worst people, but people."

"I've killed a few myself, Eliahu, and I don't even know how bad they were. At least you took out butchers and mass murderers who massacred your relatives, prime bastards. I've gunned funny little guys in sneakers, ninety-eight pound fanatics all hopped up on Marxism and nationalism and a lot of ridiculous slogans."

"What about the Palestinian guerrillas who were going to blow up the bus?"

Garrison nodded.

"Yeah, they were bastards. Dumb bastards, patriotic bastards—but bastards," he agreed. "Listen, I'm sure that you and I are both terribly interesting characters of great depth, but let's save that deep thinking for later."

"You want to talk about Sonya Brodsky?"

"Exactly, and urgently."

They discussed and tested various plans as they walked along the Quai Voltaire, then up past the bookstores and art galleries of the Rue de Seine to the Boulevard St. Germain. They finally sat down at a table outside the classic old restaurant called Lipp's, and each ordered a "serieuse, brune," a big stein of dark Alsatian beer. They were starting on their second round when a newsboy sold Garrison a copy of the *Tribune*, and the New Englander scanned it while Livneh adjourned to the lavatory. When the Israeli returned, Garrison was smiling.

"I have a plan," he announced, and then he pointed out the headline on page three.

"World Nuclear Conference Announced."

Livneh read the article carefully.

"I don't understand," he confessed.

"Let me give it to you the way The Maven would, step by step in logical sequence. One, the girl's inside. Two, we don't even know where inside she is. Three, we very probably can't go back in again to try to find her."

"Four, even if we could we might not reach her in time because we don't know how long Charles Brodsky has to live," injected the Israeli.

"Right. Five, even if we found her right away the KGB boys might be waiting for us. Six, we'd still have the problem of getting her out."

Then Garrison paused, sipped his beer.

"What about seven?" asked Livneh.

"*He's* seven," Garrison said and tapped the paper.

Livneh looked at the paragraph that Garrison had indicated, saw the name and recognized it.

"He's a very important man. Not a very good Jew but a very important man, David."

Garrison smiled at the pleasant sight of two pretty young women strolling by, shrugged.

"I don't give a damn about his piety or whether he buys Israeli bonds," he answered. "That's your hang-up. I'm leaving all the religious stuff to Talmudic scholars, friend."

"Why should this man help us? Why should you think he'd even speak to us on any subject, let alone anything as sensitive as getting a Jewish child out?"

"You don't understand. I don't intend to speak to him at all."

"Please, *b'vakasha*, explain."

It took Garrison less than thirty seconds to sketch out his plan, but then the Israeli sat silent for nearly a minute as he considered it very carefully.

"It will be difficult," he finally said.

"But not *impossible*."

Livneh shook his head.

"No, not impossible. Just extremely difficult. He is never alone. You can be sure of that. He's under continuous surveillance, day and night. He's worth more to them than an armored division, maybe five divisions."

"Good. That should make the transaction easier."

The man who killed too quickly sighed.

"It will take great precision—in both planning and execution," he calculated, "and more than a little luck."

"No, I'm not counting on luck. *Without* luck, can we do it? Can we reach him?"

"Not without violence."

"That's not my problem. That's your hang-up, and Brodsky's. My only promise was to avoid killing except in self-defense. Now answer my question, dammit. Can we do it without killing or being killed?"

Livneh pondered, shook his head.

"Not the two of us. Any plan—and we don't even have any plan—will take five or six agents, maybe ten."

"I'll get them."

"Good ones? Where?"

"That's my job. If I get them and we do a thorough intelligence job, can we develop a workable plan to reach him?"

"Maybe."

Garrison smiled.

"I only said *maybe*, David."

The American finished his beer, waved for another.

"*Maybe* is a start, a hand-hold, a place to begin. Ten minutes ago we didn't have anything. Now we've got the germ of a plan and a *maybe*."

"You seem pleased."

"A little, and I'll be a lot more pleased when we've got a plan, instead of a germ of a plan, and a team to execute it. I don't know this terrain too well, you know. I've only been here twice on leave from Germany, and only for eight or ten days each time. Do you know the town?"

Reasonably well. We . . . I . . . have conducted several operations here during the past years. One that got a lot of attention in the world press involved . . . well, the details are not relevant. I've lived here for two or three months at a time, at least six times since 1956."

1956—the year that the British and French invaded Egypt in secret cooperation with the Israelis.

"I still know some . . . people . . . who might be in a position to . . . help us secure . . . certain information . . . about the conference . . . and this man's schedule," Livneh continued cautiously.

"You mean Seven?"

Now it was Livneh who smiled.

"*Tov*, very good. Yes, you said 'he's seven'—and that would make a fine code-name. I agree, we can't use his real name anymore. Yes,

Mr. Seven's schedule and housing plans will be most important. Finding the right people to help us reach him may be much more difficult. You must realize that there will be a tremendous uproar afterwards. It will create much pressure in many security organizations and much danger for those involved with us."

The beer arrived, and the waiter departed.

"And there will be no homeland, no large apparatus to protect those who might help us, and no place for them to escape if something goes wrong."

"No embassy to take refuge in, no national airline to fly her out," Garrison continued the line of thought as he recalled the Israeli's ingenious lifting of Adolf Eichmann.

He didn't have to mention the Nazi's name.

"Yes, this would be quite different," Livneh agreed. "In any case, I think that we must be very careful to avoid the attention of all governments—including mine. We have promised not to embarrass The Maven, but that's not enough. If he knew what your plan was, he might be tempted to take advantage of it."

"*Tempted*? You've got to be kidding. If I read him right, my friend, he'd move in like gangbusters if it would help the holy homeland. That's his job."

"I'm glad that you understand. The Maven is a good man."

Garrison took a gulp of the dark brew.

"Don't worry, chum, I understand The Maven just fine. I've been dealing with that kind of wonderful, sincere, patriotic son-of-a-bitch for years. They're easy to understand, and that's why I love them. I'm really crazy about The Maven, you know. He's a prince in my book. . . . Well, we're agreed that you'll stay away from his crew up here."

Then he saw the stooped man with the scarred face walking by on the Boulevard St. Germain, and he thought of the woman in Washington. It wasn't simply that he knew that he would look like that—no, worse—if it hadn't been for her; he missed her. He missed her as a woman, not a plastic surgeon. He missed her very much, and an hour later he took the risk of telephoning her from his hotel.

"David? Is that you, David?"

"Yes, it's me and I'm fine."

"Oh my God, oh my God."

It was probably relief, he thought.

It was hard to tell, even though the connection was fairly good, but it sounded like relief rather than rage.

He was right.

"I'm okay, Honey. I'm in Paris, living like a king on the old man's money in a good hotel. How are you?"

"What are you doing in Paris, Garrison. Or shouldn't I ask?"

"Strictly business. Very grim and earnest. No broads at all. I'm being terribly faithful."

"You'd better be, you bastard . . . you sure you're all right?"

"Fine. Paris is a much cozier city than Moscow."

"Moscow?"

"Just a few days seeing the sights. Wonderful museums and that Kremlin—well, it's out of this world."

He thought he heard her sigh.

"You're crazy, Garrison. They should never have let you out of the hospital, never. . . . You're not going back to Moscow, are you?"

"No, it got kind of warm. Unseasonable, you might say."

She understood.

"Oh my God."

"You're getting very religious, Honey."

"Listen, you bastard. Stop playing your little-boy games and come home. . . . I'm scared, Garrison. *Please* come home."

"Easy, Honey. I'll be home soon. . . . I miss you. That's why I called."

She was trying to muffle her crying and she was angry and astonished to find herself reduced to this state by this man, this foolish, compulsive man.

"Easy, Honey," he soothed.

"I miss you too . . . and so do your dumb friends. I had a call from your Sergeant, the one you talked about."

"Junior?"

"Yes, Junior."

"Where is he? I may need him."

"For what? I'm sorry. I guess I shouldn't ask."

"It's probably just your professional training, Doctor."

"Stop teasing me. I know that I'm supposed to stay calm and sensible, but you're not just a patient. I don't get this emotional very often, do I?"

"Absolutely not. You're very logical, cool, and efficient and you certainly have a right to equal pay for equal work. I respect your intelligence and dignity deeply. *Now*—where the hell is Junior? Bragg?"

"Yes, Bragg," she confirmed, and was immediately annoyed with herself for surrendering to his tough tone. She wasn't one of his sergeants, and she certainly didn't have to put up with that.

"Listen, Garrison," she continued.

"Later—if you don't mind. Would you do me a favor, *please*?"

He was very devious, ruthless one moment and cajoling the next.

"What is it?"

"Phone him—right away—and tell him that I've got a deal. I need him and Mendoza for two or three weeks. It's a private deal, and the pay will be very very good, enough for the bus—don't ask what that means. He knows. Tell him that I want to meet them both at the International Motel near Kennedy at five o'clock on the day after tomorrow, and that I'll cover all their expenses. I'll explain the whole deal and the money then. . . . You got that, Honey?"

"Yes, I've got it, Captain. What is this deal? Is it dangerous? Why does it pay so much?"

You had to hand it to her.

She really hung in there.

"Honey, I'll explain the whole thing to you after I've spoken to them. I promise. Now you call Junior, and I'll phone you back in three or four hours."

"What hotel are you at—in case I have to call you?"

"I miss you, Honey. I really miss you," he answered and hung up immediately.

Bastard, bastard, bastard, bastard.

He was the prototype, she decided as she put down the phone and turned to look out her office window.

He was the original model, the classic amiable, arrogant male.

It was absolutely ridiculous to be in love with such a man, and he was insane if he thought that he was going to use her this way.

It took her eight minutes to reach Sergeant Arnold Culpepper, Jr., at Fort Bragg.

"I've just had a call from Captain Garrison," she announced after the initial amenities.

"How is he, M'aam?"

"About fifty-three percent out of his tree, in my opinion, but you might take a different point of view. He gave me a message for you, for you and Sergeant Mendoza. He said to tell you that he needs you two. He's got some kind of deal."

"Whooeee! The Captain's got a deal!"

He was obviously and illogically delighted.

"Don't you want to know what kind of deal?" she challenged.

"It'll be a good deal, a *real* good deal. He never comes up with bad ones."

This irrational confidence only added to her annoyance.

"He said it's a private deal . . . two or three weeks . . . and the pay will be very very good. He didn't give me any numbers, but he said that it would be enough for the bus. You're supposed to know what that means."

"Enough for the bus? Must be one real mother of a deal."

"What does that mean—enough for the bus?"

Sergeant Culpepper coughed, cleared his throat.

"Somethin' we've been talking about for a while," he evaded. "Enough for the bus? Man, wait till ah tell the Chief."

"Can you two get away for two or three weeks? If you can't, of course . . ."

"M'aam, we've each got thirty days leave startin' day after tomorrow."

"That's when he wants to meet you. Five o'clock at the International Motel near Kennedy. He'll pay the expenses, and he'll explain the details then."

"Fine, fine. We'll be there."

"Sergeant, I think that I ought to let you know that this deal may be extremely dangerous—*extremely* dangerous," she warned without much hope.

"Thank you, M'aam. Mighty kind of you to point that out, but ah sort of figured that. If the money's enough for the bus, it sure as hell ain't gonna be no goddamn milk run. It oughta be a gen-u-wine challenge, in a manner of speakin'."

"And that doesn't bother you?"

"No, M'aam. Not a big bunch. It's not that ah'm brave but ah'm mighty greedy."

"How about Mendoza?"

The Georgian chuckled.

"He's different. He's brave *and* greedy—specially for that bus. Well, thank you for callin'."

Thwarted, for a moment she didn't know what to say.

"Whooee," she finally replied bitterly and slammed down the telephone.

Neither of them wore a uniform, but anyone could tell from the way they stood and walked and moved that they were soldiers or athletes—and professional. They had that firmness and wariness and, at the same time, easiness. Of course, the haircuts helped. You couldn't quite call them crewcuts, but there was something sufficiently G.I. to hint at very recent military experience. The taller of the two, lean, blond haired, and adorned with the amiable boyish smile of a twenty-five-year-old whose hobbies were collecting gospel records and setting land mines, wore a light sport jacket, open-neck knit shirt and tan wash-and-wear trousers. He was graceful and good humored, and he might have been a good high school basketball player a few years earlier. In fact, the *Gainesville Times* had picked him for the All Hall County All-Stars during both his junior and senior years—about a million years ago. Well, it seemed like a million years.

The other man wore a blue shirt and a deep blue suit that emphasized his dark and dramatic good looks. He was stocky without being short, big without being fat. His hair and his eyes were black and his skin was more than bronzed, and he looked as striking as any Indian chief in the movies. He wasn't actually a chief, for it was his father who was the head of the tribe, but he was an Apache. Of that there could be no doubt. He was the essence of Apache, so classic that he might be some casting director's stereotype. Unlike the companion who walked beside him into the lobby of the International Motel, he had a limited interest in mines and booby-traps. He was a sniper and an expert in hand-to-hand combat, and he was very strong. His name was Juan Mendoza, but he'd never found any way to stop anyone from calling him Chief. After ten years in the U.S. Army, he had accepted this with the other stupidities. He had few illusions, 20-20 eyesight, extraordinary reflexes, and several dreams that he rarely discussed.

One of these involved a certain twenty-four-year-old girl who was a direct descendant of a war chief named Cochise.

Another focused on a bus.

They strode through the lobby to the desk, glancing left and right routinely before Culpepper spoke to the clerk.

"Mr. David Garrison, please?"

"311."

"Thank you, suh. Much obliged."

Waiting at the elevator door with the middle-aged couple from Cleveland, the Apache scanned the lobby again as Culpepper glanced at his wristwatch.

4:58, two minutes early.

Well, it never hurt to be early.

The door opened, and they entered with the couple. A minute later, the two sergeants stood outside Room 311.

"Man, it must be *some* deal," predicted the Georgian.

Mendoza nodded, knocked twice.

The door opened, and they stared at the man inside uncertainly.

"It's me all right," said the familiar voice in that strange face. "Hope you like what the plastic surgeons did. I think it's an improvement."

"You okay, Captain?" asked the Indian.

"Fine, and glad to see you."

"You okay, Captain?" another voice behind them mimicked.

They turned, saw the pretty young woman.

"Hello, Elizabeth," Garrison acknowledged. "I'm glad you could make it."

He spoke calmly, showing no trace of surprise or anger.

"I thought you would be, Captain. I was in the neighborhood so I thought I'd stop in for a cup of coffee."

"Come on in."

"I wouldn't want to intrude," she protested silkily.

"Not a bit. Why don't you all step in and I'll introduce you?"

The fact that he was coping so deftly didn't surprise her, for coping was one of the things that her lover did best.

"Elizabeth, I'd like you to meet Sergeant Arnold Culpepper, Jr., and Sergeant Juan Mendoza," Garrison said after the door closed behind them.

She smiled sweetly, as if she meant it.

"I do believe I've spoken to Sergeant Culpepper on the phone," she answered with substantially more Southern charm than she'd used in the past seven or eight years.

"Yes, M'aam. Twice, M'aam. You must be Dr. Clement."

"My, you've got a *wonderful* memory, Sergeant. I do declare," she continued in thickening Dixie accents, "you've got a *wonderful* memory—and you look just like you sound."

"Don't let Dr. Clement's scalpel bother you, Junior," Garrison advised as he reached for the bottle of Jack Daniels. "She's a surgeon, you know. Carries it with her all the time."

"You *okay*, Captain?" she jabbed again.

"Sit down, Doctor, and cut the crap or I'll bust your stethoscope."

The two sergeants stood there stolidly, watching and wondering.

"That's no way to speak to a Southern lady—is it, Sergeant Culpepper?"

"Cap'n?"

"Here's your drink, Junior," Garrison answered. "And here's yours, Chief. You joining us, Elizabeth?"

"Of course. Wouldn't pass up good ol' sour mash for anything, you hear?"

"I hear you, Honey. Drink up."

They all sipped, shuddered, and blinked in visceral appreciation of the powerful liquor.

"I was going to phone you," Garrison said firmly.

"From where, Helsinki or Rangoon?" she challenged.

Then she sat down in a parody of ladylike elegance, arranging her legs and skirt carefully.

"No, from here—as soon as we'd finished talking."

"Well, don't let me interrupt you, Captain. I just *love* hearing men talking business. It's so . . . virile . . . and earthy."

"You want us to come back in half an hour, Captain?" Mendoza asked.

"I'll still be here," promised the surgeon. "I'm not going to miss hearing you big strong soldiers talk about your *deal*. I've come all the way from Washington just to find out about this wonderful *deal*."

Garrison saw the question in Culpepper's eyes, shrugged.

"It's all right. I guess . . . well, maybe she has a right to know."

"Why thank you, Captain," she taunted as she finished her drink.

"Just do me one favor," he answered. "Don't mention it to the girls at the beauty parlor—or we'll all end up in jail."

"I'll keep your darling secret, Captain," she pledged. "Scout's honor. *Girl* Scout's, that is. Does that count?"

The New Englander shook his head, twice.

"How've you been, Junior?" he asked.

"Just dandy. We were a bit worried about you, Cap'n. . . . Your new face looks good, real good."

"Thank you, Sergeant," acknowledged the surgeon.

Garrison sighed patiently.

"She's right. The credit's hers."

"And the cash goes to the men. Isn't that how it goes, David?"

"You'll be going, right out on your can if you don't stop the Bette Davis bitchery. . . . How are you, Chief?"

"All right, sir. And you?"

"Fine. Complete recovery. The face is just about healed. . . . How are the others? Tom? Sandy? Bonomi?"

"The whole group's on the way back," said the Indian. "Bonomi and Tom should reach Bragg next week."

"And Sandy?"

Mendoza shook his head.

"Isn't he coming back too?" Elizabeth Clement asked archly.

"He came back a month ago—in a pine box," Culpepper explained.

She nearly dropped the glass.

"Oh my God!"

"He would have appreciated that, Elizabeth. He was a solid church-going type. His father was a minister," Garrison recalled. "Well, let's get to business. This is just that: business. Private. No connection with the Army or the U.S. Government. It's really rather simple, but dangerous. The people we're up against will be very security-conscious, and they'll be armed."

"Who're the Gooks this time?" Junior Culpepper asked from the edge of the bed where he was sitting.

"*Gooks?*" the woman asked.

"Gooks. You know, North Koreans or VC or Chicoms. There've got to be Gooks in this deal," Culpepper explained.

"It's the Russians," announced Garrison.

"Whooee! *Caucasian* Gooks! Ought to be one helluva mission!"

"It's going to be tricky, Junior."

The Georgian grinned.

"Ah don't mind, Cap'n. Never went up against Caucasian Gooks before."

"I owe a man a favor," Garrison continued, "and I promised him that I'd get one of his relatives out of the Soviet Union. A kid, a girl. Fourteen. He's financing the whole deal."

"We've never operated in Russian territory," pointed out the Apache thoughtfully.

"That doesn't matter. This operation doesn't involve Russian territory at all, just one Russian."

"The girl?"

"No, Chief, not the girl. The man we're going to trade for the girl."

"*Big* man?"

"Very *big*. King-sized, under constant guard. KGB around the clock."

"Whooee!"

"You like that, Junior?" asked the woman.

Culpepper smiled, almost roguishly.

He looked appealing, and slightly ridiculous.

"How does this Big Man feel about the trade, Captain?" questioned the Apache.

"I don't know. I haven't asked him, and I don't intend to. I mean to snatch him . . . with a minimum of violence . . . in about eight days from now."

The Indian considered this, nodded.

"Where?"

"Paris. He'll be there for an international conference. It's going to be extremely hairy. Lifting him right under the noses of an armed KGB crew will be tricky, and hiding him while we negotiate may be even worse. There's going to be a lot of heat from the French security services, from the Soviets, and God knows who else. He's very valuable, maybe priceless."

Culpepper weighed all this craftily.

"And it'll be a nine-legged bitch to swap him for the kid without getting our asses blown off, won't it, Cap'n?"

Garrison nodded.

"As usual, Junior, you've come right to the nitty-gritty in your own folksy phrasing," he agreed. "A nine-legged bitch might be an understatement. If I may quote one of your memorable remarks, this ain't gonna be no mere mother. Gonna be a genuine grandmother."

"I said *that*, Cap'n?" the Georgian asked with a shy glance at Elizabeth Clement.

"Several times."

"Perhaps in moments of frivolity. Hope I didn't offend you, M'aam."

She finished her bourbon in one gulp.

"Not a bit. It's the thought that you may all get killed that offends me, Sergeant."

Then she got up walked over to the table, and filled her glass with two ice-cubes and three fingers of liquor.

"They won't send you back in any pine boxes," she warned as she returned to her armchair. "They'll just dump you in the Seine."

It was Mendoza who broke it, who changed the subject.

"You got a plan, Sir?"

"We're working on it. There's a man who's helping me, an Israeli. He's in Paris now, scouting the set-up and trying to figure how to make the snatch. He's good. He was an agent for more than fifteen years, operated all over Europe. Knows Paris inside out, and he has connections there. Knows the Russians, too."

He saw Culpepper eyeing the bottle, nodded an invitation to have another drink.

"He was in Moscow with me. Very cool. I get the impression that he's organized quite a few jobs like this, and some hits too. Now let's get to the money. The old man who's paying for this has plenty of cash. I'm offering you fifteen thousand dollars apiece for two weeks work, plus expenses."

"That's mighty fine money, Cap'n," judged Junior Culpepper.

"Aren't you going to say *whooee*?"

"Stay out of this, Elizabeth. Yes, it's good money. Should be almost enough for the bus, Chief."

"You're one helluva salesman, Garrison," she said bitterly. "I guess I should have known that."

"Fifteen thousand won't cover the bus," said the Indian. "I just checked on the price, and it's gone up again. Twenty-two thousand, at least."

"Why don't you borrow the rest?" Culpepper suggested.

Mendoza looked dubious.

"Who's going to lend seven thousand dollars to an Army Sergeant who has no collateral so he can invest it in a bus that won't generate any income?" speculated the Indian.

Culpepper smiled that foolish boyish smile again.

"I know a big money man down in my home town who might. One of them real tycoons—with a heart of gold. You probably read about him in *Fortune* magazine and the *Wall Street Journal.*"

Garrison nodded in comprehension.

"I think I know who you mean. Yes, he's one of the giants of international finance all right. Must have at least $340 in cash."

Now the Apache understood.

"How could I ever pay it back?" he asked.

"Slowly," Culpepper answered.

"Something like fifty cents a year, I imagine," offered the New Englander.

"That's exactly it, Cap'n," Culpepper confirmed. "Let's see, that would make a nice even fourteen thousand years—say sixteen thousand with the interest."

"Right, Junior. Let's not forget the interest. Got to keep this businesslike. Is that okay with you, Chief?"

The husky Indian nodded.

"Now what the hell is this all about?"

"I guess I'd better explain, Elizabeth. Sergeant Mendoza needs twenty-two thousand dollars to buy a bus so the children on his reservation won't have to walk six miles to and from school each day, and the Chairman of the Board of Culpepper World-Wide Industries is going to lend him seven thousand," Garrison announced casually. "The Chairman is a very charitable man, gives two or three dollars every year to the Red Cross."

"Easy come, easy go," Culpepper confirmed.

"Don't look so startled, Elizabeth. Culpepper World-Wide Industries is a firm with immense assets. Two suits, several pairs of odd trousers, more than a dozen shirts, a portable radio-phonograph that must have cost $150, two or three hundred LPs, about forty-six books on the history of gospel music, and a slightly used motorcycle."

"Don't forget the $340 in cash," she advised.

"And my Confederate War Bonds."

"Right. Junior has more than $390,000 in Confederate War Bonds issued by the South back in 1863."

"They're collector's items, M'aam, and besides, someday . . ."

"The South may rise again," Garrison supplied to finish the thought.

She shook her head.

"We usually hum 'Dixie' at this point," Garrison reported. "The whole bit sounds better when we hum 'Dixie,' you know."

"A lot better," agreed Culpepper.

"You're all crazy, David, all three of you. It doesn't make any sense. Paying off a debt to a man whom you don't owe anything, and risking your neck for a bus that the government's sure to buy sooner or later."

Something happened in the Apache's eyes.

"We've been waiting for that bus for *seven* years, Doctor," he said grimly.

"This is where you're supposed to say 'Oh my God,' " Garrison advised.

She glared.

"We've *got* to do somethin' about the bus, M'aam. Chief and I . . . and the cap'n . . . been talking about that bus for a *long* time. Government doesn't seem to give a hoot in hell about those 'Pache schoolkids. Lots of promises, but The Great White Father speaks with forked tongue."

"What else would you expect from those damn yankees in Washington?" she asked.

"Glad to see you're getting into the spirit of things, Elizabeth," Garrison complimented.

"Not just the spirit, Captain."

"Now what does *that* mean?"

She smiled sweetly, too sweetly.

"Captain, that means I've decided to help you brave boys and get right into the thick of things."

There was only a moment of silence.

"Not a good idea," Mendoza judged.

"A lousy idea, Elizabeth. Out of the question."

"And what do you think, Junior?" she asked.

"Since you inquired, it's about the worst idea Ah heard in the last twenty-seven months—including New Year's Eve and the saint's days of all known faiths."

She smiled again.

"You do have a way with words, Junior. I think we're going to get along fine on this mission. How do you like my soldier talk, David?"

"I think the booze is getting to you," he replied.

"Not a bit. Not a whit. Not one goddamn iota. Not a single cell.

No, I have to go with you. I don't have all those LP albums and the motorcycle and the Confederate War Bonds, David. All I've got is you, and I can't afford to have you zapped. Zapped—that is the right word, isn't it?"

"No," said the Indian.

"No," agreed Culpepper.

"Out of the question," Garrison repeated unequivocally.

"I knew that you'd see it my way," she answered pleasantly. "After all, I'm the only one who knows how to hide him until you can swap him. Without me, you don't have a chance."

"Out of the question."

"Did I hear someone ask 'what is your plan, Doctor?' " she said softly.

Culpepper glanced at the New Englander, saw him shrug.

"We'll figure it out," Garrison assured.

"In case you don't, Captain, your adoring doctor already has figured it out—and you'll need me, for the oxygen set-up."

Garrison didn't take the bait, but Culpepper did.

"What oxygen set-up?"

"M'aam. Don't forget the old Southern charm, Junior," she reminded.

The Georgian opened his mouth to say something both rude and obscene, barely suppressed the impulse. She was the captain's woman and she had a plan that might prove useful.

"What's your plan? What oxygen set-up—M'aam?"

"You want to hide him in an oxygen-tent, Elizabeth?"

She nodded.

"Very good, Captain. You're a bright boy. Yes, that's it. We show up in Paris three or four days before you grab this Soviet superstar. We establish our identities at some deluxe hotel, an American millionaire, his valet-chauffeur and his doctor."

"He's an alcoholic, travels with his own doctor," Garrison filled in quickly.

"Exactly. Then he has a heart attack the day before the kidnapping, and he's too sick to move so we hustle an oxygen tent into the suite."

"A suite?" Culpepper mused. "I like that . . . M'aam."

"I thought you would. Then after you grab the Russian . . ."

"We switch him into the tent," continued Garrison, "and we keep him there without anyone seeing his face."

"You clever boys will have to figure how to get him in and out without being seen, but I'm sure that three professional bandits like you can handle that."

The men reflected, looked at each other.

"It might work," judged Mendoza slowly. "What do you think, Captain?"

"Not a bad idea."

"I think it's damn good," she protested.

"It just might do it," her lover admitted.

Culpepper smiled his concurrence.

"You like the idea, Junior?" she asked.

"Love it. 'Course I don't know that we need any lady surgeons for this. I took a medic course myself. I could operate the tent, I think."

"Not a chance," she answered.

Garrison shook his head.

"I don't think so, Junior. Did you ever actually handle an oxygen set-up, or was it just the field medic course?"

"Just the field medic, Cap'n."

"You'd kill him, or you'd blow the place up," she warned angrily. "This isn't like changing a fuse or changing the oil in your motorcycle. It takes a professional."

"But not a woman professional," argued Culpepper.

"Have you got something against women?"

"Hell, no, M'aam. I been married twice. I have a deep and gen-u-wine respect for the fair sex."

"Balls."

Arnold Culpepper, Jr., blinked.

"Dr. Clement just said 'balls,' Junior. It's a popular figure of speech," Garrison explained. "Like yourself, she has a wonderful way with words. You mustn't be shocked by her language, Junior. She's very modern and emancipated."

"Screw you, Captain, and all your merry men."

Garrison nodded.

"See what I mean, Junior? The doctor has a complex and colorful personality, with matching gloves and vocabulary."

She glared again.

"I think we need her—if we buy the plan," judged the Apache in matter of fact tones. "I don't know anything about where to hide somebody in Paris. I don't even speak French."

"I do," she announced.

"The doctor has many talents, Chief, and, as you said, we need her if we go this route. She has a fine mind as well as wonderful legs and a terrific sense of humor, and she does faces very well."

"You want to do this number, Cap'n?" Culpepper asked.

"Sure, unless you'd prefer my terrific medley of tropical birdcalls and Christmas songs."

"I dunno, Cap'n. There's nobody who does 'Rudolph, the Red-Nosed Reindeer' like you."

She was not amused.

"I gather that the idea doesn't quite grab you, Junior," she pressed.

He shrugged.

"To tell the truth, M'aam, I'm crazy about 'Rudolph, the Red-Nosed Reindeer'—but I'll go along."

"And you, Chief?" asked Garrison.

"Yes."

Garrison turned to the woman he loved.

"Congratulations, Doctor. You have just been commissioned Surgeon General in the Brodsky Expeditionary Force," he announced.

"The kid we're after, her name is Sonya Brodsky," Garrison explained to the others.

"What's so special about Sonya Brodsky, sir?" wondered the Apache.

"Her family. The brain surgeon who worked on Captain Garrison after the ambush was Major Bruce Brodsky," she answered for the New Englander. "The Captain feels obligated, as if it were a debt."

Mendoza nodded.

It made sense to him for a man to pay his debts..

"And all this bread's coming from Major Brodsky, Cap'n?"

"No, Junior. He has a very rich grandfather who's on his way out, maybe a couple of months to go. Department store tycoon—one helluva guy. There's only one Brodsky left in Russia, the granddaughter of the old guy's brother. The kid's in some orphan asylum and the Sovs won't let her out, so Charlie Brodsky's putting up the cash for this operation."

"I read about this Charlie Brodsky in *Time* magazine," Culpepper recalled. "Prom-i-nent and ballsy Hebrew mill-yun-aire and phil-an-thro-pist. More money than Frank Sinatra, they say. One of those wonderful American success stories, the self-made man with a steel-trap mind and a heart-o-gold. Started as a street peddler and built a vast fortune, without taking any crap from anybody. That's the part I like best. Man, this ought to be exciting!"

"As you can see, Elizabeth, Sergeant Culpepper truely digs this operation."

"I dig it deeply, Cap'n. Man, what would ole Swede Sussman say about this? Me, Arnold L. Culpepper, Jr., risking his lazy WASP ass to rescue a little Hebrew orphan girl for Charlie Brodsky!"

He saw the question in her eyes.

"I went to high school in Gainesville with Swede Sussman, M'aam. We played on the basketball team together, and he was my best goddamn friend. His daddy was a pharmacist, ran the biggest drugstore in town. Swede was . . . well, his proper name was Bert but we all called him Swede 'cause he was so crazy about those Ingmar Bergman movies. Used to drive all the way to Atlanta to see them. He had terrific hands, used to score twenty points a game."

"What's Swede Sussman got to do with this?"

"He's a rabbi now, M'aam. Sort of a shame, in one manner of speaking. He could have made it as a pro, you know. He was a star at North Carolina, one of the top scorers in the country. Great hands."

She shook her head.

"Swede Sussman, a bus, and a fanatic who has to pay a debt he doesn't owe," she summarized.

"And a stubborn incurably romantic woman who's willing to risk everything—including her life—just like in those old Warner Brothers flicks," added Garrison.

"Don't patronize me, you bastard."

The Indian sensed that it was time to leave them.

"We left our bags at the airport, Sir," he announced.

"You'd better get them. Then check in here, and phone me in about an hour."

"Two hours," corrected Elizabeth Clement in matter-of-fact tones that somehow made her carnal intentions totally clear.

"Pleasure to meet you, M'aam," Culpepper said as his eyes flicked to the bed and then back to her face.

She smiled, shook hands with the two sergeants and watched them depart.

"You should have said three hours, Elizabeth," Garrison advised as he came across the room toward her.

While they were making love, far away in Peking Colonel Feng was studying the latest despatch on Salt Fish Two. The team was in place, waiting for Olitski to arrive.

18

"High on the hawg! Hot damn!" Arnold Culpepper rejoiced as the rented Rolls-Royce halted in front of the Hotel George V, known to those who read French as the George Cinq and sometimes called the George Five by whimsical transients from Beverly Hills.

Located with a certain Gallic logic on the quietly elegant Avenue George V, the Hotel George V has excellent service, fine food, large and handsomely furnished rooms, and a lot of rich foreigners who think that the Ritz and the Crillon are a bit old fashioned and stuffy. Shahs and kings and socially ambitious book publishers favor those venerable hostelries, but famous movie figures and enormously affluent Americans—such as the playboy son of the Chairman of the Board of Culpepper Industries—gambol tastefully at the George V. It is, after all, not only a first-class hotel but also within walking distance of both Fouquet's and Prunier's—and the bar offers an endless panorama of lovely starlets and some of the best dressed courtesans in Paris. Even the "Amazons," the ladies of commerce who drive by very slowly every night, are *poules de luxe* in chic little Mercedes.

The blond-haired young man from Gainesville had good reason to celebrate.

"High on the hawg!" he repeated as Mendoza left the driver's seat to come around to open the rear door.

"Now, Mr. Culpepper, please don't overexcite yourself," urged the woman beside him on the back seat.

"Doc, I'll be good, but don't you pee on my parade," he answered.

"That last *parade* in New Orleans put you in a hospital for seventeen days," she "reminded" righteously.

"It was worth it, Doc. You never saw those girls, did you? Man, they made those fillies in the James Bond movies look like Whistler's mother," he boasted as he stepped out of the car.

"It's *your father* that I'm thinking about, Mr. Culpepper."

He smiled, helped her onto the sidewalk.

"My daddy would have appreciated them too. Satin and Cindy Sue, those fillies could really swing."

She shook her head disapprovingly.

"A couple of cheap strippers."

"Not that cheap, Doc. 'Course I didn't mind the bread. After all . . ."

"Man does not live by bread alone," she finished in bored tones. "I'm not talking about living, Mr. Culpepper. I'm talking about dying. Your dear daddy is paying me very well to prevent that."

"Keerist, and I thought you were with me 'cause you had the hots for my fan-tastic young body."

Two uniformed bellboys who'd come out for the luggage heard this last exchange, and they grinned as they took the expensive suitcases that Mendoza unloaded from the trunk of the $24,000 limousine. Five minutes later, the bellboys smiled again as they each received fifteen francs after delivering the suitcases to the suite on the fourth floor. Fifteen francs—three dollars, a promising start for the new guests.

"Easy come, easy go," Elizabeth Clement observed wryly after the bellboys had departed.

"My daddy wouldn't want it any other way, Doc."

He was probably right, she thought. Garrison had instructed them to spread a lot of money around to establish the rich Yankee playboy image, and big tips were obviously an easy way to start the talk circulating. The $3,000 in custom-made clothes that Garrison had financed in New York weren't going to hurt either. They certainly weren't injuring Arnold Culpepper's self-esteem as he studied himself in the full-length mirror.

"Groovy threads, huh?" he judged admiringly.

"Out of sight," agreed the Apache from the doorway to the adjoining room.

Elizabeth Clement looked at the Indian in surprise.

"I didn't know you spoke that way, Chief."

"I don't—not really. I just do it to amuse Junior. He doesn't talk that way all the time either."

"They are groovy threads," insisted the Georgian. "First suit worth more than ninety dollars I ever had, and I get to keep the whole kit. The Captain promised that, right?"

"Everything but the jet," she answered.

"That's only chartered, Doc, and I don't know how to fly one anyway. Real nice little bird though. Private jet from London to Paris, that's class. Wouldn't you say that's class, Chief?"

The Indian shrugged.

"A helicopter gunship might be better," Mendoza speculated.

"Better than a private jet? Man, you're one dumbass Indian. No wonder the calvary kicked the crap out of the 'Paches."

"We'll win next time."

"Only on TV, baby. You ain't mean enough, never were. You're too nice, and you trust those mother-grabbin' Yankees. You got no class, and no damn business sense either. Twenty-four dollars for a chunk of prime real-estate like Manhattan island? Just dumbass Indians!"

"How about Custer?" challenged Mendoza.

"Pure luck. Just a fluke. You're a bunch of old women now, gettin' high on mushrooms and hustlin' lousy blankets to Jap tourists."

"It's the Navajos who're selling the blankets."

She shook her head.

"That's a very weird number you two do, gents."

"Just funnin', M'aam. Chief knows I'm gen-u-wine-ly fond of Injuns. Love all them tribes. Cherokees, Sioux, Seminoles, Navajos, Black Feet, Republicans—and 'Paches most of all. When I go to the picture shows I always hiss John Wayne and root for the red mothers—I mean *brothers.*"

She turned to Mendoza.

"Why do you put up with him, Chief?"

"I need his money for the bus."

"And after that," Culpepper broke in, "he's goin' to burn my wagon train and steal my prize collection of matched Southern virgins and wreck all the toilets at Warner Brothers. He blabbed out the whole thing one night when he was sloshed on fire-water. All the tribes are going to attack simultaneously. It's a gi-gan-tic plot financed by New York radical junky perverts, creeps without faith in the future of American bowling."

"He's out of his tree?" she asked.

"About one-third of the time."

"Well, why . . . I mean . . . did he save your life or something like that?"

The Georgian laughed, pointed at his partner.

"Haw, haw, haw! Me save his life? Haw, haw, haw, haw! That dumbass 'Pache saved *my* life—*three* times!"

There was more to this and she knew it, but they weren't going to share it—whatever it was—with her now. Perhaps they might later, if there was a later.

"Why don't we unpack and go out and spend some money." Elizabeth Clement proposed.

Some 2,000 miles away, Doron turned away from his view of the Tel Aviv skyline and the distant ridge of the Jerusalem hills to look at the messages on his desk again. The Syrians were equipping another battalion of Palestinian guerrillas in a camp near the Lebanese frontier, and the Russians had just delivered ninety more medium tanks from a freighter still anchored in Alexandria harbor. "Sunburn" and "Toothache"—two of the bastards who'd been mailing timebombs from Vienna and Belgrade to Israeli officials—had been permanently "canceled" by the Shin Beth team led by "Alex."

No big surprises here.

The Syrians had always been stupid, always lacked the sense to think ahead three or four moves.

The Soviet tanks were a month late, according to the schedule in the secret agreement that a greedy Egyptian bureaucrat had sold to a "French" agent back in January.

As for the Arab saboteurs codenamed "Sunburn" and "Toothache," their training in Peking had been good but neither of them was a match for an experienced operative like "Alex." After all, "Alex" had—as they said in Hollywood—a lot of fine credits. When it came to "canceling," he was almost as expert as Livneh.

There were two other dispatches.

The West Germans were tracking down a Paraguayan typewriter dealer whom they suspected might be Martin Borman. For a few moments The Maven considered whether he ought to let the Germans know that the Shin Beth had already checked on this man, and discovered that he was only a former S.S. colonel hardly worth any serious effort. Well, the West Germans had plenty of money and they could afford to bother with such lesser war criminals.

The last message in the heap came from "Esther," the Agricultural Attaché at the Israeli Embassy in Paris. "Knife" had been seen at a small restaurant on the Rue Dragon, and "Esther" wanted to know why he hadn't been informed about this operation. What was "Knife" doing there?

The Maven puffed on his pipe, pondered.

It was a good question.

What the hell was Eliahu Livneh doing in the French capital?

The child was in Moscow, so why was Livneh in Paris?

And where was the American captain?

Paris—it didn't make sense.

"I don't like it," said The Maven who always felt uneasy when other people kept secrets from him. After all, secrets were his prerogative. Those two were up to *something*. Neither of them was the type to go to Paris for wine and women—not during a mission.

"I don't like it at all," repeated the Israeli intelligence executive. Then he called in a former paratrooper named Jacov and dictated a cable to be sent at once to "Esther." He had to know.

So did Charles J. Brodsky.

It was warm in the garden of the Manhattan town house, but the old man showed no effects of the summer heat. It wasn't the temperature that was bothering him.

"You'd better tell me, Shirley, because I don't have either the time or the disposition to cock around with you. You know what that means—cock around?"

"Something like screw around?"

The white-haired man in the wheelchair nodded.

"Very good, Miss Takeda. Now tell me what the doctor said to you on the phone just now."

"You're making a big goddamn deal out of a small phone call," the pretty nurse answered in tight almost choked tones.

"It's bad, huh?"

She stared at him, struggling to suppress the emotion.

"You wouldn't talk to me like that if it wasn't bad," diagnosed the old man. "You're a nice girl, Shirley, and you like me, and you wouldn't speak like that if it wasn't very bad. I know that."

She swallowed, crammed down the sob.

"You think you know everything, C.J.," she accused. "You may know about money and cigars and department stores, but you don't know anything about me. And you don't know anything about medicine either."

"Don't cry, Shirley. I never expected to live forever, so don't cry."

She stood there silently, tears streaming down her face.

"I'm not crying about you," she insisted.

Brodsky saw Solomon in the doorway.

"Tell her to stop crying," said the aged millionaire.

"What's she crying about, C.J.?"

"Me. Me and my few remaining months—or is it weeks?"

The black man shook his head.

"You know what the doctor told her, Solomon?"

The ex-detective nodded.

"You'd better tell me, Solomon. I've got a right to know."

"Yes, you've got a right to know. You're not doing too well, not as well as we hoped."

The old man bit off the end of a cigar, lit it, and blew a smoke ring.

"You got some numbers, Solomon? Four weeks? Four months?"

"Hard to tell. Nobody knows about these things, not for sure."

"The only sure things are death and taxes," Brodsky recited with a faint smile. "That's a cliché. Well, I've beaten a lot of taxes in my day, with the help of some expensive lawyers, but I'm not doing so well with death. The son-of-a-bitch is closing in on me. . . . Stop that crying."

She tried, failed.

"At least you're not turning weepy on me, Solomon. You're not going to cry, are you?"

"I don't know, C.J."

Brodsky puffed on his cigar again.

"That bad, huh? Must be the ninth inning all right. I guess that's why Harold was up to see me yesterday, why Ben's coming in from Los Angeles the day after tomorrow. . . . Tell that crazy shikseh to stop the water, Solomon. She's in the will, you know."

That did it.

The sobs overwhelmed Shirley Takeda, and she ran from the room.

The man in the wheelchair sighed.

"Would you like a cigar?" he asked.

"Don't mind if I do," replied the ex-detective.

He reached into the leather humidor, took out a corona, and lit it.

"I didn't know you smoked cigars, Solomon."

"Never did before."

The old man chuckled.

"Special occasion, huh?"

Solomon P. Solomon nodded.

"You like it—the cigar, I mean?"

"Fine, just fine."

The two men sat there silently smoking for thirty or forty seconds.

"I guess a man's dying is a special occasion," Brodsky reflected.

"I'd say it's unique, C.J. Nobody ever does it more than once."

The old man grinned.

"Once is enough. It's not like getting laid, you know," he answered.

"I wouldn't know. I never tried it—death, that is."

"You will, my friend."

Solomon nodded, savored the cigar.

"No doubt about it," he acknowledged.

"Doesn't seem to scare you."

The black man tried to blow a smoke ring, but didn't quite succeed.

"I'm not looking forward to it, C.J. I'm not exactly panicky, but I'm sure not looking forward to it."

Brodsky coughed, puffed on his corona defiantly.

"My feelings precisely, Solomon. How much time have I got? A month or two?"

"Maybe more."

"And maybe less. That's true, isn't it? Maybe only a few weeks, maybe ten days?"

Solomon made another attempt to blow a smoke ring.

"There's a trick to it, isn't there?" he asked.

"Yeah, I'll show it to you sometime. Meanwhile, I'm not ready to check out yet. I'm not going until that kid is out of Russia."

"If you say so. Heard anything from that Captain Garrison?"

Brodsky blew a perfect smoke ring.

"He phoned four nights ago. On his way to Paris, and he wanted me to know he had a plan he thought would work. I think he really wanted to find out whether I was still alive, but he was too polite to ask."

"He's got good manners."

"Nobody's supposed to know that he's in Paris or why."

"Never heard of him."

The old man closed his eyes for a few moments, sunk back in his wheelchair like some exhausted animal, and then braced himself again.

"That doctor isn't a complete schmuck," he admitted, "but I'm not dying before Garrison gets that kid out."

He sounded tough, purposeful, and at least three decades younger than he was. He must have been some tiger, Solomon thought.

"C.J.? Would you do me a favor?"

This thing about the child was eating at the stubborn old man, gnawing at his last days.

"What favor?"

"Teach me how to blow those smoke rings, would you?"

The old man fell for the bait, put aside his last obsession for the moment.

"Sure. Like you said, Solomon, it's a trick. Now watch how I do it."

So it was that Charles J. Brodsky taught Solomon P. Solomon to blow perfect smoke rings from $1.25 smuggled Cuban cigars. When it was all over, the old man took a nap in his chair and his friend watched him sleep.

19

Arnold Culpepper didn't sleep—at least not during the evening hours. With his bodyguard-chauffeur and his doctor in attendance, the "son of the Chairman of the Board of Culpepper World-Wide Industries" dined rather lavishly in an expensive restaurant of international repute and happily imbibed Taittinger Blanc de Blanc '64 through all seven courses.

"You're making a pig of yourself," Elizabeth Clement noted as he finished the dark chocolate mousse.

"Damn right. You say we're goin' to get zapped, M'aam. Well, if I'm goin' out I'm goin' out in style."

She sipped at her *café filtre.*

"Not if style means taste, Mr. Culpepper. It's very gauche to swill that champagne with every course, and only a hog would eat that many courses."

"He's always wanted to drink that particular champagne, Doctor."

"Just because it's the most expensive on the wine list?"

Culpepper shook his head, smiled paternally, and sighed.

"Hell, no. That's a turrible thing to say, or even think. You know money don't mean a danged thing to me. No, it was the Cap—our mutual friend from Massachusetts—who recommended it to me. Some girl gave him one of those big bottles—a magnum—for his birthday two years ago."

"Two years—that's a long time," said the Apache quickly.

"Thanks, Chief," she acknowledged. "Nice try, but I never thought our friend was a virgin."

"It might have been three years," volunteered the Georgian.

"And bless you too, Mr. Culpepper. You're a good boy, a good old boy—you hear?"

"Thank you, M'aam. . . . Say, you seem to know how to do things right around here and I'm sorry if I embarrassed you by drinkin' the wrong juice."

"Don't let it bother you. Actually there are people who might agree with you on that Taittinger '64."

"But it doesn't really go too good after dessert, does it, M'aam?"

"You might want to try some cognac. Since you're so loyal to our mutual friend, you could order some of the Remy Martin that he favors. It isn't the most expensive brandy on the wine list, but . . ."

"Money isn't everything," Culpepper agreed as he gestured grandly toward the waiter.

Twenty-five minutes and $131 later, they left a very cordial headwaiter and proceeded by Rolls to the Lido on the Champs Elysees—a large nightclub featuring healthy young women in a splendid "spectacle" that was nude and tasteful and somewhat jolly. As the Apache solemnly pointed out to Dr. Clement, they had to be healthy or else they'd catch cold in those minute costumes.

"He's right, you know, and you called him a dumbass Indian," she teased Culpepper.

"I never said he wasn't cunning, Doc. Cunning and *tricky*. Don't let him get behind you, M'aam. Don't ever let no 'Pache get behind you. Ah learned that from John Wayne."

"Screw John Wayne," Mendoza proposed cheerfully.

Culpepper shook his head sadly.

"*They* can't handle firewater," he confided.

"Without his writers, John Wayne wouldn't go three rounds. A sitting duck—just like Custer. Probably wears a truss."

His attention distracted by a new act—four naked women pretending to play a Debussy quartet—the Georgian didn't answer. The music that they elicited from the stringed instruments wasn't much, but they performed with such spirit that it was difficult if not rude to ignore them.

"He said John Wayne probably wears a truss," Elizabeth Clement repeated helpfully.

"Commie talk. Trying to tear down our faith in our national institutions, M'aam. He'd probably say the same thing about Doris Day."

"Doris Day wears a truss, too," Mendoza announced.

"Told you he'd say that," said Culpepper, and then he turned back to the meaty string quartet.

From the Lido they went to the Crazy Horse Saloon, an establishment that had two attractions. First, it had a lot more naked girls, and second, it was located on the Avenue George V less than a block away from the hotel. There was also a very sleek woman named Janine or Janette or something, about twenty-three or four and smelling of some wonderful scent. Arnold Culpepper met her at the bar about ten minutes after a yawning Dr. Clement excused herself to walk back to the George V. This Janine or Janette—it might have been Jacqueline—had long black hair and a lovely laugh and the warmth that comes from knowing she'd go home at least seventy or eighty dollars richer. She had no doubt that she was worth it, for dozens of satisfied Americans, Britons, Germans, Arabs, and Latins had told her so.

Of course, she had no illusion that she was the only pretty *putain* in Paris worth eighty dollars.

As a matter of fact, Arnold Culpepper, Jr., had no difficulty in finding two others the next evening, one called Denise, or Danielle, and a large Swedish blonde named Gunilla who stood at least five-feet-nine and smoked long thin cigars. Those two stayed over for brunch the following day and were able to give Dr. Clement some useful tips on the best boutiques, hair dressers, and leather goods shops.

"Charming girls," judged the surgeon after they'd left.

"Full of life, and they sure do know Paris, don't they?"

"That's not all they know, Mr. Culpepper, but never fear. I won't tell your daddy that you've been catting around with a couple of fancy whores."

"More than a couple," Mendoza counted and then finished his second cup of strong coffee.

"I didn't know you were mathematically inclined, Chief."

"Mr. Culpepper, I'm not so great on the long division but I can count up to twenty-two thousand without even trying."

The Georgian nodded.

"I'm thinking about the twenty-two thousand myself, friend. How about you, Doc?"

She patted her lips with the fine cloth napkin.

"I'm wondering where Our Wandering Boy is and what he's doing while we suffer in the most expensive hotels, restaurants, and nightclubs of Gay Paree," she replied.

"I wouldn't worry about him, M'aam. He's even more cunning and tricky than a 'Pache. Swift of foot, fleet of fang, quick of mind, pure of heart."

"Balls," declared Juan Mendoza.

"What did you say that for, Chief?" Culpepper asked irritably.

"So she wouldn't have to say it."

She smiled.

"You're really very sweet, Chief. Thanks, but I wouldn't have minded saying it. Not a bit."

She turned to the Georgian.

"Do you know where he is?" she asked bluntly.

"I know what he's doin'. He's collecting the hardware, cars, all the stuff we'll need."

"Recon," added Mendoza.

"That's for sure," Culpepper agreed. "He's checking out the terrain, laying out the escape route, working out all the angles. He's a real fanatic 'bout recon, M'aam."

"Then he's here?"

Mendoza and Culpepper both nodded.

"You're certain?"

"Don't sweat," Culpepper advised as he reached for the check and the pencil that the waiter had left. "Don't sweat, M'aam. He isn't."

Captain David Garrison was scanning the imposing facade of the large "contemporary" building that housed the world headquarters of the United Nations Educational, Scientific and Cultural Organization. Standing beside Livneh on the open plaza in front of the UNESCO center on the Left Bank's Place de Fontenoy, they looked back at the building they'd just left.

"That's a nice guided tour for three francs," said the American.

"Yes."

"*No,*" Garrison corrected. "No, it wouldn't work here. Too many people around, and too goddamn much traffic during daylight."

"I told you I was dubious."

"Yes, you did. But I wanted to check it out myself. This is where the conference is going to be, and it made sense to look it over first."

They turned, began to walk in the direction of the Eiffel Tower.

"Where is he going to stay?"

"Their embassy."

"Son-of-a-bitch. We'll never lift him from there."

"I think that's the idea, David," Livneh responded mildly. "It's one of their standard security measures. Their important people—especially the ones involved in military matters—always stay at their embassy whenever they go to a foreign capital. Even in Warsaw or Bucharest, it's an iron rule."

They stopped speaking for a few moments as a bus pulled up beside them, spilled out two dozen camera-decked tourists on their way to visit the UNESCO building.

"This is all new," one burly man said to his plump wife in German. "The whole city has changed since I was stationed here."

"That was a long time ago, Otto," she answered with discreet wifely hostility.

Garrison glanced at the Israeli, saw the hard look.

"Ah, the golden days of the Third Reich when our fine German boys occupied Paris," jested the New Englander.

"Not funny. Not to me, and not to the French."

"I'm sorry."

Livneh shook his head.

"Not funny to the Dutch, the Norwegians, the Poles—only to the Americans who were never occupied."

Then he turned it off, abruptly refocused on the kidnapping.

"If we can't take him at the conference or lift him from the embassy," Eliahu Livneh reasoned aloud softly, "then we'll have to seize him somewhere between the two."

"That's what I was thinking. I don't like it much."

"Do we have any alternatives?"

Garrison extracted a cigar from his breast pocket, lit it.

"None that I like any better," he admitted. "None that I like at all."

"It has to be simple," he continued and puffed on the cigar. "No James Bond crap like taking him off the UNESCO roof in a chopper."

"*Kenn.* Yes. Something simple that will work on the first try. We won't get a second."

Garrison saw the light change, halted for the flow of Citroens and Renaults.

"Let's go over it again," he calculated aloud. "Between the UNESCO building and the embassy, and at night."

"Agreed. The fewer people that know he's gone the smaller the hunt and the better our bargaining position."

"Someplace where the snatch will attract the minimum of attention. Late in the evening," the American officer reasoned. "He'll go out some night, won't he?"

Livneh nodded.

"Several state dinners have been scheduled for the senior delegates," he reported. "The French are giving the first on Tuesday night."

Garrison tapped the ash from his cigar, eyed the light impatiently.

"Too soon," he rejected. "He can't disappear that early in the conference. His absence would be noticed by too damn many people."

"Wednesday night the U.S. delegation will be the host—at your embassy."

"No deal. The Russians would be sure that it was a C.I.A. job."

"What do you care, David?"

"I care."

The light changed, and they walked on quickly.

"The Soviet banquet's on Thursday."

Garrison shook his head.

"No good. He won't go out of the embassy if it's there. How about Friday?"

"Yes, there'll be another big dinner that night," Livneh acknowledged with an odd smile.

"West Germany?"

"Good guess, my friend."

"No guess at all. That bitter look in your eyes said it loud and clear."

The man from the Warsaw ghetto didn't answer.

"Listen, dad. I may not be a soul brother, but I understand your six million reasons for not loving the Germans. The Germans have nothing to do with this operation."

"I know that."

"In your head, but not in your guts. Well, I'm not about to mix around in your guts. I could tell you that these are a whole new bunch of Germans, half of them not even born or just kids during the Nazi era, but I won't bother."

"That's very sensible of you, David."

Garrison shook his head again.

"I know about paying debts, Eliahu. That's why I'm here. The only thing that counts right now is the kid. Once we've got the kid, I don't care what you do or whom you hate. The kid comes first."

Livneh's face was a blank.

"Of course," he answered slowly.

"Okay," the American continued, "then we lift him on his way back from the West German dinner on Friday night. Let's get a street map and check the possible routes out foot-by-foot."

They turned, walked back to the Gare des Invalides and bought a *Taride-Plan de Paris* at the newsstand in the warehouse-like main hall. Ignoring the bustling throngs of travelers and the multilingual fugue of banal conversation, Livneh opened the detailed street-map in the back of the book and silently pointed to the location of the Soviet embassy.

"That's where Mr. Seven will be sleeping during his stay," he announced softly.

"During the *first* part of his stay," Garrison corrected. "Now where's the big dinner party you mentioned?"

Livneh peered at the map for several seconds, pointed again.

"Got it. Less than a mile away. Now we need a car and a stop-watch, so we can make the run and time the traffic and the lights."

"Now?"

"Maybe once just to get the lay of the land in the daylight, but tonight we'll drive it five or six times. Tomorrow night . . ."

Garrison stopped speaking abruptly, folded up the map and

turned toward the British European Airways counter. He nodded to Livneh, who accompanied him as they made their way through the knots of inbound and outbound passengers. The Israeli said nothing as Garrison nearly collided with a stocky red-headed American carrying a black leather attaché case, grunted, and then circled back through the crowd to the exit.

"You were talking about tomorrow night," Livneh said.

"Right—until I saw the red-headed fellow, Randy Andy Colton."

"Old friend?"

"Not exactly," Garrison answered as he relit his cigar. "Sort of a former colleague. A very hard customer, Randy Andy. Number Two man in the C.I.A. team in Saigon during '70 and '71."

"From his nickname I gather he's quite a ladies' man."

"Not particularly. The story is he got the nickname because he'll screw *anybody*. Not sexually, you understand. He'll use, sell-out, double-cross, rape, con, or set-up anybody. A real company man. Probably sings the C.I.A. song every morning before his ice-cold shower."

The Israeli nodded sympathetically. There were men like that in every intelligence agency in every country.

"He'd even screw his buddies in the C.I.A.," Garrison recalled as they walked.

"Did he harm you?"

"No, but the bastard gave it a real good try."

Livneh's furrowed brow announced the question.

"If this is a bad man, a dangerous and ruthless man, why did you make him notice you?"

"Just trying out my new face on him. Passed with honors. If I do as well on my next Wasserman I'll be one happy soldier-boy."

It was to be expected, reflected the survivor of the Warsaw ghetto. Garrison was very good, but he wasn't perfect. Nobody—except a few haunted paranoids—was perfect. It hadn't really been necessary for the American to test his new face on a professional such as this Colton, but perhaps it wouldn't matter.

"Maybe your Randy Andy is merely passing through Paris," speculated Livneh.

"You don't have to cheer me up. I'm in excellent spirits. Now I'm back in *my* business, the thing I know best—ambush."

"With a minimum of violence," he added, remembering.

After they'd rented the Citroen and made the short run from the West German embassy at 13 Avenue Franklin Roosevelt on the Right Bank, past the historic Grand Palais and across the Pont des Invalides, to the Soviet embassy at 70 Rue de Grenelle on the Left Bank, they made their plan and discussed what equipment they would need.

One small truck.

Two cars.

One straw laundry hamper, large.

One rope ladder.

Four bullet-proof flak vests of the type worn by U.S. military personnel in Vietnam.

Four .32 caliber pistols with silencers.

Two gas guns, ten rounds for each.

One accurate rifle, a sniper's weapon equipped with an infra-red scope for night vision, with fifty rounds of ammo.

Five good walkie-talkie radios with a range of at least 2 miles.

Six concussion grenades.

Two U.S. M-16 semi-automatic rifles with ammunition clips.

"I thought you said 'a minimum of violence.' " Livneh reminded.

Garrison shrugged.

"If everything goes well, no one will suffer any permanent injuries other than bruised egos and possible loss of some scheduled pay raise," he answered.

"But if *everything* doesn't go well?"

The captain shrugged again.

"Well, 'minimum' is a relative word—a crude measuring term at best," he evaded.

"It's the worst that I'm thinking of, and that's funny because I'm supposed to be the homicidal one."

"You think I'm turning homicidal, Eliahu?"

"No, but I believe that you're committed to getting that child out at *any* price."

Garrison considered, nodded.

"That's about it," he agreed and then he raised the question of the boat.

20

The reception was excellent, but that was hardly surprising since the government-owned French television system has higher standards than U.S., Canadian, or British TV with more dots per square inch and therefore a better definition of image. None of the three Americans watching the evening news in the George V suite cared much about the technology in question, but they appreciated the good sharp picture.

"Don't look a bit like Bela Lugosi," complained Arnold Culpepper.

"Not even like Vincent Price," agreed the surgeon.

It was true.

There was nothing of the mad scientist in the man who descended from the big Ilyushin jet. His curly graying hair was neatly combed, and the eyes that gleamed through the black-framed glasses seemed pleasant and sane. His manner was as sober as his drab suit and solid color tie. He might have been fifty-five or sixty, perhaps five feet eight, and weighing about 165 pounds.

"A middleweight," judged the Georgian.

"A heavyweight champ in the world of science," Mendoza corrected.

"And one of the beloved stars of the famous Dave Garrison Show!"

The Apache looked at her, saw that she was still troubled by the captain's absence/silence.

"Don't worry. He'll check in soon—maybe tonight," Mendoza said reassuringly.

"Written, directed, and produced by Dave Garrison," she continued bitterly.

"Now, M'aam."

"Starring Dave Garrison, with music and lyrics by Dave Garrison," she insisted.

"Don't forget the costumes, M'aam," suggested Culpepper helpfully.

"Right. Costumes and guns by Dave Garrison, Incorporated."

"Don't the Chief and me get any credit, M'aam?"

At that moment, the TV camera zoomed in for a close-up of the Soviet physicist's plump face.

"Costarring Arnold Culpepper and Juan Mendoza," she recited in an ironic imitation of the standard announcer's voice, "with a special guest appearance by Professor Josef Olitski."

Olitski smiled, glanced at the five or six men who'd followed him down the steps and now stood beside him. The Special Forces sergeants eyed the group carefully.

"Two," judged Culpepper.

"Maybe three," Mendoza warned.

"What are you talking about?" Elizabeth Clement asked over the staccato voice of the unseen TV newsman.

"KGB, M'aam. We're counting the security men in the gang."

A number of other men in the same drab suits came forward now to welcome the Soviet delegation, and the U.S. sergeants scanned them intently.

"Three more," said the Apache.

"Three more," Culpepper agreed. "That's five, right?"

"Not counting the others waiting in the cars."

"Goddamn it, Chief, you are goddamn right—as usual. No doubt 'bout it. The drivers are just about goddamn certain to be KGB too."

"Mighty sure of yourselves, aren't you?" she challenged.

"We're going by the book, Doctor," explained Mendoza. "*Our* book on Soviet security operations and methods, our training in North Carolina and Germany, all emphasized that the Sovs go by *their* book, and *their* book calls for KGB men as drivers for V.I.P. types."

Now Professor Olitski was answering the interviewer's questions in halting, concise French, uttering the standard clichés about the brotherhood of science and the road to a better life for all the world's peace-loving peoples.

The two sergeants glanced at Elizabeth Clement, who spoke good French.

"In the basic and wonderfully expressive language of the U.S. Army—just the usual bullshit," she confided.

Culpepper looked—or pretended to be—stunned.

"You know the expression, don't you?"

"Yes, M'aam," he acknowledged and then he reached for the Remy Martin bottle to pour himself a cognac.

Now Olitski was introducing some of his fellow delegates, two of whom stood up like good little schoolboys and each recited brief and obviously memorized "greetings" to "French scientists and other workers."

"*Merde*," she said a bit less hostilely.

"That means more bullshit, right?" the Georgian asked before he could stop himself.

"And you said you didn't speak French," she reproved.

"That's an historic expression, M'aam. One of our brave generals said something like that at Bastogne in World War Two, and a frog field marshal said it to the Krauts 'bout seventy or eighty years before that."

Now a French scientist and a senior official from the Ministry of Foreign Affairs intoned their welcome for the cameras, after which the TV "anchorman" back in the studio began to report on the latest promise by the Egyptian prime minister to destroy Israel by the end of the year.

"*Merde*," said the Apache contemptuously after she translated. He had little respect for politicians, even less for those stupid enough to discuss imminent military operations at a news conference.

"Chief don't put much stock in the word of Ay-rab politicians," Culpepper announced slyly.

"They're worse than those hypocrites in the Bureau of Indian Affairs," confirmed the Apache.

"Chief always roots for the Israelis in all the newsreels cause they're the underdogs, and he boos the cavalry in all those old pictures 'bout the wagon trains."

"And I root for the Union troops in the Civil War movies," Mendoza added.

The Georgian nodded several times in mock gloom.

"One real weird Indian."

She wasn't listening to the TV news or Culpepper either.

Her eyes were focused on the telephone.

"That son-of-a-bitch is probably doing it deliberately," she said.

"Ah hope so, M'aam. Easy there. Don't give me those evil looks. All ah said was ah hope he's doing this thing—this whole goddamn thing—deliberately, because it's real tricky and it ought to be done very damn deliberately."

"The Captain is a very wary and deliberate man," confirmed Mendoza.

"And that's why Chief and me and several other folks are still alive. May not seem very ro-man-tic to you, M'aam, but ah think it's tee-goddamn-riffic. Don't mean to be rude, M'aam, but it's just as easy to get zapped in Gay Paree as some stinkin' jungle, if you don't watch your security."

"That's Rule One, Doctor."

"One, two, and three," Culpepper insisted. "He'll call when he's ready—or thirty seconds before."

"Not forty-five?" she asked.

"That's not his style," replied the Apache as gently as possible.

She thought about this for several moments before she sighed.

"I guess you're right," she recalled.

"Every man—and woman, ah 'spose—has his, or her, style," Culpepper philosophized in a not very subtle effort to cheer her. "Did ah evah tell you 'bout the time Swede Sussman drove me over to Atlanta to hear this great golden-tongued ee-van-gell-ical rabbi? A real spellbinder. Sposed to be the Hebrew answer to Oral Roberts, name of Anal Abrahams."

She laughed. She couldn't help it.

"Junior, ah'd be mighty pleased," she replied in even more lavish accents than Culpepper was using, "if you'd tell me all about Anal Abrahams."

It was then that the phone bell sounded.

"Probably for you, M'aam."

She didn't hesitate.

"Hello."

The smile that suffused her face said it all.

"Yes . . . yes . . . fine . . . I'll tell them. . . . You all right?"

Ten seconds later she put down the instrument.

"He's fine," she reported, "and he wants to meet the Chief on Wednesday night at six. He didn't say where."

"I know where," said Mendoza.

"What about me, M'aam?"

She shook her head in exaggerated distress.

"No way. You're not well, Mr. Culpepper. You've been carousing too much, straining your heart. Why you might have to be put to bed any day now—maybe even tomorrow."

Garrison was ready to move.

"Don't be silly, Doc. I'm feeling jim-goddamn-dandy, and I don't care what you say," he replied with a grin. "There's about nine hundred mademoiselles and sixteen hundred bottles of champagne out there waiting for Arnold Culpepper tonight, and I'm not about to disappoint them."

His last fling before the "attack" was going to be large.

Large, lewd, and lavish. Why not?

They exchanged smiles.

"Don't worry, Doc. Nothing's going to happen to me tomorrow—or the next day either," he predicted.

Nothing did, but at four P.M. that following afternoon the assistant manager of the Hotel George V received an urgent telephone call from Dr. Elizabeth Clement. Her patient had had "another heart attack," and an oxygen tent and tanks were needed immediately. No, it would be much too dangerous to move Mr. Culpepper, for at least a week. No, there was no reason for anyone to hear of this and the idea of bringing up the oxygen gear via the rear elevator was entirely acceptable, but it had to be done immediately. Of course, if the hotel moved Mr. Culpepper out or meddled in the treatment then Mr. Culpepper's father would hold the George V responsible for any injuries. He might call his good friend, the U.S. Secretary of State, or he might sue the hotel for a million dollars—perhaps two. Mr. Culpepper, Sr., never sued for less than a million dollars, and he loved to litigate almost as much as he enjoyed drilling for oil or hunting ducks. Frankly, there wasn't that much of a chance that her patient would die, if he got rest and proper treatment. Should he perish after being moved, however, Mr. Culpepper, Sr., would probably be hunting hotel managers instead of game birds—with the same nine hundred dollar shotgun.

The assistant manager was extremely *sympatique.*

He hadn't fully appreciated the medical situation when he'd raised the question of moving the patient.

After all, the gentleman was a guest and the George V was known for its scrupulous and civilized devotion to the comfort and well-being of its guests.

It was, however, his hope that this might be managed with a minimum of distraction for the other guests.

"If you like," Dr. Clement volunteered, "we could ask the nurses to wear street clothes instead of uniforms. We could bring up the oxygen tanks inside something else—laundry hampers?"

"Whatever you think best, Doctor. I never meddle in medical matters. If there is anything that you need, please call *me.* The fewer people who know about this the better."

He might have spoken for another six minutes, but she cut him off "to call for the nurses and the tent." Within forty minutes, the oxygen apparatus had been installed in the suite and Arnold Culpepper, Jr., installed in the tent. The nurse arrived half an hour later. The play had begun. Meals were brought up three times a day, and fresh nurses appeared every eight hours.

Everything was going according to plan.

On Wednesday night, Mendoza met Garrison at six P.M. at the Gare du Nord rail terminal and followed him two blocks to the car in which Livneh waited at the wheel. The introductions were brief, the glances they exchanged wary and openly curious.

"Let's move out," proposed the New Englander, and when the Citroen was rolling he asked the Indian for a progress report on life at the George V.

"Fine, sir. Everything's going smoothly, although Junior's starting to bitch a lot."

"About what?"

"He hates using the bedpans, and now he's starting to complain about a lot of other things. He wants to know why he has to be the *son* of the Chairman of the Board of Culpepper Industries instead of the Chairman himself."

"Tell him that the Chairman would have to use the bedpan too if he had a heart attack," Garrison answered crisply. "And tell him to keep his claws off the nurses—no screwing around. I assume that he did plenty of that last week."

"Everything in sight, Captain."

"Then he won't mind doing without for a week in a noble cause. Tell him he's too damn young to pass for the head of a big company and that's why he has to play the swinging son. All he has to do is obey orders, you know."

"He knows it, too."

"Okay, we're on our way to the Avenue Franklin Roosevelt. That's where Mr. Seven's going to be on Friday night. We'll do another dry run to the Sov embassy across the Seine, and I'll show you where we're going to lift him."

They drove the route twice, with Garrison explaining exactly what he and Livneh had planned. Before they dropped Mendoza off on the Right Bank at 6:50, Garrison gave him an emergency number to telephone if anything went wrong at the hotel.

"By the way, how's she getting along?" he asked as the Apache reached for the door handle.

"Okay, now that you called. By the way, I think she loves you very much, Captain."

Garrison smiled.

"Number One woman, sir," Mendoza continued.

"At the very least. Say hello, will you?"

"You can count on that, Captain."

After setting the rendezvous for the next night, they separated three blocks from the George V. Garrison had dinner with Livneh at an obscure restaurant unlikely to attract foreigners, and was asleep in his own bed in the Hotel Royale by midnight.

At 12:40 A.M. he woke up.

Telephone.

Emergency.

Adrenaline squirted into his bloodstream and he reacted instantly.

He picked up the instrument as if it were a live grenade that he might have to throw back at some unseen enemy out there in the warm June night.

"Yes?"

"Trouble," announced the unmistakable voice of the Apache.

Garrison didn't ask whether the trouble could wait.

If the Chief called at this hour, it couldn't.

"Ten minutes. Across the street," said the man with the new face.

"Got it."

Mendoza was on time, and they walked away from the river toward the Boulevard St. Germain.

"What is it?"

"I couldn't sleep so I decided to walk the route from the West German embassy to the Sov embassy, to test it on foot. No harm in a little more recon."

"I'm listening."

"I got to less than a block and a half from the Sov building when I suddenly had this *funny* feeling."

"Jeezus Christ," said Garrison.

The Apache had had many *funny* feelings before, and he'd always been right.

"I just had this *funny* feeling that I was walking into some kind of set-up, some stake-out."

"Jeezus H. Christ."

It was a gift that the Indian had, and you couldn't argue with it. Not if you wanted to live.

"I looked all around, up and down the street. Nothing. Everything clean, but I just knew down in my gut that there was some kind of stake-out or ambush. I could taste it. Know what I mean?"

"I know. Go ahead, will you?"

"Just on a hunch, I decided to try the roofs. Take the high ground. Better visibility Bigger field of fire."

Right out of the goddamn textbooks at the Benning course for infantry lieutenants.

"So I waited until a couple came home, and when they opened the door to one of the apartment houses I slipped up behind them and got in before it closed. They were kind of drunk and, well, on their way to bed. Anyway, I got to the roof and crept out *very* carefully to scout the area—and there they were on the roof across the street."

"Son of a bitch."

"Three of them, with night glasses and a movie camera zeroed right in on the door to the embassy."

Garrison sighed, shrugged.

"Never underestimate the KGB," he said.

"I don't think you understand, Captain. These boys didn't look the least bit like Sovs to me. Sir, these little fellows looked like *Chinese.*"

Garrison stopped walking.

"*Chinese?*"

"I'm pretty sure, Sir."

The New Englander shook his head—twice.

"Jeezus H. Christ with oak leaf clusters."

"With oak leaf clusters," agreed Mendoza.

"They didn't see you, did they?"

"I don't think so—not these three. I'd bet that there are more of them in the neighborhood, or not too far away. It would depend on what they're after, I suppose. Could be anything."

"Could be *him*, dammit."

"Seven?"

"Why not? He could save them about a billion dollars and five years of sweat. Got it all in his head, the whole fucking set-up for miniature multiple warheads and lasers, too. . . . Well, they're not going to get him. He's *ours.*"

"Unless they take him first—tonight or tomorrow night."

"There's no way of telling when they're going to hit, or even if it's him they're after. My hunch says it's him. Who else is there around important enough for them to wait up for like this? And my hunch is that they're not hitting tonight, because if they were they'd have weapons and be down in the street instead of up on the roof with glasses and a camera. Maybe they'll hit tomorrow night. No way to tell."

Actually, Colonel Fent could have told him this and a good deal more about Salt Fish Two. Lacking this information, however, Captain David Garrison and Sergeant Juan Mendoza were up until near five A.M. with Eliahu Livneh. If the Chicoms meant to snatch Seven themselves, their operation had to be wrecked—quietly—so that the Sovs wouldn't increase their security. If the Chicoms had some other target, there was still the risk that they'd attack or be discovered by the KGB before Friday night, making Garrison's plan for that evening extremely hazardous if not impossible.

"Either way, it's terrible," said the Israeli.

"And it's going to get worse," predicted Garrison.

Mendoza nodded in assent, for it always did.

"Is there anyone else we could trade for the child, David?"

"We could offer Elizabeth Taylor and a complete leather-bound set of all the back issues of the Boy Scout magazine, but I don't think that they'd buy the deal."

So they went back to planning a counter-strategy, and they were still poring over the street map when the sun rose over the city. None of the plans were good, and they were all very violent. There was one that did not involve guns, and that was the one they reluctantly accepted as the stores and offices of Paris opened for another busy day.

21

"*Real* Gooks, that's better," announced Culpepper when Mendoza reported on the new development.

"With real bullets. Don't forget that," the Apache advised.

"We've played with real bullets before. This thing is really heatin' up, isn't it?"

"Don't let it steam your glasses, Junior," advised the plastic surgeon.

"What?"

"Don't let it steam your glasses or fog up your brain," she repeated.

She was angry—again.

"Now, M'aam. Don't you fret, you hear. We've got a lot of fine experience dealin' with *real* Gooks."

She turned to Mendoza.

"He isn't serious, is he?" she asked.

"Only about half."

"Half serious and half deranged. In Walter Reed we put that kind in the padded file."

"You're just funnin', ain't you, M'aam?" Culpepper chuckled.

"See, he's ready for the laughing academy right now. I'd give him a Section Sixteen in a minute."

Mendoza looked puzzled.

"Sixteen?"

"That's two Section Eights—back to back. Full disability pension."

The Georgian smiled, aware that it was only her fear that made her speak of Section Eight psychiatric discharges.

"You can't mean that, M'aam. Why this whole operation's being planned by a mighty fine officer who's a good friend of yours."

"I'd give *him* a Section *Twenty-Four.*"

"Make him famous, wouldn't it?" asked Culpepper.

"It would be a medical first," she concurred. "Be in all the journals. Yes, he'd be famous."

Mendoza glanced at his wristwatch, realized that the nurse would be returning from her lunch break in a few minutes.

"The Captain's counting on you too, Doctor," he reminded her. "Don't forget—you volunteered for this."

"A Section Twenty-Four for him, and a Thirty-Two for me," she replied. "I must be crazier than he is. I ought to commit myself."

"You did, Doctor," said Mendoza. "Back in that motel near Kennedy."

She nodded.

"Long before that, if anybody's counting," she acknowledged soberly. "Well, you'd better get back in the tent, Junior. She'll be here soon."

Culpepper started toward the bed.

"Hey, Chief, when you told the Cap'n 'bout the Chicoms, what'd he say?"

"He said Jeezus H. Christ. With oak leaf clusters."

Culpepper smiled in recognition.

"With oak leaf clusters, huh?"

"That's what he said."

The Georgian opened the oxygen tent.

"Gonna be all right," he predicted. "I'll help along. Say a couple prayers, maybe even the Hee-brew one Ol' Swede Sussman taught me. Might throw in that Buddhist chant I picked up in Cam-bodia. No point in takin' chances."

Even with the prayers, it was a long day and an even longer night. When would the Chinese attack? Garrison and Livneh followed the Soviet physicist from the embassy to the UNESCO building, sat in the gallery during the morning's plenary session, and then watched him go to the lunch sponsored by the Japanese delegation.

Nothing.

No sign of danger—yet.

Back to the conference, now divided into four committees with Olitski chairman of one of them. They wouldn't hit here, but they might on the way back to the Russian embassy when the meeting adjourned at five. It was less than half a mile, but the Chinese could do it. They were clever and daring, and they planned these things well. Without rancor, Garrison respected them for these professional skills. And he felt the tension growing within himself.

They might risk a daylight assault.

They might even try the helicopter tactic, or ambush the car carrying him back to the embassy.

They were very good at ambushes, lots of experience.

"Bastards," said Garrison as he waited.

"Half an hour," the man who gave flute lessons answered.

It was 4:30, and a warm afternoon.

It seemed very warm.

Finally—somehow—it was five o'clock, and ten minutes later Olitski and another Russian emerged from the building. There were three men with them, one an Indian delegate and the others husky Sovs who had to be KGB agents. They stood together in the bright sun, chatting as if there were no Sonya Brodsky. The Russian embassy car pulled up, and one of the security men opened the door.

Olitski waved it away, said something.

"He's got to be crazy," Garrison thought aloud.

The KGB man obviously felt the same way, but Josef Olitski had made up his mind to walk back to the embassy through the balmy June afternoon and he wasn't about to be dissuaded by any obsessive policeman. The security officer tried to reason with him, but Olitski just smiled and loosened his tie and set off toward the Rue de Grenelle. With the two unhappy KGB agents behind him and three other armed security men in the car that followed twenty yards behind, he strolled along the Avenue de Suffren in animated conversation with the Asian scientist.

Any time now.

From any direction.

In nineteen different ways, the Chinese could move to take him.

But they didn't. The Indian shook hands with Olitski and left him a block away from the Soviet embassy, and the Russian physicist entered the building ninety seconds later without incident.

Livneh and Garrison walked away, found a café, and each drank a properly potent yellow Pernod. "Our luck's holding," the U.S. captain admitted in response to Livneh's silent toast, "but I'm not going to count on luck tonight."

"It would be most unfortunate if they plan to attack tonight also."

"I think I can find out," Garrison speculated, "and as a precaution we'll have your stunt-driver friend Léon in reserve. He's ready?"

"With the truck, David. He knows exactly what he must do—and nothing more."

Garrison explained how he meant to check out the plans of the Chinese, and then phoned Mendoza to meet him in forty minutes on the Seine bridge called the Pont D'Iena. That would give Livneh enough time to get the rifle and the radio, and return.

It was a lovely old bridge, a gently sculpted span within rifle range of the Tour Eiffel on one side and the green Trocadero Park on the far bank.

"You all set for tonight, Chief?" Garrison asked when the Apache joined him there above the tranquil river.

"All set. Is something wrong?"

"I'm not sure. I've got to find out if those Chinese are up on that roof again tonight. If they are, we're probably okay. If they're not, it could mean that they're going to make their move tonight too. I want you to find out, and to cover them."

Cars streamed past them as Garrison spoke, and now he stopped speaking as a young mother and two pretty twins—perhaps nine years old—approached on foot. Garrison chatted briskly about the art wonders of the Louvre until they had moved out of earshot, then returned to his plan.

"I want you up on the high ground again—higher this time, Chief.

Get above them on some nearby roof—if they're up there. If they are, report by walkie-talkie and keep them out of our hair."

Mendoza nodded.

"By whatever means may be necessary," Garrison continued.

Livneh pulled the Citroen up beside them, and the U.S. captain took out the small suitcase on the front seat.

"Only if necessary. It's got a sniper-scope," he said as he handed the canvas bag to Mendoza. "Oh yeah, we'll need a radio call sign, Chief."

"How about Fat Freddy, sir?"

That had been the call sign on that last ambush in the U-Minh Forest.

Was it sentiment, or some Apache thing to exorcise the ghost of that brush with death?"

"If you like," Garrison replied without asking the question.

He slid into the car beside Livneh, and Mendoza started walking toward the Soviet embassy. He reached the Rue de Grenelle ten minutes later, strolling along slowly with a casual window-shopper's gait. He scanned the brocades and china displayed at Au Vieux St. Germain in 4 Rue de Grenelle, then crossed the street and wandered on to Japanese and Khmer art objects in the window of the Josette Schulman shop at Number 17. There were some fine antique clocks for sale at the establishment at 39 Rue de Grenelle, and the elegant etched glass in the Hautinguiraut store at Number 48 gave another opportunity to dawdle. It took him sixteen minutes from the quay to the embassy at Number 70, but the Apache was in no hurry. *They* wouldn't be up on the roof before darkness, for they too were practical enough not to strike during daylight.

He ate dinner in a small neighborhood restaurant two blocks away, and at 7:30 reached the roof of the tallest building in the area. Crouching low, he opened the suitcase and assembled the rifle. Then he screwed on the sniper sight. The last step was to load the weapon.

At 7:35, Dr. Elizabeth Clement told the nurse that she could go out—or rather, down—for dinner. The nurse was delighted, for eating the George V cuisine was one of the fringe benefits that she especially appreciated. Only a rich *Americain* would feed a mere nurse in this deluxe hotel, of course. Five minutes after the nurse left the suite Arnold Culpepper, Jr., also departed—in a laundry hamper. The overall-clad men who carried it were not employees of the oxygen supply firm. One was a former Israeli agent with a gift for the flute, and the other a U.S. Army captain with a talent for ambush.

They loaded the straw hamper into the rear of the van, and Garrison helped the Georgian out a few seconds after Livneh had closed the door from the outside. Culpepper blinked under the impact of the beam from Garrison's flashlight, sighed.

"Thank you, Cap'n. Kind of cramped in there. Not that I'm complaining."

"Mendoza says you're bitching all the time," Garrison replied as the truck began to move.

They both sat down on the floor.

"That's a typical goddamn Apache lie, Cap'n. I didn't exactly enjoy the bedpans and I might, just might, have said a word or two about that mother of a plastic tent, but I never bitch."

"Wouldn't do no good if you did, son," Garrison said wryly in his own version of a Southern drawl.

"It was kind of-sort of boring in that see-through enema bag," admitted Arnold L. Culpepper, Jr., in confidential tones, "but I'm reckonin' tonight will be a bit livelier."

"At least. In case the merriment gets out of hand, Junior, you'd better put on the flak jacket."

Culpepper reached into the canvas duffel bag, pulled out one of the armored garments.

"Real Gooks with real bullets," he muttered in enthusiastic anticipation. "Say, Cap'n, where's the Chief? I've got to take care of that wild 'Pache, you know. Look after him, so to speak."

"He's up on a roof with a sniper rifle, covering one of our flanks—so to speak. Fine, Junior. You look like a real dude in that flak jacket."

Now Livneh banged on the metal partition, and they knew that they were approaching the West German embassy.

"Mr. Seven should be starting on his first course in a little while," Garrison estimated after glancing at the fluorescent face of his wristwatch. "Probably finishing his champagne—maybe his second—any minute now."

"Taittinger '64, Cap'n?"

"You're getting to be a real man about town, aren't you?"

"Up to my ass in gracious living," Culpepper admitted with unabashed pride. "The lady was a big help. She taught me a lot."

"Me too."

For a moment she filled his consciousness, and then—without warning or premeditation—his attention shifted to Mendoza on that rooftop. It happened instantly, like a sudden jump cut in some fast-paced action film. *Bam*—there he was, the Apache with the rifle. He was damn good with a rifle, even without the scope.

"You don't think she's right, do you, Cap'n?" Culpepper broke in abruptly. "You don't think we're going to get zapped, do you?"

Garrison shook his head.

"What about the kid, sir? Think they'll swap her?"

"No doubt about it."

"You don't think they might try to double-cross us, do you?"

The Special Forces captain looked amused.

"No doubt about that either, Junior. To quote that big country and western hit you used to sing a couple of years ago, just as sure as little green apples."

"You got a plan for that, Cap'n?"

Garrison nodded.

"I *knew* you had a plan. I told the lady this afternoon. Don't sweat it, Doctor, the Cap'n has it all figured out. He's got a *great* plan. That's what I told her."

There were two more thumps, and Garrison flicked off the flashlight before he slid open the panel behind the steering wheel.

"Radio message from Mendoza," said Livneh. "Want to talk to him?"

"Yes."

Garrison reached forward, took the walkie-talkie.

"Hello, Fat Freddy-One," sounded the plastic box. "This is Fat Freddy-Two up on the mountain."

It was Mendoza all right.

"Fat Freddy-One here. How's the view? Repeat, how . . . is . . . the . . . view?"

"View is terrible. . . . Nothing to see. . . . Excellent line of sight, but nothing to see. . . . Tourists have moved on. . . . Maybe they're coming to your party tonight. . . . I'd like to come myself."

There were no Chinese on any of the roofs near the Soviet embassy, and Mendoza's guess that they might make their own move to take Olitski tonight could well be correct. In that case, every skilled man and gun might be needed.

"You are welcome to the party, Fat Freddy-Two. Come on back to your hotel and we'll pick you up in twenty minutes."

At 8:10, Garrison deftly slid the rented Citroen in along the curb twenty yards from the George V. and Mendoza immediately put the suitcase on the rear seat.

"Get in," ordered the captain with a touch of impatience.

"Okay, let's have it," he continued a few moments later as he put the car into gear.

"Just what I told you, sir. Not a trace of them. Maybe Charlie's over here somewhere."

Just a habit. Charlie—short for Victor Charlie or VC—was the enemy.

"We'll drive around and look, just as soon as you get into the flak jacket. It's on the floor behind you, Chief."

They didn't find any sign of the Chinese, not by nine or ten or eleven. They checked with Livneh by radio twice, and he hadn't seen Feng's team either.

"I don't like it, Chief. How about you?" Garrison asked as he stopped for traffic at the corner near the Theatre Marigny.

"They're here. My gut tells me they're here—now, Sir."

"My gut says the same thing. . . . Well, we'd better stop the cruising and move back into position near the German embassy. Our friend should be coming out any minute."

It was 11:48 when Professor Josef Olitski was ushered out of the elegant building at 13 Avenue Franklin Roosevelt. Two waiting Soviet security men escorted him to the big limousine, where another armed agent sat beside the chauffeur.

"Stand by to roll," Garrison said into the walkie-talkie.

"No escort car. That's good," Mendoza calculated aloud beside him.

The Russian Zis sedan moved out into the traffic.

"Here we go," began the U.S. captain.

Another voice broke in almost instantly.

"*Ici, Léon. Ici, Léon. Vos amis sont arrivés. Vos amis sont arrivés.*"

The man whom Livneh had recruited was reporting that he'd seen *them.*

"*Attention, Léon. C'est Charles?*"

"*Oui, c'est Charles.*"

The Chinese.

"*Bon soir, Léon,*" said Garrison in the preagreed code phrase.

The Russian car was passing the Grand Palais when Léon began to pick up speed in the truck.

"About time," Garrison thought aloud. "They're almost at the river."

The Chinese driver was warily laying back, using three vehicles between his car and Olitski's limousine to screen it from the KGB guards.

"Now, *now*, dammit."

It was as if Léon had heard Garrison's plea.

The truck accelerated, began to circle the carload of Chinese as if to pass, and then swerved suddenly. The Renault carrying Feng's strike force began to turn, but not fast enough. The heavy *camion* smashed into the left rear of the car, sent it careening off diagonally with a metallic crash. Then there was another loud ugly sound marking the second impact—the Renault plowing into a parked gray Fiat and crumpling it up like a ball of paper.

"Beautiful, *beautiful*," Garrison celebrated as he watched the truck pull back into the flow of traffic leading to the Pont des Invalides.

In three or four minutes police cars would reach the site of the accident, and the Chinese—those too badly hurt to flee—would have to cope with them. But in three or four minutes it wouldn't matter. It would be all over.

"Ninety seconds. Stand by," Garrison said tensely like some television director.

In the laundry van waiting just off the Rue de Grenelle on the opposite bank of the Seine, Arnold L. Culpepper, Jr., sat beside the Israeli—a concussion grenade in one hand and the walkie-talkie in the other.

"Stand by, Fat Freddy," it sputtered. "On the bridge and closing fast. On the bridge and closing fast."

"Standing by. We are standing by," answered the blond Georgian.

The Russian chauffeur was driving slowly and carefully, conscious of the importance of his passenger and the creativity that Parisians displayed behind the wheel. He wasn't about to match egos with any of them, and he let them pass without any sense of competition or resentment. He was on the Rue de Grenelle, only two blocks from the embassy, when a large dirty truck tooted and rolled past noisily.

Then he hit the brakes, jamming the pedal to the floor.

The grimy *camion* had cut across his lane without warning, and the Russian cursed as he fought to avoid a collision. He failed. The front of the big limousine—both fenders and the radiator—were bashed in, and everyone in the Zis was hurled forward by the impact. One of the guards beside Olitski groggily opened the rear door nearest the sidewalk, and that was when Mendoza hurled the first concussion grenade. It was still in the air when the van pulled around the corner, and a moment later Culpepper threw the second. It was a perfect pitch, right through the open window beside the Soviet driver.

The first blast stunned the KGB operative who'd opened the rear door.

The second knocked out both men in the front seat.

There was still one guard unaccounted for—but not for long. He was groggy but courageous, and he could still think. He had enough sense to know that he had a much better chance inside the armored body of the car. He pushed the scientist to the floor, then drew his automatic to fire back. He squeezed off two shots, one wrecking the windshield of the Citroen only three inches from Garrison's face.

"Gas. Use the gas," the captain told Mendoza and then leaped from the Citroen and dropped into a combat crouch.

The Apache flung two grenades, and then Culpepper tossed two more. As the acrid blinding fog swirled up around the Renault, the KGB agent leaned forward to close the windows.

That was when Garrison shot him twice—once in the shoulder and once in the upper chest.

"Let's go," ordered the ambush expert.

The three men raced toward the damaged Zis. Junior Culpepper got there first, jerked open the rear door to drag out Olitski. The wounded security agent fell out, rolled over and shot Culpepper in the stomach at almost point-blank range. The Georgian collapsed backwards. Garrison fired again, punching three holes in the guard's arm and abdomen. The man dropped the gun, twisted away moaning.

"Get Junior," Garrison ordered as he pulled out the dazed scientist.

Olitski's face was cut, one lens of his eyeglasses was cracked, and a tiny stream of blood dribbled from one ear. All predictable effects of the concussion grenades, and the coughing from the tear gas didn't amount to much either. The merchandise was in good condition, suitable for barter.

They hurried Olitski and Culpepper into the back of the laundry van, and Livneh drove off immediately with the crash expert, Léon, beside him. Fortunately the Rue de Grenelle was no main thoroughfare and there was almost no traffic this late at night, so they were able to escape from the area without delay.

"What about Junior?" Garrison asked the Apache. "You think he's going to make it?"

Culpepper groaned, still clutching at his abdomen.

"He'll be walking tomorrow, sir. The flak jacket took all the impact."

"Right in the gut," Culpepper gasped painfully. "That mother shot me right in the gut."

"No, right in the armor. Bet it hurts like hell," Mendoza said sympathetically.

"Jeesus Christ, it's like I was hit with a baseball bat."

"You're right, Chief," Garrison said. "He's bitching all the time. One lousy little nine millimeter slug that didn't even break the skin, and he's pricing tombstones. You ought to see the other guy, the one that shot you. He's got five slugs in him—*five*."

"Teach that mother a lesson. Goddamn hero. Hope they bury him upside down in a leaky coffin. . . . Ooooh, that does smart, Cap'n."

Now Olitski said something. It was more of an incoherent mumble, not enough to make sense but more than enough to remind them that they'd be at the George V in less than five minutes. Garrison opened the first-aid kit, took out the prepared hypo, and knocked Olitski out with a squirt of morphine.

Everything moved according to his plan. They put the physicist in the hampeı, and eleven minutes later Olitski was sleeping in the oxygen tent at the hotel.

"You may want to clean him up a bit when you get a chance," Garrison told Elizabeth Clement.

"He looks terrible. What did you do to him?"

Garrison shrugged.

"Nothing much. Wrecked his car, knocked him silly with concussion grenades, choked him a tiny bit with tear gas, and put five slugs into the cowboy sitting next to him."

"You're a tender type, aren't you?" she challenged.

"You ought to know, Doc," he replied.

He kissed her, first cupping her face in his big hands and then again after she was in his arms.

"Gotta go," he announced. "I really ought to ravish you right now—the way they do in dirty books—but we gotta go. By the way, we also gave your patient a shot of morphine. Take good care of him. I'm going to need him to trade in a couple of days."

She looked up at him.

"You still think you're going to get that girl out, Dave?"

His answer didn't make much sense at first.

"Masada shall not fall again," he told her.

She hardly slept at all that night.

22

The battered Chinese—one with four broken ribs—had all fled from their wrecked Renault before the Paris police arrived and the KGB men had used their diplomatic immunity to avoid telling the *gendarmes* anything, and the silenced .32s that Livneh had bought had made so little noise that no one on the Rue de Grenelle knew for certain that there had been a gunfight. Several people thought that they'd heard a shot or two—one old lady claimed it was a machine gun—but it was all rather vague and irritating. There was a damaged Zis limousine, an abandoned *camion* and a Citroen that had been rented by a man using what proved to be a false passport.

On the surface, it was all confusing.

Nevertheless, within seven hours after the kidnapping intelligence organizations of four major powers were aware that Professor Josef Olitski had been lifted. It is to their professional credit that no one panicked, but it is also a fact that everyone concerned was quite disturbed. They were also surprised, especially Stanley Harper.

In fact, Colonel Stanley B. Harper, a trim forty-one-year-old Kansan who had been Assistant U.S. Air Attache in Paris for seventeen months, was more than surprised. He was astounded, indignant, and somewhat sleepy when Berlov awoke him at six o'clock. He often ran into Ivan Berlov at six o'clock, but usually P.M., not A.M. Colonel Ivan Berlov was Harper's opposite number, the Soviet embassy's Assistant Air Attache, and a man of considerable grace on the diplomatic cocktail party circuit. There was nothing graceful about Berlov this dawn, however.

"Shtennley Harper? This is Berlov, Colonel Berlov," the Russian singsonged into the phone.

The Kansas wheat farmer's son sat up in bed immediately.

"Harper here," he acknowledged in the approved Pentagon ritual.

"I have been instructed to inform you that incidents such as last night's obscene affair are *intolerable.* I'm sure you know what I mean."

"Don't have the foggiest goddamn notion what you mean. What're you talking about?"

Berlov's reply was a meaningful and plainly hostile combination of a sniff and a grunt, another first for Russian creativity.

"Your denial was not unexpected, Harper, but that's routine, of course. Now to the gritty nitty, as you say, you've got to give him back, and at once."

"Give *who* back?" asked the U.S. colonel, and immediately wondered whether it should have been "whom."

Berlov made that special sound again.

"Give him back now, and there'll be no retaliations. Tell your people that. And please, no fairy tales about him wanting political asylum. He's no defector. We all know that, and that brutal ambush on the Rue de Grenelle only confirms it."

Someone important—presumably Russian—was missing, and the reference to the Rue de Grenelle indicated that the disappearance had taken place in Paris. The KGB apparently thought that a U.S. intelligence unit had taken the man. It had to be a man, for Berlov had spoken of "him" repeatedly. But who was he and had some American cloak-and-dagger service seized him? Colonel Harper had no idea.

"Berlov, I don't think this is the sort of thing we ought to chew on the phone. In half an hour I'll be awake enough . . ."

"In half an hour I'll pick you up outside your building."

"What's up, Honey?" Sallyanne Harper asked her husband after he'd placed the telephone back in its cradle on the bedtable."

He reflected, yawned.

"Something—that's for damn sure. That was your friend, Colonel Ivan Berlov—the slick dancer I've noticed you and Gladys Nippey ogling at all the parties."

"Don't be silly, Hon," protested the messy-haired blonde beside him.

"Berlov thinks Our Side's grabbed some Hot Pistol from Their Side. He's probably crazy, but maybe the C.I.A. did it. They're crazier than Berlov, you know. Jeezus, maybe that Berlov thinks *I'm* with the C.I.A.?"

"Are you, Stanley?"

Harper rubbed his scratchy beard, looked at her pityingly.

"We've been married for almost eighteen years, parented four kids. Don't you think *you'd* know if I was one of those Spooks?"

Was or were? It was damned irritating.

"I might not, Stan. You're a very clever person."

He shook his head back and forth, as if testing whether it was firmly attached.

"Even if I was—which I'm not—you shouldn't ask, Sallyanne. Jeezus, I thought you understood about security."

She apologized, got out of bed, and made coffee as he showered and shaved. It was good-American-instant coffee, none of that bitter stuff the French swilled so stubbornly. The embassy PX made life in Paris quite bearable, for you could always get your favorite brands of deodorant, coffee, or canned chili. Stanley B. Harper wasn't much of a dancer, but he was a good provider.

At 6:30 that morning, he provided Colonel Ivan Berlov with an opportunity to explain how unpleasant and violent the Cold War could become again if Professor Josef Olitski didn't return to the

Soviet embassy within forty-eight hours, Monday, when the conference resumed. Shortly before nine A.M., Harper provided a full and somewhat grim report of his talk with Berlov to Brigadier General Wally Tom Partridge, and Partridge promptly relayed the information/threat to a certain Second Secretary named Colton who was the C.I.A. "station officer" at the embassy. Randy Andy Colton listened craftily, nodded just as if he knew all about it, and sent a Priority One cable to somebody code-named "Klondike" at the Agency's headquarters in Virginia.

"Klondike," who savored crises almost as much as he enjoyed a vintage Pommard, almost purred. He discussed the news with a Deputy Director in the Operations Division, and they called an emergency meeting of Working Group Six. Six was a very hush-hush interdepartmental intelligence committee that furtively functioned under the cover name of the Joint Task Force on Frozen Foods, having abandoned the camouflage of the Cold Weather Research Studies Group in 1969. Within four hours after Colton's cable left Paris, a number of earnest and guileful middle-aged men assembled in a "secure" room in the D ring of the third floor of the Pentagon. There, with the confidence that came with the knowledge that this chamber was "swept" for electronic bugs each week, they explored The Olitski Affair.

And its possibilities.

First, of course, the recriminations.

Why hadn't *we* taken Olitski, and—for that matter—Walchek too?

Perhaps we could have persuaded them both to defect, pointed out the skinny captain from O.N.I., if "Colonel Nelson" had been on the ball. Nelson, who was not a colonel and used at least four other names, was the C.I.A.'s expert on arranging defections, and this jab by the Office of Naval Intelligence simply reflected internecine jealousy at his many successes. Why the O.N.I. captain didn't even know Nelson's real name, but there was no point in bringing *that* up now. After the way that O.N.I. had botched that routine thing in—well, never mind.

The chairman of Six, a pragmatic Air Force general who hated meetings, brought the conversation back to the three "hard" questions.

Who had Olitski?

Why were the Sovs blaming us?

Would they really retaliate that savagely?

After the usual ninety-three minutes of cool and slyly unpleasant dialogue, it was decided that the Russians were blaming the U.S. because they couldn't think of anyone else to blame, and that there was undoubtedly a possibility that brutal acts of misguided retaliation might follow. With unconcealed reluctance, the five American intelligence organizations represented agreed that the C.I.A. network in Paris should try to find Olitski and—if necessary—return him to the Sovs. It was ridiculous, but no other course seemed open.

The question of who had lifted Olitski remained unanswered.

"It was a first class professional job," concluded the C.I.A. delegate after he described the kidnapping details Berlov had given.

"If you find them, maybe you ought to hire them?" suggested the O.N.I. captain.

"I would in a minute. The character who planned this is a goddamn wizard. I'd sign him up anytime—at top wages. He's a nifty operator, tough and nifty."

By the time the meeting broke up, the D.S.T.—France's internal security and counterespionage organization—was already searching for Olitski. The Direction de la Surveillance du Territoire had not discovered the kidnapping. Another French unit roughly similar to the American C.I.A.—the S.D.E.C.E.—had been monitoring Harper's phone routinely, and the wiretapper had reported Berlov's conversation to the Night Duty Officer. In response, the energetic Service de Documentation Exterieure et de Contre-espionnage had assigned a full surveillance team to cover the meeting of the two foreign colonels. When that team's sensitive eavesdropping equipment picked up the references to Olitski, the S.D.E.C.E. prepared to launch an immediate search for the missing physicist. It was over the angry protest of the S.D.E.C.E. that the Minister of Defense turned "l'affaire Olitski" over to the D.S.T. instead. The D.S.T. had much greater manpower available in the Paris region, reasoned Monsieur le Ministre, and this was no time for petty rivalries. With any luck at all, *la belle France* might seize Olitski for itself.

Two major Soviet intelligence organizations with active *apparats* in Paris—the civilian KGB and the military G.R.U.—were also hunting for the scientist, and in Moscow a Red Army marshal was telling a Deputy Minister of Foreign Affairs how tough and angry he should be when he spoke to the U.S. ambassador at noon. In Peking, Colonel Feng was neither tough nor angry as he scanned the report from the French capital. He was thoughtful, almost bemused.

Salt Fish Two had failed, and now the Chinese could do nothing until Olitski surfaced again—somewhere, sometime. He would, sooner or later. It didn't matter that much where he was for the moment, for the Chinese could wait. Yes, they would try to find out what had gone wrong with Salt Fish Two—and they would wait.

After all, Olitski was worth waiting for.

23

There were nine D.S.T. agents in the Tuileries Gardens when Berlov met Harper that Saturday afternoon, and the French operatives were an appropriate assortment of males and females, old and young, "rich and poor" in diverse costumes—and they didn't hear anything. The two colonels spoke tersely, softly, and allusively, without mentioning names or other specifics.

"None of our people know anything about this," assured the Kansan.

"That's impossible to believe."

"We've checked every unit here and every agency back home. Zero. Nothing."

"Rubbish. Not acceptable."

"Look, they've told us to help you find him. All our people here will be working on this for you."

Berlov eyed him skeptically.

"That's right out of Walt Disney."

"What?"

"A fairy tale—like Peter and the Wolf. We don't want fairy tales, Harper. You'll have to do better."

"We're doing our best—with very little, dammit. You haven't told us very much, not enough anyway. Four or five male Caucasians—one sort of swarthy—between twenty-five and forty years old. No good descriptions, no clue to nationality—nothing."

"One of them was shot in the stomach twice. That's something."

"Okay, that's something tangible. We'll check out all the hospitals."

Berlov, weary after a sleepless night, fought down a yawn.

"Don't bother. We already did that. Just give him back."

"Jeezus. Look, maybe the French police found something in that car they left."

The Russian shook his head.

"We do not wish to involve them. This is between you and us."

"You and somebody else," Harper corrected. "*We're* just innocent bystanders."

"You'd better not stand-by too long. There are only thirty-five hours left. After that, it will be extremely unpleasant."

Then he let his tired eyes wander over the mothers and children, the pink-faced little governess from Normandy and the ice cream vendor at his wheeled cart.

"Beautiful afternoon, isn't it?" Berlov said wistfully as if in remembrance.

Then his focus and concentration returned to the Cold War.

"I expect to hear from you this evening, Shtennley Harper. I'll be at the embassy."

By the time Berlov had returned to 70 Rue de Grenelle, the package had already been delivered and the Soviet ambassador had opened it. Olitski's watch, his spectacles with one cracked lens, and a note—the traditional kidnappers' package. The message, typed in French by Livneh, announced that "he" would be returned unharmed in exchange for Sonya Brodsky, a fourteen-year-old girl in Moscow's Ostankin School for wards of the state. If the Russians were willing to make the swap, they should signal this by having a man carrying three umbrellas standing at the Aeroflot ticket counter at the Invalides air terminal from ten A.M. until noon on Sunday.

The last sentence warned that if there was no exchange "he" would be sold to *the Chinese.*

It was insane.

That was the first reaction of the ambassador and the KGB *rezident* who directed Soviet espionage in France.

The second reaction was to telephone Moscow, using a scrambler to insure privacy. It didn't take the KGB direktor in the Russian capital very long to locate the child, and to learn that an American named Garrison, a suspected agent, had visited her there two weeks earlier. This Garrison had claimed to be a friend of a distant relative, one Charles Brodsky of New York City. According to the Ministry for Foreign Affairs, that Charles Brodsky had four times sought permission for the child to emigrate to the United States. Garrison had said that he ran a bookstore in Pittsfield, a city somewhere near Boston. That might be untrue, however, for he had visited the U.S.S.R. on a forged visa—an expertly forged visa.

"The importance of the child is incomprehensible," judged the direktor in Moscow, "but this Garrison is probably an American agent in any case."

"The Americans have offered to cooperate, Comrade."

"You certainly don't believe those bastards, do you?"

The KGB executive in Paris hesitated.

"Well . . . I'm not sure. . . . Normally I wouldn't, Comrade, but there was one more thing in the ransom note. If we don't agree to deliver the child . . . well . . . they say they'll sell him to the *Chinese*!"

"That's completely crazy. Not even the Americans could be that crazy. It's ridiculous. Can you make any sense out of it—any sense at all?"

"None at all, Comrade—from an official point of view. But if the Americans are telling the truth and it is some other group that has taken him . . ."

"It's crazy. The child is meaningless—just another child."

"Comrade, it may be . . . perhaps . . . that she is not just another child to someone."

"That is obvious, although I don't understand why. I don't even care. What I do care about is this attempt to blackmail and humiliate the Soviet Union. We will not be intimidated by thugs."

"Then you don't wish to trade the girl?"

Some of these men in the field were incredibly dense.

"Of course, we'll trade her for Olitski. We'd give them a dozen orphans for him—a hundred. No, we'll make the exchange if we have to. Send your man with the umbrellas. We'll fly the girl in on a special flight. Even more important, see how sincere the Americans are about helping. Ask them to find this Garrison, David Garrison. Tell them that we believe he was part of this kidnapping, and let them deliver him to us."

Thanks to the wonders of modern communications, this message reached "Kondike" at C.I.A. headquarters outside Washington at eleven P.M. on Saturday night. To be precise, the message came in about an hour earlier and he was summoned from a Georgetown party to cope.

C.I.A. to State: require immediate biography and address on David Garrison carrying U.S. passport. Priority computer run imperative.

State to C.I.A.: Captain David O. Garrison, U.S. Army, hometown Stockbridge, Mass., departed U.S. for Tel Aviv in May. Returned in June for five days. Current whereabouts unknown.

A U.S. Army captain?

C.I.A. to Military Intelligence, G-2 Night Duty Officer—Pentagon: Urgently need military record, biography, and current location of U.S. Army Captain David O. Garrison. WG-6 priority project. Reply soonest.

It was 3:25 A.M. when a Military Intelligence major named Fusco telephoned with the answers. "I don't know what the hell you guys are up to," he told "Klondike," "but you sounded hysterical and the WG-6 priority didn't hurt either. What is this, World War III?"

"It may be your ass, Fusco. Where's Garrison?"

"According to Walter Reed, he's out of town on a sixty day leave."

"What is he, a doctor?"

"A patient. Big combat type. Caught a grenade in Vietnam and they brought him back to fix his face. Two operations, according to the nurse I talked to. What's he done?"

"Just answer my questions, Fusco. Give me some kind of a description."

The G-2 major complied with the vital statistics on age, height, weight.

"What about his M.O.S.?"

"Lots. He's hot stuff. Paratrooper, demolition man, sharpshooter rating with all U.S. and Sovblock small arms, frogman, guerrilla warfare pro. You name it, he does it."

"Special Forces?" Klondike speculated.

"One of the best. A fistful of decorations—almost all for classy ambushes. I phoned Bragg for you, and they say he's a superstar in the ambush game."

"That figures. It certainly figures."

"You going to hire him?" asked Fusco. "I don't think that the Army would be too crazy about that. He's very popular in certain circles. They wouldn't give him up."

"Don't pry, Major. If we were going to, we certainly wouldn't talk about it to you—and not on the phone. Godalmighty, you got as much sense of 'security' as a meatloaf."

Fusco thought of several tart answers, decided to save them for his memoirs.

"Anything else?" he said.

"Family. Wife? Kids? Parents?"

"Wife, negative. Children, negative. Father in Stockbridge, Mass."

"You wouldn't have a fairly recent picture of him, would you?"

"Negative. Try Walter Reed in the morning."

The man code-named "Klondike" did that, sent a courier to the hospital at eight o'clock that Sunday morning. It would be interesting—as well as useful—to see what this slick superstar looked like, "Klondike" thought as he finished his fourth carton of black coffee since midnight.

They were embarrassed and puzzled at Walter Reed, reported the courier by telephone. The photos of Captain David O. Garrison's new face were not in the file. They were supposed to be there, but no one could find them. This was because Dr. Elizabeth Clement had removed them but the courier didn't know that, so all he could do was report his failure.

"Very *nifty*," Klondike said to himself as he put down the phone.

He thought about the meticulously planned and adroitly executed ambush on the Rue de Grenelle, and he concluded that it wasn't at all surprising that the pictures were gone. It figured. A nifty son-of-a-bitch such as this one thought ahead, as they'd trained him to do.

Garrison would plan for every contingency, try to cover every angle. You had to admire his professional competence, brooded the red-eyed C.I.A. executive.

"Brodsky," thought the man known as "Klondike."

He put in a call to the New York City residence of Charles J. Brodsky, was pleased to find that the multimillionaire's number was listed. If Garrison had actually represented the aged tycoon on that trip to Moscow, Charlie Brodsky might know where the Special Forces captain was now.

"Hello," said a voice that was male and somewhere over forty.

"Is this the Brodsky residence?"

"It's one of the residences of one of the Brodskys."

"Charles J. Brodsky—that's whom I want."

"He's having breakfast," answered Solomon P. Solomon. "Could you call back in an hour?"

"This is very important. This is the Central Intelligence Agency, and we'd appreciate his cooperation. We're trying to reach a man named Garrison, and we think that Mr. Brodsky may have his address."

"I don't think so," the former detective responded with a smile.

"What?"

"I never heard of this Garrison. It wouldn't be Gurtman, would it? Max Gurtman? Has a big store in Phoenix?"

Deadpan. Sincere voice.

No sign that he was putting on one of the most powerful agencies of the government.

"No, not Gurtman. David Garrison, Captain David O. Garrison."

"Never heard of him. Of course I don't travel by ship much. My stomach won't take it."

Somehow "Klondike" controlled his temper.

"He's an *Army* Captain. Please, I'd like to speak to Mr. Garrison—I mean Brodsky—himself."

"I'll ask his nurse."

Thirty seconds later Shirley Takeda came to the phone.

"Yes?"

"Is this Mr. Brodsky's nurse?"

"I hope so. What can I do for you?"

Klondike repeated his litany.

"This isn't a fund raising thing, is it?" she inquired sweetly. "If it is, you'd better check with the Brodsky Foundation."

"Miss, the C.I.A. does not raise funds privately. We are financed by the Congress. Surely you've heard of the C.I.A.?"

"Oh—the C.I.A.? Certainly, heard a lot about you. Mostly good things. I must have misunderstood. Well, I'm sure that Mr. Brodsky would be glad to cooperate with the government. He's very patriotic. He's an old man and not well, but very patriotic. Now who is this Donald Garrison?"

"David. Captain David O. Garrison, U.S. Army."

"I'm sorry about the confusion," she apologized in adroit non-sequitur. "We get a lot of calls from charities, mostly Jewish. Mr. Brodsky's very philanthropic. Gave one hundred thousand dollars last year to the U.J.A.—that's the United Jewish Appeal."

Was she really that scatter-brained?

"Nurse . . . please . . it is both important and urgent that I speak to Mr. Brodsky. I must locate Captain Garrison immediately."

"He's not here. You can look for yourself. We always cooperate with all government agencies. Health inspectors, men from the Fire Department, we let everyone in to check on things. You won't find Garrison here. Frankly, I'd doubt that Mr. Brodsky ever heard of him. I've been his nurse for more than a year, and I never heard of this Garrison. . . . Say, did he ever work at any of the stores? Maybe the personnel department knows something about him. They keep terrific files."

It had to be malice. Nobody could talk like that by accident.

"Klondike" refused to submit.

"Listen, the Sovs say this man was in Moscow a couple of weeks ago and he said that Mr. Brodsky had asked him to visit a distant relative, a girl named Sonya Brodsky."

"It's a common Jewish name," fenced Shirley Takeda briskly. "This Garrison isn't Jewish, is he?"

"What the *hell* has that got to do with anything?"

"Don't get fresh, Mister. Just because you're with some big government outfit doesn't mean you can talk to me like that. I'm a taxpayer, and Mr. Brodsky is a *very large* taxpayer. Just watch your language, Buster."

Either she was crazy or she read too many short stories.

"I'm tired and I'm sorry and I want you to ask Mr. Brodsky two questions."

"Of course. Always glad to cooperate, so long as you're courteous. A little common courtesy always helps, you know."

"You're absolutely right. Now here are the two questions."

"Should I get a pencil?"

"I don't think that will be necessary. First question: Did Mr. Brodsky ask Captain Garrison to visit anyone in Moscow? Second question: Where can Captain Garrison be reached right now?"

"Gotcha," Shirley Takeda announced, and then she recited the questions word for word to demonstrate that she understood.

"Fine. You'll ask him now?"

"Not now. He's eating his breakfast, and then he'll go to the potty. Prunes every morning. But when he's off the potty—if he doesn't fall asleep—we'll call you. Give me your name and number."

"Nurse, this may be a matter of life and death."

"Honest?"

"You have my word."

"You're not just crapping me, are you?"

"Not even a little bit."

"Just a minute."

She put down the phone, took a lipstick from the pocket of her snug-fitting white uniform, and redecorated her lips. She studied the results in the wall mirror, flicked off a tiny red speck from a front tooth, and returned to the conversation.

"I asked him just what you said," she reported in the tones of a conscientious schoolgirl.

"And what did he say?"

"He doesn't remember any such person. Actually, he said that he'd never heard of the goddamn idiot—but that's age. He's a bit senile. *They* get that way after seventy. Not all of them, but a lot of them. Memory comes and goes. Anyway, he said to tell you that he doesn't recall ever meeting anyone by that name and he has no idea where you could find this person. He also said to tell you to keep up the good work. He's a great fan of the C.I.A., loves spy movies."

Something was wrong.

If Brodsky didn't know Garrison, why would the ambush expert use the old man's name to visit the girl in Moscow? How would

Garrison even know that anyone named Sonya Brodsky existed, and why would he care?

"Nurse, do you know whether Mr. Brodsky does have a relative—a girl about fourteen—in Moscow? A kid named Sonya Brodsky?"

"That's the name you mentioned before. Nothing wrong with my memory."

"Well?"

"I think he does. I'm not his secretary or anything, I'm a nurse, but I seem to recall a letter about her. Maybe you'd better ask Mrs. Nafkawitz. She handles the correspondence."

"May I speak to her?"

"Sure. On the 8th of July. She'll be on vacation until then."

It wasn't worth it.

You just couldn't get anything from these people.

"I'll call back," he concluded, "and thanks for your cooperation with the government."

"What else would you expect? We're not hippies, you know!"

She walked out into the garden where she found the old man at the breakfast table.

"Niee fellow. Works at some government agency. Wanted to ask about some Army Captain named Garrison," she reported nonchalantly as she resumed her seat.

"I heard—on the extension phone. That was some number you did for him, chatchka."

She poured herself another cup of coffee from the elegant silver pot.

"Well, C.J., I was only trying to do as well as Solomon did. He's a tough act to follow."

"You didn't have to tell the man I was senile, Shirley," Brodsky pretended to grumble.

"I didn't think you'd want me to tell him to go screw himself, C.J.—that was my first idea."

Brodsky considered the choice.

"You did the right thing, Shirley. No point in being discourteous to civil servants. They lead a dog's life as it is."

He looked over at the black man.

"What do you think, Solomon?"

"I think Garrison's made his move. He's done something that's got them bothered—something big."

"How do you figure that?" wondered the man in the wheelchair.

"Well, the C.I.A. doesn't call about double-parking, Charlie."

Brodsky nodded.

"True. You have a good analytical mind, my friend. The C.I.A. doesn't phone up about double-parking, or littering either."

He spoke slowly, with some effort.

Not much time left now. All three of them in the garden knew it.

"C.J., why should our government care about what he does to get the girl out of Russia?" asked the nurse.

"I guess that depends on what he did. Whatever it was, it's caused some excitement."

"And trouble," Solomon added.

Shirley Takeda took another bagel, applied the cream cheese, and topped it with a generous portion of smoked salmon.

"Trouble isn't going to bother *him*, not *him*," she predicted before she bit.

"It bothers *them*," responded the aged millionaire.

"We're not finished with them," Solomon concurred. 'That story about a senile old man on the potty—they won't buy it. The C.I.A. isn't that dumb."

"I hope not, Solomon. If they are, I've been paying hundreds of thousands in taxes to support a bunch of schmucks."

"Maybe they are schmucks, C.J.?" she suggested hopefully.

Brodsky shook his head.

"Maybe bastards sometimes, but not schmucks. No, they're not going to give up on this. They'll be tapping this phone, right?"

"In about an hour and a half," calculated the ex-detective.

"Watching the house?"

"No doubt about it. That man who called was in a sweat, a cool controlled sweat, but he was sweating, C.J., and he meant business."

"Anything else they might do, Solomon?"

"Everything else—everything they can think of. They know this game pretty well, and they're good thinkers."

On the second floor of the huge office building in Virginia that houses the Central Intelligence Agency global headquarters, "Klondike" was peering blankly at the opposite wall and thinking about those missing photos. He couldn't force as rich and influential a man as C.J. Brodsky to tell him where Garrison was, but he could get pictures of the new face to send to Colton in Paris. There had to be a way.

State.

There would be a duplicate photo of the new face in the passport files at State. There was no way of guessing how long it might take for those genteel mediocrities at State to locate the file—or even whether they could do it at all before Monday morning. Well, they'd just goddamn had to. This was a top priority WG-6 project. Once they got the picture, the Agency could wirephoto it by cable to Colton. In the meanwhile, Colton had already been instructed to look for Captain David O. Garrison in all the hotels favored by foreigners.

The hunt had been on for hours.

As for Solomon P. Solomon, his prediction that the C.I.A. would be tapping the Brodsky phone within an hour and a half proved incorrect.

It took one hour and fifty-five minutes.

24

"I am *not* a warlock, wizard, sorcerer, or voodoo priest," Colton announced as he peered out the window of his office in the American embassy on the Place de la Concorde.

During the past dozen years, a lot of people in a lot of countries had called Andrew Colton a lot of things—almost all of them unpleasant and more than half of them true. There was a shocking variety of pejorative terms that could be legitimately applied to this ruthless Cold Warrior, but he certainly wasn't a warlock, wizard, sorcerer, or voodoo priest. He was a hard-working and practical man who enjoyed serving a large tough organization run by hard-working and practical men.

That was why the order to find Garrison bothered him.

"I am *not* and *have never been* a warlock, wizard, sorcerer, or voodoo priest," he repeated, "so how am I going to find Garrison if he has a whole new face?"

No one answered.

There was no one else in the room.

Colton often talked to himself, in part because so few other people would speak to him. He was, to be sure, not typical of all the employees of the Agency. Most of the others were less barbarous and more humane, and he was one of the few who always sympathized with the vampires and zombies in the horror films. It was, however, untrue that he had pulled the wings off flies as a child. He had smashed them with a hard rubber hammer that didn't hurt the walls.

Forty-one years old and frustrated, he now wanted to smash something else but he didn't know what. He had sent out sixteen of his "people" to cover 103 hotels on the chance that someone named David Garrison might be registered at one of them, and the results had been—as expected—modest. They had found a Buick dealer from Scranton, Pa., but his name was Fred Gunderson and he was sixty-two years old. The only Garrison was a music appreciation teacher from Spider Crotch, Oklahoma, a woman who'd come to Paris with her toothy sister. Colton hadn't even hoped that Garrison would be foolish enough to use his own name and passport on a clandestine operation such as this, but making the check was routine.

"Maybe . . . maybe the French might do better," he calculated aloud.

He had an "informal working relationship" with the Number Three man at the D.S.T., but Colton didn't trust the D.S.T. people. He didn't trust the U.S. Air Force's A-2, the American Army's G-2, or the Navy's O.N.I. either, and, as a matter of fact, wasn't that sure about the International Red Cross, UNICEF, or the Cannes Film Festival. Still, the D.S.T. had a lot more bodies available and perhaps he could snow them with some not-too-elaborate yarn.

He telephoned Marcel Perrier at the D.S.T. official's unlisted home number, went through the customary three minutes of conversational preliminaries.

"By the way, Marcel," he continued with forced nonchalance, "somebody over here asked me if I'd help find a friend of his who's supposed to be in town."

Perrier didn't ask whether it was urgent.

It had to be for Colton to call him at home on Sunday.

"An American?"

"Yes, name of David O. Garrison. That's G-A-R-R-I-S-O-N. I don't have any idea where the hell this guy might be, probably shacked up with some girl in a hotel. Think your people could get us an address for him?"

"Right now?"

"*Tout de suite, mon ami.* Want to reach him before he blows town."

"There are a lot of hotels. That would be a big job."

Perrier was pricing the deal.

A big job would require a lot of manpower and effort, and the D.S.T. would expect to be repaid with a favor just as large and probably with interest. If the British were a nation of shopkeepers, Colton thought irritably, then the French were a nation of bookkeepers.

"Put it on my tab," replied the American.

"Is this a rush *affaire*?"

Pricing and testing, nudging to see how much the market would bear.

"I wasn't kidding when I said *toute de suite.* Time is a very important factor."

Perrier thought about all the men already tied up hunting for Olitski, wondered whether the Americans had him and were trying to distract the D.S.T. from that crucial search. It was extremely difficult to be more devious than Andrew Colton, calculated the D.S.T. executive, for Colton had a passion for convoluted conspiracy and deception that was almost oriental in its complexity. Still, in this duel the French had the advantage for Colton couldn't know that the French knew about Olitski.

Or could he?

Maybe some louse, some jealous louse at the S.D.E.C.E., had leaked it to the Americans just to hurt the D.S.T.?

It was unlikely, and the D.S.T. could always spare a few agents for such a chore. If they succeeded, the C.I.A. would owe them "one" and if they failed it wouldn't matter that much.

"We shall look into this at once," Perrier promised.

Colton gave him a general physical description of the David Garrison whom he remembered, and some two dozen D.S.T. operatives joined the scores of U.S. and Soviet agents already hunting for the "faceless" Special Forces captain. It was an odd sensation for the ambush expert to hear one of the searchers asking the room clerk of his own hotel about *Monsieur Garrison, un Americain* as Garrison walked through the lobby. Of course, they weren't going to find anyone by that name registered at the Royale—thanks to the forged Canadian passport that Livneh had provided for "Jeffrey Green of Toronto." He made a mental note to thank the Israeli, who would undoubtedly be amused by the incident.

Livneh didn't look the least bit amused.

Even Culpepper, who was sharing the Israeli's hotel room now, managed to smile from the bed on which he was recuperating, but Livneh didn't react at all. He nodded, walked into the bathroom to pour himself a glass of water.

"Something's bothering him, Cap'n," the Georgian said softly.

"I can see that. What the hell is it?"

Culpepper shrugged, winced from the abdominal pain.

"You're not bleeding, are you, Junior?"

"No, but it hurts all the time."

"How long has he been like that?"

"Since we took Seven. He doesn't say much, just sits there with a mean-mean look on his face. Sometimes he gets up and paces around a mite, and then he sits down again and hates the wall."

Livneh came out of the bathroom.

"Your friend will be all right, David," he predicted with a glance toward Culpepper.

"How about you, Eliahu?"

"All right."

"Something bothering you?"

"A personal problem."

His expression showed nothing, but the eyes belonged to a man properly code-named "Knife."

"I want you to get a car and take Mendoza out to the country somewhere," Garrison said as if he hadn't noticed. "He's going to need some target practice with the rifle. He's got to get used to it. We can't afford a miss on the bridge."

"Why don't you take him?"
"Because I don't know where to take him. What's wrong?"
Livneh shook his head.
"I have some personal business," he answered. "You don't need me now—not anymore."
What was it?
"None of us has any personal business until we've got the kid," Garrison said firmly. "You gave me your word. We shook hands on it. We're all counting on you."
"I understand."
"What do you want me to say—that the kid's counting on you?" challenged the New Englander. "That this unfortunate little Jewish orphan is counting on you? Well, I won't."
"Thank you."
"I won't because it would be a lot of crap. She never heard of you, and we don't even know whether she wants out anyway. I'm saying that I gave my word to Brodsky and you gave your word to me. That ought to be enough. Hearts and flowers isn't my tune, dammit, and I'm not going to pretend that it is."
"David, this is a private thing and . . ."
"Private? What the hell do you think our mission is—a U.N. project? Keeping your word or saving the kid out of the goodness of your heart, I don't care which you pick. Well?"
Livneh stood there stolidly for what must have been fifteen seconds but seemed a lot longer, with sweat glistening on his forehead.
"After the child is safe . . . after that, I will attend to my private matter," he said slowly.
Whatever it was, it wasn't flute lessons.
It had to be the other thing, the problem that The Maven had discussed so frankly.
That other thing was unspeakable, so Garrison didn't even try to help.
"That'll be fine," he replied with a calmness that he didn't feel. "After we've got the kid, you can go into business for yourself. You'll have the money too. I haven't forgotten my promise either."
Livneh didn't answer.
"Right," continued the New Englander. "You'd better get moving. He's waiting in front of Notre Dame on the Isle de la Cité,

or will be in about five minutes. Get back before eight. It's on for tonight, if they can fly her in."

"They did the umbrella bit this morning?" Culpepper asked.

"Right on time."

The man from the Warsaw ghetto slipped on his jacket, departed without a word.

"You wouldn't have any idea—I mean, did he say anything?" Garrison asked a moment later.

"About what's bugging him? Not a clue. He took good care of me . . . real gentle and kind. He knows plenty about wounds, I'd bet."

"Junior, what the hell did you talk about? It couldn't have been cuts and bullet holes all the time. Did he say anything about Seven or the Sovs or even the kid?"

Culpepper shook his blond head carefully.

"Only kid he talked about was his sister. Talked about her quite a bunch, Cap'n. A beautiful girl, he said. A sweet and beautiful girl. Showed me an ole faded snapshot. She was about nine or ten. Probably forty by now."

"No, she isn't forty."

"You know her?"

"Know about her. She's dead. They gassed her."

Culpepper sat up in bed, startled.

"*Gassed* her?"

"With a lot of other kids, and then they tossed her body into a furnace. One of those fucking Nazi death camps—a long time ago."

It was a rare event.

Arnold L. Culpepper, Jr., was at a complete loss for words.

"They wiped out his whole family, mother, father, aunts, uncles, cousins—everyone," Garrison said grimly.

"Must have been some experience."

"You could say that. Didn't you ever see those old newsreels, the film our Army photo crews took when we overran some of those camps?"

The Georgian shook his head.

"Not as I remember, Cap'n. I'm only twenty-three though. Maybe they don't show those pictures anymore."

"*He* remembers all right. A lot of people who saw those films may not remember, but he remembers."

"No goddamn way he could forget, Cap'n."

"You're right again, Junior. No goddamn way he could forget. . . . Well, that doesn't answer my question. Maybe he'll say something to Mendoza."

The Apache returned just before eight P.M., put down the suitcase that contained the dismantled sniper gun.

"Where's Livneh?" Culpepper asked from the bed.

"Parking the car. Should be up in a couple of minutes."

"Rifle okay?"

"Sure. I've got it sighted-in now. Fired about forty rounds. How about you?"

"Comin' right along. She still hurts like hell, Chief, but not all the time anymore."

Mendoza nodded.

"Never thought I'd see the day I'd bless Yankee ingenuity," rambled the Georgian, "but that flak-jacket sure saved my gut."

"Maybe it was invented by somebody from Florida, or even South Carolina?"

Culpepper's face brightened at the thought, and he slowly raised himself to his feet.

"Wanna help me get into that mother again, Chief? It's on for tonight, you know."

"The swap?" Mendoza asked as he handed Culpepper the armor vest.

"Yeah, three o-goddamn-clock in the morning. Cap'n set it up by phone while you were out. . . . Easy . . . easy there, son. I'm still sort of tender in the lower ab-do-men. Not too tight. . . . Thank you. Say, you picked out your roof?"

The Indian nodded.

"You're not sayin' much tonight, Mighty Chief."

"I was thinking about something that happened this afternoon."

"Hey, the Cap'n wanted me to ask you about Livneh. He was acting sort of funny, as if he had something bothering him a lot. Might have something to do with his sister whom the Nazis killed. He was talking about her today."

"He told me about her, too."

Mendoza went on to describe how Livneh had hurried back from the country to get to a strange underground crypt behind Notre Dame cathedral before it closed at seven o'clock. They'd entered through a garden, descended a flight of steps, crossed a courtyard walled in granite, and finally reached a Y shaped crypt. In small niches in each of the two shorter legs of the Y were sealed handfuls of earth and ash, each from one of the fifteen Nazi death camps. The only light came from black overhead "fixtures," replicas of the fake "shower faucets" used in the gas chambers of the Third Reich. The walls of the stem of the Y were lined with tiny illuminated crystals, one hundred thousand on each wall. This was Paris' Monument to the Deported, the two hundred thousand French—mostly Jews—who never returned from those camps. On the way out, the Apache had noticed an inscription chiseled into the stone above the doorway.

"Forgive . . . do not forget," Mendoza reported. "He translated it for me. Then we found a café and had a drink, and he told me about his sister and the rest of the family. Tomorrow would be her birthday. . . . When he finished talking, he cried."

"Rough," commiserated Culpepper.

"Rough. I cried too. . . . I'm not ashamed of it. I cried."

"You got nothing to be ashamed of, Chief."

Mendoza didn't answer. He walked to the window, then back to the middle of the room and finally hung up his jacket on the back of a chair. Then he unbuttoned his collar and sat down on the edge of the brass bed.

"I'll tell you one thing, Junior. I've been thinking about his sister, and I've made up my mind. There isn't a damn thing we can do about his sister, or all the others, but we can do something about Sonya Brodsky."

"It isn't the same thing, Chief. The Sovs aren't shoving people into gas chambers."

The Indian shook his head angrily.

"There's some kind of principle involved here. All I know is that we've got to get that little girl out tonight."

"Then it isn't just the bus anymore?" Culpepper asked.

"Not anymore."

Then the door opened, and Livneh entered the room.

25

There are more than twenty bridges across the Seine in Paris and one might argue, as people often do, as to which is the most beautiful, but no one could dispute which is the oldest. It is the Pont Neuf, whose first stone was ceremonially laid by Henry III of France on May 31, 1578. This old "new bridge" is adorned by a bronze statue of Henry IV on horseback, hardly surprising since it was Henry IV who sat on the throne when the multi-arched span was completed and politicians have never hesitated to steal credit for other people's works. It is a handsome bridge, even if, perhaps, less elegant than the Pont du Carousel or the Pont Alexàndre III. Say what you will, it is certainly more attractive than the Pont des Arts that straddles the river less than a quarter of a mile downstream.

Questions of relative beauty were not prominent in the minds of the men in the two cars, but that may be because they were not French. They were KGB agents, four in one sedan on the Left Bank's Quai des Grand Augustins and a similar number in another auto on the Right Bank. There were also nine other armed Russians on foot, covering both approaches to the bridge. They were waiting for the men who would bring Professor Josef Olitski. If it seemed feasible, they would ambush the kidnappers and rescue the scientist before he ever reached the Pont Neuf. If this looked too dangerous, they would wait until after the exchange to kill the foreign thugs.

The orders were clear: the kidnappers must die.

The man who'd given these orders was standing near the middle of the bridge, close to where it lofts over one tip of the Ile de la Cité, nearer the Louvre side of the Seine. He was a large balding man of substantial experience in these matters, and at The Center he was spoken of as Andrei. That wasn't his real name, but security was rigorous at The Center—the KGB headquarters in Moscow. Andrei was the KGB *rezident* in Paris. He had not originated these orders, but was merely relaying them for the smaller sharp-faced man who'd come in on the special flight. As the KGB chief for Western Europe, that man had considerable authority and a number of names—among them, Matsesta. This was an inside joke, for that was the name of a health resort on the Black Sea.

There was a third man on the Pont Neuf, Colonel Berlov.

And there was a fourteen-year-old girl, very stiff and quite silent. She was tired too, for it was three A.M. and she'd never been up this late in her life. Berlov started to move forward to comfort her, decided that Matsesta might not approve. He had a bad reputation, that one.

"Where are they?" demanded the man from Moscow testily.

The Assistant Air Attache glanced at his watch, saw that it was only two minutes after three. This was typical KGB crap, two lousy minutes. Two minutes off schedule. Why it sometimes took Berlov two minutes to finish peeing, and this desk-jockey was raising a stink because The Other Side was that much late.

It was stupid and unnecessary, like the ambushes that Matsesta had so lovingly planned. You couldn't say it though, not even today. Even now, tangling with the KGB could be hazardous to your health—like smoking cigarettes.

"They're probably cruising the area, Comrade," Andrei answered in matter of fact tones. "After all, people capable of this sort of sophisticated operation would have the sense to check out the neighborhood for traps."

The *rezident* was right, but Berlov wasn't about to get into this sort of squabble.

"What people—the invisible men you and the Americans couldn't find?"

"Yes, those people, Comrade," Andrei replied to his superior.

"I think you give those hoodlums too much credit."

"I didn't *give* them anything. They *took* it."

There was very little traffic, only an occasional car floating past and even fewer pedestrians. A hobo-beggar shuffling along, a pair of slightly tipsy adolescents who were probably Sorbonne students, a sullen Algerian in laborer's clothes walking slowly toward the Arab quarter in the nearby Fifth Arrondisement—no one who resembled the kidnappers. Berlov saw a tallish man with a small suitcase approaching on foot from the Left Bank, then turned his attention away to look for the car in which *they* would arrive with the physicist. Matsesta looked at his watch again, saw that it was 3:08.

"I don't like waiting," he announced testily.

"Sorry I kept you," said the man with the suitcase as if in reply. He spoke in English.

They all stared at him, studying his face as if to memorize it.

"I've come to make the exchange," Garrison declared.

"I don't see the merchandise, Mister?"

"Dupont. You can call me Dupont. I'm in the bridge business," he told the man from Moscow.

"Spare me your cheap humor, Mister. Where is the merchandise?"

Garrison shook his head.

"Quite near, and I'll produce it when I'm satisfied that you've brought my package for the swap. Fair is fair, to quote Voltaire."

For a moment, Colonel Berlov tried to recall the quotation and then decided that this foreigner was probably being ironic.

Matsesta gestured toward the girl, and the *rezident* brought her closer.

"Don't say anything," Garrison told her. "Well, just yes or no."

He didn't want her to mention his name, for even now the Sovs couldn't be sure who he was. To make their task more difficult, he was wearing the plain-glass spectacles and the pasted-on mustache he'd bought in a costume shop and he didn't want this weary child to fix his identity.

"Are you Sonya Brodsky?"

"Yes."

She was worn, uncertain.

"I'm taking you with me, away from these people, but I'm curious about something. You don't have to answer if you don't want to, Sonya. Sonya, do you wish to leave Russia?"

She looked at him, then at the KGB men, and then back to Garrison.

"Yes!" she said in much stronger tones than he'd ever heard her use.

"Yes, yes, yes," she repeated defiantly.

She was a Brodsky all right.

"Okay. I'm ready to deal," acknowledged the American.

He opened the suitcase, took out a walkie-talkie unit.

"Gonna get your package," he told Matsesta. "Couldn't bring it in with me because of those gunmen you've got staked out on both ends of the bridge. They *are* gunmen, aren't they?"

The KGB executive didn't respond.

"I hope they are," Garrison continued, "because my men who're covering them with machine guns from the roofs are. Okay . . . your package."

He raised the radio to his mouth.

"Fat Freddy One to Fat Freddy Two . . . Fat Freddy One to Fat Freddy Two . . . Bring up the package. Repeat, bring up the package."

He put down the walkie-talkie, extracted a bundle from the suitcase.

"Don't look around for cars, Comrade," he advised cheerily. "It's such a nice June night that we decided not to drive."

Then they all heard the sound of a motor from somewhere below.

"Perfect weather for a boat ride," Garrison noted as he unwrapped the bundle.

They turned toward the noise, saw the shape of a small launch, riding without lights, closing from a few hundred yards away. Garrison unrolled the escape ladder, hooked its two metal clamps over the rail and lowered it down to the water. The boat slowed to a near stop below, and maneuvered for a moment. Thirty seconds later, Eliahu Livneh climbed onto the Pont Neuf.

"That's not him," said Andrei.

"He's next," the New Englander promised.

He was. Shakily but not surprisingly so for a man of his age and his recent experiences, the scientist managed to ascend and, with some effort, reach the stone railing. The Israeli helped him over, and the Russians stared at him very carefully. He rubbed his eyes with his right hand, uncomfortable without his glasses.

Matsesta said something in Russian, and the physicist responded in the same tongue. Then Andrei said something in English.

"The case?"

There was a small attaché case chained to Olitski's left wrist, not too heavy but enough to have made his ascent a bit clumsy.

"The case? That's our ticket out of here. Maybe I misjudge the KGB," Garrison apologized, "but it occurred to me that we might have some trouble leaving after we'd made the exchange. There's a bomb in the case, a radio controlled bomb. We need an hour. You're going to sit here like patient comrades for sixty minutes. Talk about the Bolshoi Ballet or the Dynamo soccer team. You can tell dirty jokes if you like, but sit here for an hour. If you make any move to come after us, we'll blow your scientist into dog meat. There'll be chunks of him all over the Pont Neuf."

Matsesta shook his head.

"You don't believe me? You don't think we've got somebody watching, somebody who could set off the charge after we've gone? Well, Comrade, let me put your mind at rest. I'll do my famous William Tell number for you, free of charge."

Garrison now took an apple—covered with some luminous paint—from the suitcase and placed it on the rail about five feet from the man from Moscow. The New Englander picked up the walkie-talkie.

"Shoot!"

The Apache on the Left Bank rooftop squinted through the sniper-scope, aimed very very carefully and squeezed the trigger.

The apple shattered into pieces.

"A difficult shot for most men," Garrison noted, "but not for him. Pressing a button to set off a charge is a lot easier, of course."

"You won't get very far, Mr. Garrison," promised Matsesta.

"The name is Dupont. . . . Okay, let's move out."

He started toward the rail, stopped.

"Where's her bag?"

The man from Moscow shrugged.

"You said the child, not her clothes," he answered smugly.

"Cheap. You're a real cheap bastard, aren't you, Comrade?"

There was no answer.

"Her passport?" asked Livneh.

The senior KGB executive shrugged again.

"No Soviet citizen can leave without a passport," insisted the Israeli. "He must have her passport."

"You'd better produce it, Comrade," Garrison advised.

Matsesta moved suddenly toward his pocket, and a .32 bloomed miraculously in the Israeli's left hand.

"Nice trick, huh? He does magic shows for children's parties. He saves his right hand for his knife," reported the American.

Now there was a knife in Livneh's right hand—just like that.

"Okay, let's see that goddamn passport. Get it out very slowly, terribly slowly unless you enjoy major surgery."

The fear in Matsesta's face made Berlov smile—for just a second before he suppressed it. Livneh moved forward, took the passport and then jerked the pistol from Matsesta's belly-holster.

"You were very close to one of those posthumous medals they give heroes, Comrade."

"Very close," confirmed the Israeli tautly.

"Your lucky night. All right, let's get down to the boat. You first, hen the child," ordered the American.

"I'll cover the rear," insisted Livneh.

He might still kill them, but there was no point in arguing. Garrison helped the girl to the rail.

"You'll be hearing from us, Mister Dupont," threatened Matsesta.

"I hope not—for your sake. You don't know who we are, or how many, or where we are. If you come after this kid, comrade, you'll find out that my friends can shoot more than apples. You may get the top of your head blown off one night five weeks from tomorrow, or maybe somebody will burn out your embassy in Rome in a couple of months. There might be a bomb in your military attache's car in London, or a little accident that would sink one of your freighters."

"You think you're clever, don't you?"

Garrison smiled.

"That's the dumbest thing you've said," he answered. "Would a clever man do all this to rescue one fourteen-year-old orphan?"

He swung himself over the rail, descended three steps and reached up to help the child follow.

"Leave them alone. Let the child go," said Olitski weakly.

He had more to say, but he staggered instead. Berlov and the *rezident* rushed to his side, and even the man from Moscow turned his attention to the important scientist. They were supporting him as Livneh followed the others down.

"I'm all right, just tired," the Israeli heard him say in Russian.

The boat pulled away ninety seconds later, and the four men on the Pont Neuf waited for an hour. At ten minutes after four, a taxi pulled up and a uniformed bellboy stepped out smiling. He had every reason to smile, for he'd been tipped generously by that American woman doctor before she'd left the George V.

"Professeur Olitski?" he asked as he thrust forward the envelope

Berlov took it, tore it open, and found the key.

It worked.

They removed the handcuff, and then the Soviet colonel noticed the second key. It had to open the case. Berlov picked up the case, walked twenty yards away so that no one else would be injured if it were booby-trapped. Slowly and warily, he inserted the key and opened the leather case.

"No bomb," he called out to the others.

"What is it?" asked the *rezident.*

"Come and see."

Olitski burst into laughter when he looked into the case, and even Berlov had to cough to muffle his amusement.

No bomb.

One bottle of Remy Martin cognac and four brandy snifters neatly cushioned in layers of paper tissue.

"You have a remarkable sense of humor, Professor," grumbled the man from Moscow.

"Not usually. This is probably just joy to be alive and free, and that is something to celebrate. At the risk of poor taste and immodesty, shall we drink to my health?"

So they did—at 4:15 in the morning as the sky began to turn rosy over the roofs of Paris. It was excellent brandy, they all agreed, and they all felt a little better afterwards. Matsesta's face wasn't entirely cleansed of that troubled angry look, however, for he would have to make the report to The Center.

There was no predicting what might happen after that—or to whom.

Perhaps even to the head of the KGB's Western European desk.

As he contemplated this disturbing prospect, Andrew Colton was contemplating the photo of Captain David O. Garrison's new face that had just arrived by cable from "Klondike." The D.S.T. labs could run off a hundred prints within a few hours—by nine o'clock at the latest.

By sunset, they would have Garrison and his friends.

26

The prints were ready by nine A.M., but neither the D.S.T. nor the C.I.A. found David Garrison. He wasn't in Paris. He wasn't even in France. The chartered jet had taken off on schedule at 3:55 A.M., and had delivered them to the commercial field at Prestwick, Scotland in time to catch the regular Monday morning Air Canada flight to Montreal. This was all as planned, with one exception. Livneh was with them. Garrison had expected him to leave them at the airport in Paris, but the Israeli had surprised him by announcing his wish to go on with the child. They seemed to get along quite well on the transatlantic leg, and while Dr. Elizabeth Clement slept with her head on her lover's shoulder Livneh and Sonya Brodsky spoke softly, almost intimately, in Russian by the hour. Behind them, Culpepper and Mendoza talked about the bus as they looked at the checks that Garrison had given them.

"Don't drink too much of that champagne," the Indian advised when Culpepper signaled the stewardess for a refill.

"Drink all I damn please. Just completed a hee-ro-ic and highly profitable mission, made a sack of money, and I'm comin' home with a load of groovy threads. Man, wait till Swede hears about this."

"I don't think we're supposed to tell anyone, Junior."

"Then I got a reason to drink. Frustration. Going to soak up a whole bottle, and I just may ravish the stewardess—maybe twice. Don't argue with me, Redskin. I ain't signed over that seven thousand yet."

"I think success has gone to your head."

"That's a fair estimate. Just humor me for a while, and you'll get your money when we reach Montreal."

Neither Culpepper nor Mendoza ever reached Montreal. They got as far as that city's Dorval Airport, but they never went downtown because Garrison wouldn't let them.

"It's time to split," he advised. "It may be tricky crossing the border, and I don't want you to be parties to any breaking of U.S. laws. Eliahu can probably buy a forged visa for the kid and one for himself—since he knows how to find such things—but there's no reason for you to get involved."

"You expectin' trouble at the other end, Cap'n?"

"Maybe. Could be. Maybe those boys we left on the bridge got through to Moscow and Moscow may have screamed about all the illegal and immoral things done to liberate one Sonya Brodsky, relative of C.J. Brodsky of New York City."

Arnold L. Culpepper, Jr., rubbed the side of his nose thoughtfully. "You think the cops or the C.I.A. might have the Brodsky house staked-out?"

"That's just what I'm thinking. There's one last thing that you can do for me, since you'll be passing through New York in about two hours anyway."

He explained what was to be done, and at ten that night Culpepper telephoned Garrison at Montreal's Chateau Champlain hotel with his report.

"Did exactly what you said, and it's just the way you figured," he announced. "Called the house and talked to that Solomon feller. Told him I was a true buddy of his friend from Washington, the one he drove to the airport. Arranged to meet him in a bar. That house is hotter'n a pistol, Cap'n. Phones tapped, full surveillance. It's the Spooks all right. They called up to ask about you two, three days ago, you and the kid. Solomon and the nurse gave them a load of prime eagle shit, Cap'n, and after that . . . *pow* . . . the whole neighborhood went. Spooks in all the cellars and trees, swinging by their tails like monkeys in the jungle. They're really out to rip your ass, Cap'n."

"From ear to ear. Listen, did you give my message to Solomon?"

"Sure did. He's gonna tell the old man about it. Seems to think they can handle it. Only problem's gonna be the phone, but he's got an idea about cutting a tape of the old man with the instructions."

"Thursday afternoon at three o'clock—you told him that?"

"Yessir."

"How is the old man, Junior?"

"Not good. From what Solomon says, he could check out next week."

Garrison looked across the room at Elizabeth Clement and the girl watching television.

"I don't think so," he answered. "If he knows that she's on her way, he's going to hang in there—maybe for months. That's not your problem anyway. Deposit the checks and buy that bus. That's an order."

"Yessir."

"And clear out of New York. Go home for the rest of your leave. That's another order."

"I'll remember that, Cap'n. Oh, Cap'n, Chief and I were talking, and he reminded me that we forgot to thank you."

"For what? Not for the bus, I hope. You earned that—the hard way."

He could hear Arnold Culpepper, Jr., clearing his throat.

"Not for the bus, Cap'n. It got bigger than the bus. For the chance to do something . . . well, something *noble.* Christ almighty, we might never get another. This was kind of almost . . . religious. We won't forget this, Cap'n."

Garrison wondered whether he'd say it.

"Take care of yourself, Cap'n, and *watch your ass*—sir. They may be coming up from behind."

You could count on Culpepper. He was reliable.

"And give our best to that fine lady," concluded the Georgian gallantly.

"Send mine to the Chief, and mail me a picture of the bus. If I'm not at Leavenworth you can reach me at Walter Reed."

"You ain't going to no federal prison for what you did, Cap'n. You're going to get a medal."

"With oak leaf clusters?"

"With oak leaf clusters."

Now it all depended on the old man. On Wednesday, they took a bus from Montreal into Albany and the forged visas were not detected. On Thursday, Garrison rented a car and they set off down the New York State Thruway to Manhattan. It was as they crossed

Ninety-fifth Street that the Special Forces captain asked Livneh the question.

"Eliahu, there's something I'd like to talk to you about before we reach Brodsky's house."

"The personal business in Paris?"

Garrison nodded.

"If it's still that personal . . ." he continued tentatively but didn't get to complete the sentence.

"Not any more, David. There was a man in Paris whom I wanted to kill. You probably didn't even notice him, but I did and I recognized him. The West German security agent who let Olitski out the door of their embassy that night—I remembered him. He was one of the SS monsters in Warsaw. They probably don't know that, but I remembered him and I wanted to kill him."

He paused, glanced at the young girl.

"I changed my mind," Livneh announced, and Garrison understood. "He isn't my problem, not my *personal* problem. I sent The Maven a cable about this man from Montreal. Now it's his problem. I have other things to do."

"Flute lessons?"

"Exactly."

"And Hebrew too," interrupted Sonya Brodsky. "You promised me both."

"Don't worry about it," advised Garrison. "He's a man who keeps his word."

No one said anything about Sonya Brodsky going to Israel after the old man died, but no one had to. No one would mention it, Garrison speculated, although it might actually please C.J. to know that she would live in The Holy Land. It would certainly please Livneh, who had no family of his own left.

"Eighty-eighth Street," announced Elizabeth Clement.

'Don't sweat it," he advised.

"God, you sound like that G.I. Cracker from Georgia! I'm sweating because I'm frightened, Dave. Is that weak or something?"

"It's fine, just fine, Honey."

She sensed that he wasn't even listening to her now, that his focus was somewhere ahead on Eighty-second just off Fifth.

"Three minutes to three," she said after checking her wristwatch.

"What have you got, Eliahu?"

"Same thing."

It was probably some sort of extraordinary omen—two different watches showing the same time—but was it a good omen or a bad one?

"You know what to do," reminded Garrison as they drew abreast of the big art museum.

They stopped for the traffic light, and when it turned green Garrison swung the rented sedan around the corner to stop directly in front of 3 East 82nd Street. He flicked off the motor, and they all poured out of the car. At that instant, three P.M., the door of the Brodsky town house opened and the four fugitives sprinted inside. Garrison was aware of another car pulling up—Spooks, no doubt—but he didn't look back. Junior would not approve.

Solomon P. Solomon closed the door quickly behind them.

27

They shook hands.

"Company's coming," said the New Englander.

"You're not company, Captain. You're practically part of the family, and this young lady *is* part of the family."

Garrison jerked a thumb toward the street door.

"I mean company-company, Solomon. Super-spooks representing your irate Uncle Sam. Well, we've got about two and a half minutes before they start pounding on your portcullis so I might as well make the introductions. This is Eliahu Livneh and this is Miss Sonya Brodsky, Charlie's *great-niece*. . . . I think that's right, and the larger lady is Dr. Elizabeth Clement."

"Is someone ill, Captain?"

"No, I just like to keep a plastic surgeon around all the time. She goes with me."

"All the time, Captain," she confirmed.

"Not if I go to Leavenworth."

"All the way, Captain."

"He's waiting in the garden," reminded the ex-detective.

"Come meet him," said Garrison as they started up the hall. "He's really something. You've got one remarkable old great-uncle, Sonya. As Junior would say, definitely outstanding."

They entered the garden, and everyone there beamed. Shirley Takeda beamed, a man whom Garrison recognized as the distinguished lawyer who'd drafted the contract beamed, another man with a very familiar face—a public face—beamed and C.J. Brodsky glowed as if he were twenty-five again. Garrison made the introductions, and the girl moved toward the old man in the wheelchair cautiously.

Then she ran, and they embraced.

Shirley Takeda cried, of course, as quietly as possible.

"Stop that, stop that," ordered Brodsky. "Go get some milk and cookies. You like milk and cookies, don't you, Sonya?"

"Oh yes, but we had a big lunch."

"Bring a *lot* of cookies. I may eat some myself," insisted the aged tycoon.

Still clutching the girl's left hand, he turned to his lawyer.

"Would you like some cookies, Judge?"

"I haven't eaten cookies for at least nine years, Charlie. They're fattening."

"Today we're having cookies and milk. We've got all kinds, don't we, Shirley? You did what I said?"

"Oatmeal cookies, lemon cookies, chocolate chip—I bought nine different kinds, and Solomon baked a cake," she reported as she wiped her eyes.

"Cookies all right with you, Marty?" Brodsky asked the other man.

"Why not? I judged a pizza contest last week, so why not cookies—unless you've got strudel? I'm very fond of Solomon's strudel."

The doorbell rang twice, and they all knew who it was.

"Any strudel left from last night?" Brodsky asked evenly.

"I think so."

Now the nurse was weeping again.

"Shirley, Shirley—go bring the cookies, and the strudel."

The doorbell sounded again.

"You'd better get that, Solomon," advised Brodsky.

The black man walked to the street door, opened it to face two neatly dressed men in their late twenties. They weren't as neatly dressed as F.B.I. agents, but neat enough for most purposes. They could have been I.B.M. executive trainees. They weren't.

"Is Captain Garrison here?" one of them asked politely.

Solomon P. Solomon considered the inquiry.

"His car's double-parked outside," said the other one.

"You going to give him a ticket?" Solomon questioned.

"No, we're not the police. We're with the Central Intelligence Agency."

"That's nice."

"Mv name is Dillon, Arthur Dillon, and this is Mr. Hacketts."

They each produced plastic-sheathed identity cards.

"That's nice," Solomon reiterated noncommittally.

"Well," said Dillon, "we'd like to see Captain Garrison and the little girl."

"She's not so little. She's fourteen."

Dillon refused to lose his temper.

"You're right. We'd like to see Captain Garrison and the fourteen-year-old girl, who just came in with him. *We saw them enter.*"

"That's nice. I think they're busy. They're having milk and cookies."

"We *love* milk and cookies," announced Hacketts.

"Why didn't you say so? We've got plenty—nine different kinds of cookies, and strudel, too. Come on in."

They followed him into the garden.

"This is Mr. Dillon and Mr. Hacketts of the C.I.A.," Solomon announced routinely. "They say Captain Garrison's car is double-parked outside."

Charles J. Brodsky laughed loudly.

"I don't believe it," he said.

"You said that the C.I.A. wouldn't call about double-parking," he reminded Solomon.

"That's not exactly why we're here. We want to talk to Captain Garrison and the little . . . Miss Sonya Brodsky."

The millionaire glanced at his attorney.

"You got a warrant? Search warrant?" tested the lawyer.

"No, sir."

"*Any* kind of warrant?"

"No, sir."

The attorney sniffed contemptuously.

"They don't even have any legal right to be here. You can throw them out, Charlie," he advised.

"They like milk and cookies," reported Solomon P. Solomon gravely.

"The chocolate-chips are very good, gentlemen," invited Brodsky.

"I can recommend the oatmeal," added Garrison.

The two agents looked at him studiously.

"Captain Garrison?"

"Right. You're going to be crazy about the oatmeal."

It was going to be very difficult to describe all this in the report.

"You armed, Captain?" asked Hacketts.

"To eat cookies? Hell, no, I use my fingers."

Dillon's eyes wandered to Livneh.

"Is he armed?"

"I never asked him, but I doubt it. He's a flute teacher."

"I'll bet."

"Milk, gentlemen?" offered Shirley Takeda.

"Keep an eye on her," advised the Special Forces officer. "*She* may be armed to the teeth."

"Milk or no milk?" the nurse demanded impatiently.

They took the milk, sipped.

Then Dillon recognized the man with the public face.

"Senator Jacobs?"

"Everybody knows you, Marty," complimented the man in the wheelchair. "Those hearings on TV did you a world of good."

"You up here for the milk and cookies too?" wondered Dillon.

"The strudel," replied the Honorable Martin A. Jacobs of the Senate Foreign Relations Committee. "I always enjoy some strudel with my old friend and distinguished constituent when I'm in town."

"You know Mr. Brodsky for a long time?"

"About thirty years. That right, Charlie? You contributed to my first campaign for the House back in '42, didn't you?"

"Maybe. I guess so."

"Mr. Brodsky's a very generous man," Jacobs added, "and he has *a lot of friends in Washington*. . . . Have you tried the strudel?"

"I'm sticking with the chocolate-chips for the moment, Senator."

"Don't pass up the strudel. As a fairly senior senator—eighteen years on The Hill—I recommend the strudel."

The two C.I.A. men exchanged glances, and Dillon reached for a piece of strudel.

"Good?"

"First class, Senator. You ought to try it, Ted," he advised his associate.

Hacketts looked at him uneasily, tasted a bite.

"First class—I guess. I never tried strudel before."

They finished their strudel and their glasses of milk.

"Thanks. We came here to talk to Captain Garrison about the Olitski business," explained Dillon.

"What?"

"The *Olitski* thing, Captain?"

"What's that?"

"How about some milk, gentlemen?" urged Brodsky amiably. "Make you big and strong. Good for your teeth."

"Very good for your teeth," confirmed the nurse, "especially if you're pregnant."

"Do I look pregnant?" asked Dillon irritably.

"No, but you could lose fifteen or twenty pounds," advised Elizabeth Clement.

"Who's she?"

"She's a doctor," Garrison responded. "Now what were you talking about?"

"Olitski."

"Is that a person or a place?"

"A Soviet scientist."

"Never heard of him. Maybe the doctor has. She keeps up with these things. You ever heard of him, Doc?"

"I don't think so. I only know about the medical people. Is he medical?"

Dillon shook his head.

"In Paris," he pressed.

"Last week," added Hacketts.

"We were in Israel last week, visiting the holy places. Pilgrimage."

"I'll bet."

"You ought to try the oatmeal now," suggested the surgeon.

The C.I.A. men looked at each other again.

"Could I see your passport, Captain?"

"You don't have to show them anything," advised the attorney.

"I don't mind. One should cooperate with the Spooks. They work for us, you know."

Garrison handed over his passport.

There was nothing in it that indicated he'd been in Paris during the previous twenty-seven months.

There was an Israeli exit-visa less than four days old—forged.

"What about her?" Hacketts demanded as he returned Garrison's passport.

"She's got a Russian passport."

"With a valid U.S. entry visa?"

The senator put down his glass of milk.

"I knew there was *something* I'd forgotten, Charlie," he apologized. "Picked it up at State this morning, and stuck it in my pocket. . . . Here it is."

He gave it to Brodsky, who handed the sheet of paper—unread—to Dillon.

"Six months visa. All clean and proper," acknowledged the C.I.A. agent twenty seconds later.

He returned it to the man in the wheelchair.

"Would anybody like to explain how Sonya Brodsky got out of the Soviet Union?" he invited.

There was no answer.

"Very tidy. I've never seen better. Would you mind if I used your phone to call my boss in Washington? We'll pay for the call."

"Use this phone, if you like," Brodsky proposed, "and have some more cookies."

Dillon called "Klondike" and explained in stiff, guarded language what had faced him.

"He wants to talk to you, Captain," he said.

"Garrison here."

"Captain, I want to tell you that this is just about the *niftiest* operation I've heard of in five years. It was beautiful, absolutely beautiful."

"I don't know what you're talking about."

"The whole thing, fantastic! A work of art. The way you lifted him, the way you made the swap, the way you bugged out. Very classy. Very creative and classy. You know, a man with your talent is wasted in the Army."

"I still don't know what you're talking about."

"I'm talking about a job, a whole career—with us. I'm going to make a star out of you. I'm going to get you your own show. Prime time. You can set up your own team, pick your people and your missions. What kind of crappy money does an Army captain make? Peanuts, and you have to take all that crap from boob majors and colonels."

"You're offering a different brand of crap?"

"Precisely. No illusions, I like that. Now listen, Captain, when you get back to Washington I want to see you. A nice lunch somewhere. French food, good wine. Man to man talk. I'll tell you all about it."

"I don't think so."

"Just listen to my pitch. At least you'll want to hear about the cables from Colton. He's half-crazy that you got away."

"Colton is a bastard."

"Klondike" chuckled.

"Of course he is. You're a good judge of character, Dave. We're going to get along fine."

"Then you're not going to arrest me or the girl?"

"For what? Something somebody no one can identify for sure did in a foreign jurisdiction when you were in another country 1,000 miles away? Boy, that was *nifty*!"

Garrison sighed.

"No, I'm going back to Walter Reed."

"Sure, get some rest. I'll catch you there."

"You want to say anything more to Dillon or Hacketts?"

"You'd better put Dillon on again."

When Dillon put down the phone a minute later, he looked at Garrison and then C.J. Brodsky.

"Thanks for the milk and cookies, Mr. Brodsky."

"My pleasure. How about a cigar?"

"They're Cuban," warned Garrison.

"Doesn't surprise me a bit."

He took the cigar, lit it, and puffed.

"See you in Washington, Captain."

"Don't hold your breath."

Dillon puffed again.

"Honor to meet you, Senator."

"I'll go out with you. I'm flying down on the four o'clock shuttle from La Guardia."

"We'll give you a lift."

The lawyer exited with them, and everyone relaxed.

"Is it all right now?" asked the girl.

"Just fine, thanks to C.J. Brodsky and his friends."

"Now, Davey, you're supposed to call me Charlie. You too, Sonya."

She nodded and smiled and yawned, and Shirley Takeda led her off to her room.

"Thank you, Mr. Garrison," she said before she left the garden.

"You're welcome."

After she'd gone, Brodsky took an envelope from the pocket of his silk dressing robe.

"Here it is, boychik—$225,000. Certified check."

"Thanks."

"You must be feeling pretty good, huh? You screwed *three governments*, three big-fat world powers, made $250,000 and found yourself a very pretty doctor."

"I paid my debt and I brought out a nice young girl. . . . Of course, I'm not knocking the money, you understand."

"I understand. What about Mr. Livneh here?"

"He's a flute teacher."

"Oh, maybe Solomon could find him a flute. There must be an instrument shop open somewhere in the neighborhood."

"Two flutes, Charlie," corrected the Special Forces captain. "He's promised to teach Sonya how to play—that and Hebrew."

"Do you work for Doron?"

"I did, Mr. Brodsky—a long time ago."

No more questions, please. It was written all over his face.

"How would you like to stay here—for a while?" the wise old millionaire suggested. "That would certainly make the lessons easier, and you could talk to me about Israel."

"You're very kind."

"No, very selfish. . . . Now, what about you, Davey? What are you going to do?"

Garrison sensed that she was watching him intently.

"My best—whatever it is."

"It ought to be pretty damn good," judged Brodsky. "You don't have to stay in the Army, do you?"

"No, he doesn't," she answered for him.

Brodsky looked at him, chuckled.

"Harold is going to have a *fit*, Davey. He never believed that it was possible. . . . Say, what about Brucie? Can I let him know?"

"Just tell him that he's free of me now, because I don't owe anyone anything anymore."

Brodsky noted the look in Elizabeth Clement's eyes, realized that she'd soon set David O. Garrison straight on that. She'd give it one very large try; that was for sure.

"What else can I do to thank you, Davey?"

"How about a cigar?"

They each took a cigar, and Garrison ignited both with his lighter.

"Come by and see me sometime, Davey."

"I will," he promised.

"You'd better make it soon, Captain. That's what they tell me."

Garrison puffed on his corona, blew a perfect smoke ring.

C.J. Brodsky blew another one, and the New Englander nodded in acknowledgment.

"You've had a good run for your money, Charlie."

"The best. You will come see me—both of you?"

"You've got my word."

They shook hands with him, then with Livneh, and a minute later Dr. Elizabeth Clement and Captain David O. Garrison stepped out into the late afternoon sun.

"What are you going to do, Dave?" she asked.

"Pay the ticket."

The New York City Police had been less charitable than the C.I.A., and there was a summons for double-parking tied to the windshield wiper. He removed it, shoved it into his pocket before opening the car door for her.

"As I understand it, we can drop this machine off at the airport," he told her.

"Where are we going, Dave?"

He started the car, drove east to Park Avenue and turned south.

"You haven't answered my question, or Charlie Brodsky's question either. What are you going to do?"

"Deposit the check and get you into the sack. No, the banks are closed. Reverse order. . . . Oh, you mean next month or next year? We could travel some. . . . I never did get to see Masada. Maybe later I'll open that bookstore up in Pittsfield. You'd like it up in the Berkshires. Top hospital, too. Berkshire Medical Center. Might need a plastic surgeon to fix up the half-ass skiers. I know two fine doctors on the staff up there, Bob McInerney and Clem Curd. They might get you a job—if you're good enough."

"I was good enough for you, you bastard. You really mean that about leaving the Army?"

He jerked the car suddenly to avoid hitting a sky-blue MG that switched lanes without warning, and then he flipped down the visor to protect his eyes from the late afternoon glare.

"Leaving the Army? Maybe. I can give you a definite maybe. I had a swell offer from the C.I.A., just fifteen minutes ago."

"That's even wilder than the Army," she protested. "Are you crazy, Dave?"

"A little—but not that crazy. Seems a shame to waste my wonderful talent for ambush though."

"You can ambush me—every night and twice on Sundays. Isn't that enough?"

"Why don't we find out?" he replied, and then he flipped on the radio to fill the car with music.

At least one thing was over, he thought contentedly. The Olitski matter was closed.

This judgement was not entirely correct, however, for in Paris, Moscow, and Washington the D.S.T. and the KGB and the C.I.A. were still making analyses, filing reports, and apportioning blame.

In Peking, Colonel Feng was considering an entirely different question.

Which should it be now? Salt Fish Three. Or Four?

In his office on the nineteenth floor of the Shalom Tower in Tel Aviv, Issachar Doron had no such problem in making up his mind. Glancing at the cable from Montreal again, it seemed clear that the obvious thing to do was to notify the Shin Beth supervisor in Paris about the man at the West German embassy. This was an unexpected bonus, but Livneh would explain it all when he returned from Canada. It had apparently gone well. They had brought out the

Brodsky girl, and now Israel had settled its obligation to the tough annoying American captain. Of course, the supervisor in Paris would want to know how they'd discovered the Nazi war criminal at the German embassy—but it wasn't really necessary to supply him with such details.

He didn't have to know everything, Doron decided as he relit his pipe.

After all, *he* wasn't The Maven.

J. BARNICOAT
CASH SALES DEPT
P.O. BOX 11
FALMOUTH
CORNWALL TR10 9EN

Please send me the following titles

Quantity	SBN	Title	Amount
________			________
________			________
________			________
________			________
________			________
			________
		TOTAL	________

Please enclose a cheque or postal order made out to FUTURA PUBLICATIONS LIMITED for the amount due, including 10p per book to allow for postage and packing. Orders will take about three weeks to reach you and we cannot accept responsibility for orders containing cash.

PLEASE PRINT CLEARLY

NAME...

ADDRESS...

....